Teaching with Authority

A Theology of the Magisterium in the Church

Richard R. Gaillardetz

A Michael Glazier Book
THE LITURGICAL PRESS
Collegeville, Minnesota

THEOLOGY AND LIFE SERIES
Volume 41

A Michael Glazier Book published by The Liturgical Press

Cover design by David Manahan, O.S.B. Church dignitaries at the Second Vatican Council, 1964.

1   2   3   4   5   6   7   8

Library of Congress Cataloging-in-Publication Data

Gaillardetz, Richard R., 1958–
    Teaching with authority : a theology of the magisterium in the church
/ Richard R. Gaillardetz.
        p.   cm. — (Theology and life series   ;   v. 41)
    "A Michael Glazier book."
    Includes bibliographical references and index.
    ISBN 0-8146-5529-7
    1. Catholic Church—Teaching office.   I. Title.   II. Series.
BX1746.G326   1997
262'.8—dc20   96-36775
                                                     CIP

To Brian Thomas Gaillardetz,

a sacrament of God's love.

Contents

Abbreviations

Documents

AA	*Apostolicam actuositatem*	Vatican II's Decree on the Apostolate of the Laity
AG	*Ad gentes*	Vatican II's Decree on the Church's Missionary Activity
CD	*Christus Dominus*	Vatican II's Decree on the Pastoral Office of Bishops in the Church
DH	*Dignitatis humanae*	Vatican II's Declaration on Religious Freedom
DV	*Dei verbum*	Vatican II's Dogmatic Constitution on Divine Revelation
EN	*Evangelii nuntiandi*	Pope Paul VI's Apostolic Exhortation on Evangelization in the Modern World (1975)
FC	*Familiaris consortio*	Pope John Paul II's Apostolic Exhortation on the Family (1981)
GS	*Gaudium et spes*	Vatican II's Pastoral Constitution on the Church in the Modern World
LG	*Lumen gentium*	Vatican II's Dogmatic Constitution on the Church
NA	*Nostra aetate*	Vatican II's Declaration on the Relation of the Church to Non-Christian Religions

PA	*Pastor aeternus*	Vatican I's Dogmatic Constitution on the Church of Christ
PO	*Presbyterorum ordinis*	The Decree on the Ministry and Life of Priests
SC	*Sacrosanctum concilium*	The Constitution on the Sacred Liturgy
UR	*Unitatis redintegratio*	The Decree on Ecumenism
UU	*Ut unum sint*	Pope John Paul II's Encyclical on Ecumenism (1995)

Other Abbreviations

AAS	*Acta apostolicae sedis*
ARCIC	Anglican–Roman Catholic International Commission
CDF	Congregation for the Doctrine of the Faith
CLSA	Canon Law Society of America
CTSA	Catholic Theological Society of America
ITC	International Theological Commission
Mansi	J. D. Mansi, ed., *Sacrorum conciliorum nova et amplissima collectio*
DS	Denzinger-Schönmetzer, *Enchiridion symbolorum: Definitionum et declarationum de rebus fidei et morum,* 32nd edition.
NCCB	National Conference of Catholic Bishops
NCWC	National Catholic Welfare Conference
USCC	United States Catholic Conference
WCC	World Council of Churches

Introduction

The Second Vatican Council was the most significant event of the century for the Roman Catholic Church. There is perhaps no better example of the way in which, within a broad religious tradition characterized by profound continuities, so much real change is possible. Over the last few decades the Roman Catholic Church has already reaped the fruit of the renewal initiated by the council. This is evident in the flourishing of lay ministries, a more active participation of all the baptized in the life of the Church, a greater appreciation of the Bible among Catholics, a reinvigoration of liturgical life, a more profound sense of our real if imperfect communion with non-Catholic Christian traditions, and a more positive engagement with the issues and concerns of the world at large.

Since the council, Church authority itself has experienced renewal. Vatican II nudged the Church away from a more autocratic and papocentric exercise of authority to one that was more collegial and consultative in character. This new direction was reflected in a number of important developments after the council. In 1965 Pope Paul VI established the world synod of bishops in the *motu proprio, Apostolica sollicitudo,*[1] thereby providing an institutional structure that could put into action council teaching on episcopal collegiality. Regional episcopal conferences, newly empowered by Vatican II, took on ever-greater pastoral initiatives. Within the local Churches pastoral and presbyteral councils were often enthusiastically established. And in the pontificate of Paul VI there were hints of a new way of exercising ecclesial authority. Rather than acting peremptorily on the question of artificial contraception, the Pope first established a study commission, which included the laity in its membership. Decades

[1] *Apostolica sollicitudo,* AAS 57 (1965) 775–80.

later the American bishops would make this kind of consultation a permanent feature of the process by which they developed pastoral letters. Pope John Paul I refused a papal coronation, symbol of the imperial and monarchical trappings that had for centuries obscured the role of the bishop of Rome as servant of the servants of God *(servus servorum Dei)*. Pope John Paul II dispensed with the use of the papal "we" in ecclesiastical documents. Indeed, in his *Crossing the Threshold of Hope,* the Church's first Polish pope warned of the danger of misunderstanding the sometimes lofty titles attributed to the bishop of Rome.[2] Finally, one must acknowledge the important efforts made by both Paul VI and John Paul II toward curial reform.[3]

Yet in spite of real progress many of these developments have not fulfilled their original promise. While Paul VI established the world synod of bishops, the synod was not granted deliberative power, as many bishops at the council had hoped. The authority of episcopal conferences has been challenged by the Roman curia. Pastoral councils, eagerly established in the 1960s and 1970s, have too often been marginalized in the 1980s and 1990s. Symbolic gestures suggesting a renewed vision of ecclesial authority have frequently been undermined by undue curial interventions in matters pertaining to local Churches, questionable litmus tests for the appointment of Church officeholders, and an intolerance for responsible theological dissent. It is difficult to avoid the conclusion that, in spite of important developments, the ecclesiological renewal brought about by the council has been only partially realized in the area of Church authority.

Recent papal actions suggest that the time may now be ripe for attending more directly to questions of ecclesial authority. As we approach the coming Jubilee Year celebrating two millennia of Christianity, John Paul II has focused his considerable energies on the cause of Christian unity. In his 1994 apostolic letter reflecting on the coming jubilee, the Pope sought a fuller implementation of the teaching of Vatican II and a renewed commitment to Christian ecumenism.[4] Six months later came an apostolic letter on Roman Catholicism's

[2]John Paul II, *Crossing the Threshold of Hope* (New York: Knopf, 1994) 4–14.

[3]Cf. *Regimini Ecclesiae universae, AAS* 59 (1967) 885–928; *Pastor bonus, AAS* 80 (1988) 841–932.

[4]John Paul II, "As the Third Millennium Draws Near" *(Tertio millennio adveniente), Origins* 24 (November 24, 1994) nos. 20, 34.

relationship to the Churches of the East.[5] Less than a month after that came a major encyclical on ecumenism. In that encyclical the Pope specifically called for a further study of five fundamental topics with a view toward achieving a "true consensus of faith" (*UU* 79). The fourth of these topics was "the magisterium of the church, entrusted to the pope and the bishops in communion with him, understood as a responsibility and an authority exercised in the name of Christ for teaching and safeguarding the faith." Later in the encyclical he singled out the problematic issue of papal primacy, noting the obstacle to formal Christian unity it represents. In a remarkable gesture the Pope committed himself to finding a way to exercise that primacy, which is "open to a new situation," and invited other Church leaders and theologians to join in a dialogue with the goal of surmounting this ecumenical obstacle (*UU* 95).

In this volume I have tried to combine two central features in the Pope's agenda for the Jubilee Year preparation: a fuller implementation of the teaching of Vatican II and a reassessment of ecclesial teaching authority. I do not propose some wholly new, constructive theology of teaching authority. Rather I have set for myself the more limited task of reconsidering the nature and exercise of doctrinal teaching authority in the Roman Catholic Church in the light of three basic theological insights or principles that emerged out of Vatican II. They are as follows:

1. *Vatican II taught that the Church, that is, the whole people of God, has been addressed by the word of God, incarnate in Jesus Christ and dwelling in the Church by the power of the Holy Spirit.* The council's personalist theology of divine revelation stood in contrast to a more propositional view of divine revelation which understood revelation primarily as a collection of doctrinal statements. In the theology of Vatican II, Jesus Christ, as both the mediator and sum of divine revelation, is God's personal address to not only the whole Church but the whole human race. Firmly rejected is the view that God communicates divine revelation primarily to the hierarchy, who then transmit that revelation to the rest of the Church. Rather, the word of God emerges within the whole Church through a complex set of ecclesial relationships in which all the baptized, professional theologians, and the college of bishops play important roles.

[5] John Paul II, "The Light of the East" (*Orientale lumen*) *Origins* 25 (May 18, 1995) 1–13.

2. *The Church is a communion, a sacramental sign and instrument of communion with God and the unity of the whole human race* (cf. *LG* 1). The vision of the Church developed at Vatican II represented a decisive move away from an excessively institutional view of the Church and toward an ecclesiology grounded in the concept of communion, which, as we shall see in chapter 1, has its roots in the biblical notion of *koinonia*. *Koinonia,* or "communion," as a concept, underlies many different metaphors and images of the Church (e.g., body of Christ, vine and branches). It is an elastic concept oriented toward the idea of participation and relationship. It suggests that the Church is constituted by a set of relationships that possess a particular character. Furthermore, as Walter Kasper has observed, "the communion of the Church is prefigured, made possible, and sustained by the communion of the Trinity."[6] Consequently, one can say with Bruno Forte that the Church is an "icon of the Trinity."[7] That is to say that the life of communion actualized in the life of the Church mediates the life of Trinitarian communion. If this assertion is valid, it follows that *all* ecclesial relationships will be governed by principles drawn from theological reflection on the triune life of God. This means that, as with the Trinitarian relations, all ecclesial relations will be 1) egalitarian yet differentiated and 2) mutual and reciprocal. This has significant implications, needless to say, for the exercise of power and authority in the Church.

3. *The universal Church is realized and manifested in the local Churches.* Vatican II took important if only initial steps away from the highly pyramidical and institutional view of the Church that dominated Catholic theology in varying degrees from the Council of Trent to the mid-twentieth century. No longer would the universal Church be seen as a large corporate structure subdivided into ecclesial units with bishops functioning as little more than vicars of the pope. Vatican II recovered an ancient theology of the local Church that viewed the universal Church not as an institutional superstructure but as the *communio ecclesiarum,* the communion of local Churches. Similarly, it explicitly affirmed that bishops function not as delegates of the pope but as themselves vicars of Christ responsible for pastoring those local Churches.

[6]Walter Kasper, *Theology and Church* (New York: Crossroad, 1989) 152.
[7]Bruno Forte, *L'Église: Icône de la Trinité* (Paris: Médiaspaul, 1985).

I believe that these three insights, developed in varying degrees in the documents of Vatican II, provide the foundation for a theology of teaching authority that is both faithful to our doctrinal tradition and responsive to the unique situation of the Roman Catholic Church as it looks to the beginning of its third millennium of existence.

The focus of this book is on the doctrinal teaching authority of the ecclesiastical magisterium. While it is the responsibility of every baptized believer to pass on the faith, it is the particular task of the bishops, under the headship of the bishop of Rome, to pass on the faith *authoritatively* in *doctrinal* form. This volume will examine the relationship between the broader teaching responsibility of the whole Church and the particular task of authoritatively proclaiming the faith as doctrine which is the special responsibility of the Church's bishops under the headship of the bishop of Rome.

The structure of this book is largely drawn from the traditional threefold distinction between the *subject* of doctrinal teaching, the *object* of doctrinal teaching, and the *exercise* or act of doctrinal teaching. However, the developments of the Second Vatican Council remind us of the importance of a fourth category, namely the *reception* of doctrinal Church teaching by the whole people of God. While this structure offers the advantage of considering the Church's doctrinal teaching authority from several different perspectives, it will be impossible to avoid a certain overlap of material.

Part 1 consists of two chapters that explore the subject of doctrinal teaching authority. Chapter 1 addresses the Church itself, the concrete, historical subject of Church teaching (as Yves Congar reminded us, it is the Holy Spirit who is the *transcendent* subject),[8] giving special consideration to the ecclesiological contributions of Vatican II. In the second chapter attention shifts to the formal subject of doctrinal teaching, the college of bishops, often referred to today as the ecclesiastical or hierarchical magisterium. In this chapter I will consider the ecclesiological opportunities for a renewed ministry of the college of bishops with the pope as its head, in the light of the teaching of Vatican II.

Part 2 is concerned with the *object* of Church teaching, namely, the word of God. Chapter 3 explores the broad outlines of a theology of revelation reflected in Vatican II's Dogmatic Constitution on Divine

[8]For Congar's treatment of the subject of tradition, see *The Meaning of Tradition* (New York: Hawthorn, 1964) 48–78.

Revelation, *Dei verbum*. A consideration of the diverse functions of creedal statements in the early Church will provide a helpful horizon for understanding the functions of dogma/doctrine in the Church today. Chapter 4 attends to the way in which the Roman Catholic tradition acknowledges a real gradation in Church teaching; not all Church doctrine possesses the same degree of authority or is related to the word of God in the same way.

Part 3 addresses the important cluster of issues connected with the manner of exercising doctrinal teaching authority in the Church. Consequently, in chapter 5 I explore the unique shape of ecclesial authority suggested in the life and teaching of Jesus of Nazareth. In that chapter I also explore the way in which the Holy Spirit assists the authoritative teachers of the Church in the performance of their ministry. Chapters 6 and 7 correspond to the traditional distinction between the ordinary and the extraordinary magisteria and consider in some detail the concrete forms of exercise of those different modes of doctrinal teaching.

In Part 4 I devote two chapters, 8 and 9, to those questions connected with ecclesial and personal reception of the Church's doctrinal teaching. Where chapter 1 begins with the whole Church, which is in some sense a teaching Church, chapters 8 and 9 bring us back to the whole Church as a learning Church. How does the whole Church make Church doctrine its own? Finally, in the Conclusion I end with a brief reflection on the future of the Church's teaching ministry.

While I have written this book for a broad readership, some of the material does explore questions of a relatively technical character. I have tried to keep these technical discussions to a minimum while providing adequate documentation for scholars in the notes. Many important questions could not be considered, nor could every view on a given matter be represented. I have also included at the end of each chapter a select bibliography of English language resources for the nonspecialist interested in pursuing a particular topic in more depth.

While it is my hope that this book might contribute in some small way to further scholarly discussion of the subject matter, I have a particular interest in aiding ministry students and the many faithful Catholics in pastoral ministry, ordained and nonordained, who desire a better grasp of the nature of the Church's doctrinal teaching authority. It is only when the Church's pastoral ministers adequately understand the nature and exercise of the Church's doctrinal teaching authority that they themselves can faithfully echo God's word. I believe there is also a real value in all the baptized having a more developed sense of the character of doctrinal teaching and its place in the faith of the believer. A healthy exercise of doctrinal teaching authority will occur only when the whole Church recognizes itself as both a teaching and learning Church. Finally, I am convinced that there can be little further progress toward formal Christian unity until we Roman Catholics have considered more fully a number of internal questions regarding the nature and exercise of doctrinal teaching authority in the Church. I hope that this volume will provide a modest contribution toward the discussion of those questions.

In conclusion, I would like to acknowledge the many who have assisted me in this project. I should begin by thanking Mark Twomey and the editorial and marketing staff at The Liturgical Press for doing everything that was necessary to bring this work to print. To those who read versions of this manuscript I owe a special thanks: Nancy Dallavalle, Sandra Derby, Michael Fahey, Mark Miller, Thomas O'Meara, and Donna Teevan. Mary Hurter provided helpful input at the early stages of this project. My colleagues at the University of St. Thomas School of Theology, Chester Borski, Louis Brusatti, Jack Gallagher, Sandra Magie, Seán Charles Martin, and Michael Prokurat have been most helpful conversation partners. Special thanks must go to the University of St. Thomas for providing supplemental research funds. Sean Horrigan, who worked for one semester as a research assistant, deserves thanks for his generosity and good humor in undertaking some of the less-appealing tasks associated with bringing any manuscript to publication. The contributions of the students who have taken my courses in ecclesiology, revelation and faith and the documents of Vatican II have found their way into these pages as their questions and probings have done much to clarify my own thought. Finally, I owe a special debt of gratitude to my wife, Diana Horadam Gaillardetz, who had to stand by and watch as an originally modest summer project grew over a period of three years to eat up more family time than it ought. That she, with amazingly few exceptions, sustained an attitude of support and patience is a much greater credit to her than this book is to me.

Part One

The Subject of Doctrinal Teaching Authority

1

The Renewal of Ecclesiology
at the Second Vatican Council

Pope John XXIII took much of the Church by surprise when, within months of his papal election, he announced plans for a new ecumenical council. Both ecclesiastical insiders and professional Vatican watchers were largely caught off guard. The crucial question for many concerned the actual agenda of the council. Some immediately saw in a new ecumenical council the opportunity to remake the face of the Church in accord with the more enlightened values of modernity.[1] Others saw it as an opportunity to condemn the evils of communism and dangerous theological developments occurring within the Church.[2] The Pope did not immediately show his hand, but as the council approached he spoke more insistently of the need for an *aggiornamento*, a bringing-up-to-date of the Church. This theme was affirmed in his address at the opening of the council. On that occasion he stated that the purpose of the council was not simply to re-state and defend Church teaching. Rather, the times demanded a new exploration of Church teaching in order to better address the challenges of the age. One must distinguish, he insisted, between the substance of the deposit of faith and its manner of presentation. He also challenged the defensive posture that had gripped the Church for well

[1]This view would be reflected in the optimistic agenda for a council offered by Hans Küng in *The Council and Reunion* (London: Sheed & Ward, 1961).

[2]Cardinal Ottavianni, prefect of the Holy Office and a key player in the events of the council, was noted for pushing this more conservative agenda.

over a century. Where in the past the Church was quick to condemn dangerous or even erroneous positions, now the Church must use "the medicine of mercy." The Church must learn to *persuade* the world of the truth of the gospel.[3]

The significant contributions of Vatican II may be attributed to both this call for an *aggiornamento* and the contributions of many French and German Catholic theologians during the 1940s and 1950s. These theologians were engaged in what came to be known as *ressourcement* theology,[4] a return to biblical and patristic sources as an alternative to the often rigid and ahistorical neo-Scholastic theology that had dominated modern Catholicism. The significant ecclesiological shifts that transpired over the course of the council were the product of these twin tasks of *aggiornamento* and *ressourcement*. These ecclesiological shifts will serve as the starting point for my reconsideration of the nature and exercise of doctrinal teaching authority in the Church. While it will not be possible to consider all the important topics addressed at the council, it will be necessary to review, at least briefly, some of the more important elements in the council's ecclesiological renewal.

The Ecclesiological Renewal of Vatican II

In a sense, all the documents of Vatican II were concerned with ecclesiology. However, in this chapter I will focus on the most important ecclesiological document of the council, the Dogmatic Constitution on the Church, *Lumen gentium*. The preparatory draft on the Church was, like many of the preparatory drafts, reflective of the preconciliar, neo-Scholastic theology generally taught in seminaries. The emphasis was on an institutional structure that presupposed a rigid distinction between clergy and laity and considered the mission of the Church in light of the siege mentality that had become prevalent. The principal mission of the Church was to defend itself against the evils of Protestantism, secularism, communism, and indeed, modernity it-

---

[3]These themes were all developed in his address at the opening of the council. For an English translation of the text of that address see, Floyd Anderson, ed., *Council Daybook, Sessions 1 and 2* (Washington: NCWC, 1965) 25–29.

[4]For Yves Congar's classical articulation of *ressourcement*, the return to sources in the study of the Church, see his *Vrai et fausse réforme dans l'Église* (1950; reprint Paris: Cerf, 1969) 301–17.

self. During the first session of the council Bishop de Smedt of Bruges summarized well the shortcomings of this draft when he accused it of triumphalism, clericalism, and juridicalism.[5] The bishops eventually sent the draft back to committee for a comprehensive rewrite.

The subsequent draft was quite different from the original. It largely eschewed neo-Scholastic language in favor of a description of the Church that drew considerably from both Scripture and the early Church writers. Strikingly absent was the preparatory draft's preoccupation with matters of institutional structure; the second draft presented the Church as an event of divine grace. As the constitution took shape, the bishops abandoned any attempt at producing a rigorously systematic ecclesiological tract of the kind common to the manuals. The council members instead chose to explore a rich plurality of images and concepts in order to highlight key aspects of the life of the Church.

The Trinitarian Foundations of the Church

In the preparatory draft, the first chapter of the constitution on the Church was entitled "The Nature of the Church Militant." In the final form of the constitution the first chapter is entitled "The Church as Mystery." The shift from the category of nature to that of mystery indicates the turn away from a long-standing preconciliar emphasis on law and institutional structure. Four centuries earlier Martin Luther had drawn on Augustine's distinction between the visible and the invisible Church to relativize the former in favor of the latter. After two centuries of corruption and abuse in many of the Church's visible structures, it was not surprising that Luther and the other reformers would downplay the significance of these structures. Ecclesiastical law, sacraments, and offices, Luther contended, could have only a functional value. It is also not surprising that Roman Catholicism would react to this by defending precisely those visible aspects of the Church that were under attack. The great Catholic apologists like Robert Bellarmine insisted that the visible attributes of the Church in its law and hierarchical structure were integral to the Church's true identity. Certainly Bellarmine and others never denied the transcendent

[5]Gérard Philips, "History of the Constitution," in *Commentary on the Documents of Vatican II,* ed. Herbert Vorgrimler (New York: Crossroad, 1989) 1:109.

inner reality of the Church, but their fundamentally defensive posture did, over time, lead to its neglect.

The rejection of the initial preparatory draft on the Church reflected the council members' determination to reassert that the reality of the Church goes beyond its structures and laws to participate in the ineffable presence of God. Drawing on St. Cyprian, the council writes that the Church "appears as 'a people made one by the unity of the Father and the Son and the holy Spirit'" (*LG* 4).[6] The innermost reality of the Church, its participation in the triune life of God, shifts from background to foreground.[7]

As Karl Rahner emphasized in his theology, God's mystery is not a mystery in the sense of a puzzle to be solved; God is not mystery simply because of human limitations. The divine mystery refers to God's being precisely as incomprehensible.[8] To speak of God as absolute mystery is to make a claim not about human finitude but about God. In this context, to describe the Church as mystery is to say that the Church too is ineffable, a spiritual reality that cannot be reduced to its visible structure. The Church's reality must be understood in the light of God's saving work through Christ and in the Spirit. The Church shares in the mystery of God to the extent that it participates in God's saving work on behalf of humankind. Through Christ and by the power of the Spirit we are invited to become adopted sons and daughters of God. This invitation to divine communion is offered through the mediation of the Church. "*Lumen gentium* declares that the primordial elements of the Church are not structures, laws, doctrines, sacraments, or hierarchical ministers, but the mysterious presence at its core of the God who is triune communion and who calls men and women to communion with one another and with God."[9] The Church is not an autonomous entity; rather, its very existence depends on its relationship to God through Christ and in the Spirit.

---

[6]Unless otherwise specified, I will be using the English translation of the conciliar texts taken from Norman Tanner, ed., *Decrees of the Ecumenical Councils* (Washington: Georgetown Univ. Press, 1990).

[7]Walter Kasper, *Theology and Church* (New York: Crossroad, 1989) 151.

[8]See Karl Rahner, "The Concept of Mystery in Catholic Theology," in *Theological Investigations* (Baltimore: Helicon, 1966) 4:36–73.

[9]Michael G. Lawler and Thomas J. Shanahan, *Church: A Spirited Communion* (Collegeville: The Liturgical Press, 1995) 6.

The Church as Sacrament

While the Church is a transcendent, spiritual reality that participates in the divine life of God, it is also a historical reality. It is visible, tangible—it exists in space and time. This visibility was in fact what the ecclesiologists of the Counter Reformation wished to preserve in their description of the Church as a *societas perfecta,* a perfect society. The visible elements of the Church did not possess a mere functional value, they signified or manifested the spiritual reality of the Church. However, the Church as *societas perfecta* also suggested an ahistorical and static perspective. Consequently, the council members chose to avoid this image. Instead, its positive contributions to ecclesiology were integrated into a concept that would play a more significant role at the council, namely the understanding of the Church itself as sacrament.

In the Catholic tradition sacraments are visible signs that effect or mediate God's transforming grace. As such, sacraments possess an outer and an inner dimension.[10] They are finite, visible realities (the outer dimension) that mediate divine mystery (the inner dimension). Insofar as they are sacraments, the outer dimension of the sacraments stand in relation to or serve the inner dimension. The council fathers used the language of sacramental theology to express this joining of the visible/historical and transcendent aspects (or, the outer and inner dimensions) of the Church. "[T]he church is in Christ as a sacrament or instrumental sign of intimate union with God and of the unity of all humanity" (*LG* 1). The long-standing restriction of the term "sacrament" to the seven sacraments of the Church gave way before this claim that the Church itself was inherently sacramental. It is the visible, human dimension of the Church that becomes the efficacious sign of God's saving presence in human history.[11] This understanding highlights the proper relationship between the Church's outer, historical reality—the realm of human activity, institution, structure, office, law, and doctrine—and the inner reality of the Church as a

---

[10]This paragraph draws on the helpful treatment of this topic in Lawler and Shanahan, *Church,* 38–42.

[11]The council members again were influenced by the work of Karl Rahner along with that of Otto Semmelroth. Both theologians had written of the Church as a "primordial sacrament." See Karl Rahner, *The Church and the Sacraments* (New York: Crossroad, 1963); Otto Semmelroth, *Church and Sacrament* (Notre Dame: Fides, 1965).

participation in the mystery of the triune life of God. The visible dimensions of the Church are not functionalized, yet neither are they seen as ultimate realities in themselves. The visible humanity of the Church is not opposed to or even paired with the Church's transcendent inner reality; rather, the humanity of the Church itself *opens out into* that transcendent reality.

The Church as Communion

It is as a sacrament, a visible and effective sign of the divine life offered to humanity, that the Church draws the believer into communion with God. This notion of "communion" played a central role in the ecclesiology of the council. Pope John Paul II, in his apostolic exhortation "On the Laity," affirmed the judgment of the 1985 extraordinary synod when it referred to the notion of communion as the central and fundamental idea of Vatican II.[12] Even when the term "communion" does not itself appear, a careful reading of the principal conciliar documents suggests that the concept was among the most influential at the council.[13] The council retrieved this notion of

[12]*Christifideles laici, Origins* 18 (February 9, 1989) 570 (no. 19).

[13]The council was indebted to several important studies on the biblical and patristic concept of communion: Jérôme Hamer, *The Church Is a Communion* (New York: Sheed & Ward, 1964); Ludwig Hertling, *Communio: Church and Papacy in Early Christianity* (Chicago: Loyola, 1972, originally appeared in German in 1943); Yves Congar, "Notes sur les mots 'confession,' 'église,' et 'communion,'" *Irénikon* 23 (1950) 3–36; idem, "De la communion des églises à une ecclésiologie de l'église universelle," in *L'épiscopat et l'église universelle,* ed. Yves Congar and B.-D. Dupuy (Paris: Cerf, 1960) 227–60; M.-J. Guillou, *Mission et unité. Les exigences de la communion* (Paris: Cerf, 1960). Since the council the literature has grown considerably. For some of the more significant works see Lawler and Shanahan, *Church;* Medard Kehl, *Die Kirche: Eine katholische Ekklesiologie* (Würzburg: Echter Verlag, 1992); Hervé-Marie Legrand, Julio Manzanares, and Antonio García y García, eds., *Iglesias y catolicidad: Actas del Coloquio internacional celebrado en Salamanca, 2–7 abril, 1991,* (Salamanca: Universidad Pontificia, 1992); J.-M. R. Tillard, *Church of Churches: The Ecclesiology of Communion,* trans. R. C. De Peaux (Collegeville: The Liturgical Press [A Michael Glazier Book], 1992 originally, *Église d'Églises: L'ecclésiologie de communion* [Paris: Cerf, 1987]); Robert Kress, *The Church: Communion, Sacrament, Communication* (New York: Paulist, 1985); James H. Provost, ed., *The Church as Communion* (Washington: CLSA, 1984); Antonio Acerbi, *Due ec-*

communion from the biblical and patristic concept of *koinonia*, or *communio*.

In order to appreciate the council's appropriation of the term *koinonia*, it may be helpful to review briefly how the word functioned in the Second Testament and early Church literature. *Koinonia* is usually translated as "fellowship," "communion," or "participation." The biblical authors employed the word *koinonia* primarily to describe humankind's participation in the divine life of God: "God is faithful, and by him you were called to fellowship with his Son, Jesus Christ our Lord" (1 Cor 1:9). "The grace of our Lord Jesus Christ and the love of God and the fellowship of the Holy Spirit be with all of you" (2 Cor 13:13). Indeed, St. Paul's use of the term *koinonia* suggests an incipient Trinitarian theology in which it is through the Son and Spirit that God invites humankind into divine communion.[14] It is in the incarnation, the pinnacle of the economy of salvation, that God makes definitive the divine offer of communion. By our sharing in the death and resurrection of Jesus, celebrated sacramentally in baptism (Rom 6:3f.) and in the Eucharist (1 Cor 10:16-17), we are brought into this divine communion.

---

clesiologie: Ecclesiologia giuridica ed ecclesiologia di communione nella "Lumen Gentium" (Bologna: Dehoniane, 1975); Ferdinand Klostermann, *Gemeinde—Kirche der Zukunft: Thesen, Dienste, Modelle*, 2 vols. (Freiburg: Herder, 1975); E. L. Dóriga, *Jerarquia, infallibilidad, y communiòn intereclesial* (Barcelona: Herder, 1973); Pier Cesare Bori, *Koinonia: l'idea della communione nell' ecclesiologia recente et nel Nuovo Testamento* (Brescia: Paideia, 1972); Joseph Ratzinger, *Das neue Volk Gottes: Entwürfe zur Ekklesiologie* (Düsseldorf: Patmos, 1969).

[14]Michael Fahey has noted that for all the attention that has been paid to the redemption and expiation motifs in St. Paul's soteriology, one should not overlook the fact that the Eastern tradition's doctrine of *theosis*, or divinization, has its origins in Paul as well. This tradition would be developed in Irenaeus, Athanasius, Gregory of Nazianzus, Gregory of Nyssa, and Maximos the Confessor. Michael Fahey, "Ecclesial Community as Communion," in *The Church as Communion*, 12. For more on Eastern soteriology and theological anthropology see Panayiotis Nellas, *Deification in Christ: The Nature of the Human Person* (Crestwood: St. Vladimir's Seminary Press, 1987); Constantine N. Tsirpanlis, *Introduction to Eastern Patristic Thought and Orthodox Theology* (Collegeville: The Liturgical Press [A Michael Glazier Book], 1991) 61–80.

While Paul uses the word *koinonia* to describe the believer's participation in the life of God, this usage does not support any privatized understanding of communion with God. This is evident in Paul's understanding of the Church as the body of Christ. One had fellowship with God through Jesus precisely in and through fellowship in the Christian community. The term *koinonia* expressed the fundamental connection between participation in the life of God and participation in Christian community. Paul's whole ecclesiology presupposed a fundamentally organic view of the Church that suggested not just complementarity and diversity within the Church but coexistence.[15] For Paul, life in Christ meant life in the body of Christ, the Church. The Church was no mere aggregate of individuals. Rather, by baptism into the Christian community one participates in a new reality, one is a new creation. Individual believers do not *make* a Church, initiation into the Church through faith and baptism *makes* the believers; it introduces them into a new mode of existence. This vision of the Church is further evident in Paul's understanding of charisms. For Paul charisms were not spiritual gifts given to an individual but gifts manifested in an individual believer *for the sake of* the Church (1 Cor 14:12).

Koinonia also appears in the Acts of the Apostles where it expresses the communion or fellowship of believers (Acts 2:42), and again, there is a union of the vertical and horizontal dimensions of communion. In Acts the fundamental ecclesial event is Pentecost, an event that expresses the central role of the Holy Spirit in drawing all believers into spiritual communion. J.-M. R. Tillard sees Pentecost as comprised of three constitutive elements: the animating presence of the Holy Spirit; the apostolic witness centered on the Lord Jesus; and the communion of the human multitude, whose very diversity in the power of the Spirit manifests a unity of faith.[16] Tillard observes that while the term *ekklesia* is never used in Luke's Gospel, it will appear in the Acts of the Apostles only after Pentecost, and then sixteen times. We are drawn into communion by the Spirit and are thereby constituted as Church. Luke's appreciation for the pneumatological conditioning of the Church is vital. It is the Spirit that transforms a

---

[15]Jerome Murphy-O'Connor, "Eucharist and Community in I Corinthians," in *Living Bread, Saving Cup,* ed. Kevin Seasoltz (Collegeville: The Liturgical Press, 1982) 4.

[16]J.-M. R. Tillard, *Church of Churches,* 8.

collective of individuals into a living communion of believers. Without this pneumatological dimension there is a danger of the concept of communion degenerating to secular conceptions that ignore the way the believer is reconfigured in his communion with other believers and with God.

From a rather different biblical perspective we find in the Johannine tradition a similar appreciation for the simultaneity of communion with God and communion with one another. "[W]hat we have seen and heard/ we proclaim now to you,/ so that you too may have fellowship with us;/ for our fellowship is with the Father/ and with his Son, Jesus Christ" (1 John 1:3-4). For the author of the first Johannine epistle there is a profound unity between love of God and love for one another. "God is love, and whoever remains in love remains in God and God in him. . . . If anyone says, 'I love God,' but hates his brother, he is a liar; for whoever does not love a brother whom he has seen cannot love God whom he has not seen" (1 John 4:16, 20). By recognizing the inseparability of the life of love and communion with God, the Johannine tradition, in its own way, affirms the unity of the so-called vertical and horizontal dimensions of communion. Human communion is not simply a moral imperative flowing out of divine communion, it is integral to it.[17]

In summary, the Second Testament understandings of communion are grounded in convictions regarding the gracious God who has come to us in Christ and in the Spirit as revealed in the economy *(oikonomia)* of salvation. The communion that we are offered is a gift of God. It is grace, but it is not a private grace; it is a gift realized and nourished in human communion and preeminently in the communion of believers.

Theologians from the East and West have developed from these biblical texts an actual "ontology of communion."[18] Just as communion

---

[17]Jérôme Hamer, *The Church Is a Communion,* 159–64. More recently, in an instruction to the bishops on the ecclesiological notion of communion, the CDF wrote: "If the concept of communion, which is not a univocal one, is to serve as a key to ecclesiology, it has to be understood within the teaching of the Bible and the patristic tradition, in which communion always involves a double dimension: the vertical . . . and the horizontal." "Some Aspects of the Church Understood as Communion," *Origins* 22 (June 25, 1922) 108.

[18]For an example from Greek Orthodoxy, see John Zizioulas, *Being as Communion* (Crestwood: St. Vladimir's Seminary Press, 1985). For a recent attempt to explore an ontology of communion from a Roman Catholic perspective,

is an apt expression of the very being of God as life-giving personal relationality, so communion also names the proper modality of all authentic human existence. We are made for communion with God, and no earthly reality in and of itself will satisfy. But this spiritual communion with God does not constitute an escape from our daily world. Rather, we come to this communion with God in large part through our embrace of others. Every authentic act of love is an event of communion, and as such it is at the same time an event of grace.[19] It is this life of communion that the Church sacramentalizes. In the Church this life of communion, to which all humanity is called, is celebrated in word and sacrament. The Church both points to this life of communion and actually effects it through the realization of its life and mission.

The council incorporated this biblical view of communion in the first chapter of *Lumen gentium*. Attending to the vertical dimension, the council affirms that it is through the mediation of Christ's Church, by the power of the Spirit, that we are drawn into the triune life of God. By the power of the Holy Spirit, God the Father "restores life to human beings who were dead through sin. . . . The Spirit . . . prays in them and bears witness to their adoption as children. . . . Through the power of the gospel he [the Spirit] rejuvenates the church, continually renewing it and leading it to perfect union with its spouse" (*LG* 4). In that same article we find attention to the horizontal dimension: "He [the Spirit] leads the Church into all truth and he makes it one in fellowship and ministry *[in communione et ministratione unificat]*." In the Church believers experience, most profoundly, the life of communion into which all humanity is invited.

It is as a union of the vertical and horizontal dimensions that we can understand ecclesial communion as a sacrament of our salvation:

> Consequently, this messianic people, although it does not include everybody, and more than once may appear as a tiny flock, nevertheless it constitutes for the whole human race a most firm seed of unity, hope and salvation. It has been set up by Christ as a communion of

---

see Catherine Mowry LaCugna, *God for Us: The Trinity and Christian Life* (San Francisco: HarperCollins, 1991).

[19]See Karl Rahner, "Reflections on the Unity of Love of Neighbour and the Love of God," in *Theological Investigations* (New York: Crossroad, 1982) 6:231–52.

life, love and truth; by him too it is taken up as the instrument of salvation for all, and sent as a mission to the whole world as the light of the world and the salt of the earth (*LG* 9).

This ecclesial communion is further developed in the council's recovery of the Eucharistic foundations of the Church. The celebration of the Eucharist effects a communion among those believers gathered at each Eucharistic celebration as all are united in the breaking of the bread. Echoing St. Paul (cf. 1 Cor 10:16-7), the council writes that "through the sacrament of the eucharistic bread, there is represented and produced the unity of the faithful, who make up one body in Christ" (*LG* 3). This is reaffirmed in article 11: "Indeed, refreshed as they are by the body of Christ in the sacred gathering, they show forth in a concrete way the unity of the people of God, which in this most noble sacrament is both suitably symbolized and wonderfully brought about." Finally, the centrality of the Eucharist in the life of the local Church is evident in article 26, which states that the faithful gathered together in the Eucharist under the ministry of the bishop are

> the new people called by God in the Holy Spirit and with full conviction. . . . In these [local Churches] the faithful are gathered together by the preaching of the gospel of Christ, and the mystery of the Lord's Supper is celebrated "so that the whole fellowship is joined together through the flesh and blood of the Lord's body." In any community of the altar, under the sacred ministry of the bishop, there is made manifest the symbol of that charity and "unity of the mystical body without which there can be no salvation." In these communities . . . Christ is present by whose power the one, holy, catholic and apostolic church is gathered together. For "participation in the body and blood of Christ has no other effect than to make us pass over into what we are consuming."

In the Eucharistic *synaxis* the Christian community proclaims in word and celebrates in ritual and symbol its most profound reality, its truest identity as a people whose lives are being conformed to that of Christ by the celebration of the paschal mystery.

However, the nature of the Church as communion is not limited to the *communio* that exists among the members of a particular Eucharistic community. Soon after the period of the Second Testament the notion of communion was extended to describe that spiritual bond that existed among all local Eucharistic communities. There was a common conviction that all Eucharistic communities abided together

in shared ecclesial communion.[20] For the early Church the sacrament of the Eucharist brought about not only the communion of those gathered at each altar but the communion of all local Churches. This followed from the emerging Eucharistic theology of the time. Wherever the Eucharist was celebrated the body of Christ was actualized in a sacramental fashion. But the body of Christ is one and cannot be fragmented. Therefore one must be able to speak of a unity, a communion, existing among all Eucharistic communities.[21] The one Church, Christ's body, is actualized wherever believers gather for the breaking of the bread. Patrick Burns succinctly captures this Eucharistic perspective of the Church, which had fully developed by the third century:

> The basic unity of the church in the third century was the local eucharistic congregation, united under one bishop and the college of presbyters and college of deacons who assisted him in his pastoral ministry. Such local churches were not substations of the church universal or branch offices of a world-wide organization. Rather the local Christian community, united in faith in the saving word and in eucharistic fellowship in the body of the Lord, was the church of God for its locality, the effective presence of the whole Christ in its concrete life and worship. Yet precisely the principle of unity of this local church, the saving presence of Christ in word and sacrament, made it aware of its essential relationship to the other local Christian communities throughout the world (where the same Lord and the same Spirit

---

[20] Cf. Ludwig Hertling, *Communio: Church and Papacy in Early Christianity;* Werner Elert, *Eucharist and Church Fellowship in the First Four Centuries* (St. Louis: Concordia, 1966); Kenneth Hein, *Eucharist and Excommunication: A Study in Early Christian Doctrine and Discipline* (Frankfurt: Lang, 1975).

[21] This Eucharistic theology is particularly profound in the Orthodox tradition. See Nicholas Afanassieff, "The Church Which Presides in Love," in *The Primacy of Peter,* ed. John Meyendorff (Crestwood: St. Vladimir's Seminary Press, 1992) 91–144; idem, "Una Sancta," *Irénikon* 36 (1963) 436–75. For a contemporary treatment of Eucharistic ecclesiology from an Orthodox perspective see Zizioulas, *Being as Communion.* Perhaps the most influential Eucharistic ecclesiology in the West is that of the French Jesuit Henri de Lubac. Cf. Henri de Lubac, *Les églises particulières dans l'Église universelle* (Paris: Aubier-Montaigne, 1971). For a helpful comparison of Zizioulas' Eucharistic ecclesiology with that of de Lubac, see Paul McPartlan, *The Eucharist Makes the Church: Henri de Lubac and John Zizioulas in Dialogue* (Edinburgh: T. & T. Clark, 1993).

brought about the same ecclesial reality). The local church, without ceasing to be fully church, existed only in a world-wide communion of churches which constituted the church universal.[22]

Vatican II retrieved this extended understanding of ecclesial communion in its treatment of the ministry of the bishop and the relationship between the local Churches and the universal Church: "The individual bishops . . . are the visible principle and foundation of unity in their own particular churches, formed in the likeness of the universal church; *in and from these particular churches there exists the one unique catholic church"* (*LG* 23, my emphasis). And again in the Decree on the Pastoral Office of Bishops in the Church, *Christus Dominus,* we find this passage:

> A diocese is a section of the people of God whose pastoral care is entrusted to a bishop in cooperation with his priests. Thus, in conjunction with their pastor and gathered by him into one flock in the Holy Spirit through the gospel and the eucharist, they constitute a particular church. *In this particular church the one, holy, catholic and apostolic church of Christ is truly present and at work* (*CD* 11, my emphasis).

These texts reflect a move away from that preconciliar universalist ecclesiology that viewed the diocese as little more than an administrative subset of the universal Church. Vatican II represented an at least tentative return to an ecclesiology in which the one universal Church is manifested in the communion of local Churches.[23] As the famous Protestant ecumenist Jean Jacques von Allmen put it, the local Church "is wholly Church, but it is not the whole Church."[24]

---

[22]Patrick Burns, "Communion, Councils, and Collegiality: Some Catholic Reflections," in *Papal Primacy and the Universal Church,* ed. Paul C. Empie and T. Austin Murphy (Minneapolis: Augsburg, 1974) 152.

[23]I say tentative because the council was not always consistent in this matter. Often texts that supported a *communio* ecclesiology were simply juxtaposed with texts that continued a more universalist ecclesiology. For more on this juxtaposition of two ecclesiologies see Antonio Acerbi, *Due ecclesiologie: Ecclesiologia giuridica ed ecclesiologia di communione nella "Lumen Gentium";* Herve-M. Legrand, "The Revaluation of Local Churches: Some Theological Implications," *Concilium* 74 (1972) 53–64.

[24]Jean Jacques von Allmen, "L'Église locale parmi les autres églises locales," *Irénikon* 43 (1970) 512.

In this relationship between the universal and the local it should be apparent that neither can be given priority over the other.[25] To grant the priority of the local Church would be to suggest that the universal Church is little more than a confederation of autonomous local Churches. To give priority to the universal Church is to risk reverting

[25]A theology of communion cannot be properly Trinitarian if it gives priority to either the universal or the local; this would violate the perichoretic relationship of the particular Churches as the manifestation of the universal Church. This is the principal shortcoming of the CDF instruction "Some Aspects of the Church Understood as Communion." In no. 9 the instruction quotes John Paul II from his September 16, 1987, address to the American bishops when he asserts, rightly, that "the universal cannot be conceived as the sum of the particular churches, or as a federation of particular churches." However, the instruction then goes on to a more problematic claim, "It [the universal Church] is not the result of the communion of the churches, but in its essential mystery it is a reality ontologically and temporally prior to every individual particular church." It then employs the mother-daughter image to describe the relationship of universal to particular. This application of the parental analogy is no less open to misunderstanding than was the father-son analogy in the Trinitarian battles with the followers of Arius and Eunomius in the fourth and fifth centuries. Both Arius and Eunomius interpreted the father-son analogy such that the procession of the Son was a creation in time. This flawed view continues as the instruction justifies this priority by characterizing the birth of the Church at Pentecost as the birth of the universal Church. One could easily claim, as did a recent ecumenical document, that the gathering at Pentecost was also the manifestation of a particular Church inasmuch as it was a concrete gathering of believers in one place. See *The Church: Local and Universal* (Geneva: WCC, 1990) no. 22. The CDF makes one final questionable move when it joins the principle articulated in *LG* 26 that the universal Church is formed in and out of the Churches (*ecclesia in et ex ecclesiis*) with a postconciliar principle first enunciated by John Paul II, namely that the Churches are also formed in and out of the universal Church. "Address to the Roman Curia," *AAS* 83 (1981) 745–47.

The claim that either the universal or the local Church possesses a temporal or ontological priority can suggest an understanding of *communion* as a mere accidental quality of the Church rather than as a concept reflective of a fundamentally relational or communal ontology. For important ecumenical responses to this document from theologians representing the Orthodox, Methodist, Reformed, and Anglican traditions see *Catholic International* 3 (September 1992). For an appraisal by a Roman Catholic theologian see Walter Kasper, "The Church as Communio," *New Blackfriars* 74 (May 1993) 232–45.

to a preconciliar ecclesiology that conceives of the Church as an international corporation subdivided into ecclesial departments or "branch offices." Only by accepting the radically relational character of the one Church understood as a communion of Churches can these two extremes be avoided. This view of the relationship between the local Churches and the universal Church will provide the indispensable foundation for a theology of the episcopate and papal primacy to be developed in the next chapter.

The Church as the Body of Christ and People of God

The council attempted to develop further the Trinitarian and Eucharistic foundations of the Church in *Lumen gentium* by juxtaposing two biblical images, the body of Christ and the people of God. Pope Pius XII had already contributed to the renewal of Catholic ecclesiology by reappropriating the biblical image of the Church as the body of Christ in his encyclical *Mystici corporis*.[26] Not surprisingly, the council continued to make use of this biblical image. The metaphor of the body of Christ aptly expresses the organic dimension of the Church's life, its close relationship to the Eucharist, and its origins in Christ. As Christ's body, the Church exists in dependence on Christ.

However, many Protestant theologians have raised concerns regarding both the notion of Church as sacrament and the use of the metaphor, body of Christ.[27] The close unity with Christ that this image suggests makes it difficult, they contend, to take seriously the

---

[26]One should note that the application of the biblical metaphor, the body of Christ, to the Church has a long and complicated history. Joseph Ratzinger has identified three distinct historical applications of the metaphor: (1) the biblical-patristic understanding of the Church as body of Christ, which stresses the Eucharistic foundations of the Church, (2) the medieval understanding, which was more corporatist in its conception; and (3) the modern usage in the nineteenth and twentieth centuries, which emphasizes the more organic and mystical connotations of the metaphor. Joseph Ratzinger, *Das neue Volk Gottes,* 99.

[27]These concerns are reflected in the writings of Wolfhart Pannenberg, *Thesen zur Theologie der Kirche* (Munich: Claudius Verlag, 1970); Eberhard Jüngel, "Die Kirche als Sakrament," *Zeitschrift für Theologie und Kirche* 80 (1983) 432–57; Ulrich Kühn, *Sakramente* (Gütersloh: Mohn, 1985). A good summary of the various positions on this more sacramental view of the Church can be found in Wolfgang Beinert, *Die Sakramentalität der Kirche und Sakrament* (Zürich: Benziger, 1980) 13–66.

human and sinful dimensions of the Church. This conception of the Church is in danger of usurping the divine initiative in the work of salvation. The unity of Christ and Church must not obscure the important differences between the two. The Church is not just a sacrament of grace, it is also a recipient of grace, a community of sinners that always stands in response to God's divine initiative. The Church is not only the body of Christ, it is also the bride of Christ, radically dependent on its bridegroom. The Reformed tradition's pneumatological emphases lead it to look with suspicion on an ecclesiological image that appears to give little place to the ongoing work of the Spirit in the Church. Beyond these Protestant concerns it must be noted that the Christological foundation of this view of the Church also downplays any anticipation of the Church in the history of the people of Israel. These concerns may shed some light on the council's decision to augment this image of the Church with another biblical image, the Church as the "people of God."

The image of the people of God is rich in biblical resonances, suggesting divine election and consecration. Just as the people of Israel were God's chosen people, so the Christian community of believers is constituted not merely as an aggregate of individuals but as *a people* consecrated to God through the saving work of Christ. This image effectively highlights the historical journey of God's people, Jew and Gentile, in covenantal relationship with God. As God's people, we are by that very fact a pilgrim people. At the close of the first chapter of *Lumen gentium,* the council states:

> While Christ "holy, blameless, unstained" knew no sin, and came only to expiate the sins of the people, the church, containing sinners in its own bosom, is at one and the same time holy and always in need of purification and it pursues unceasingly penance and renewal (*LG* 8).

We are a people *on the way* who have the promise of God's presence and guidance but who still await the consummation of God's plan. In the seventh chapter of *Lumen gentium* the council develops this more eschatological vision of the Church:

> The church to which we are all called in Christ Jesus and in which through the grace of God we attain sanctity, will reach its completion only in the glory of heaven, when the time for the restoration of all things will come and along with the human race the whole universe, which is intimately united to humanity and through it attains its goal,

will be established perfectly in Christ. . . . Already, therefore, the end of the ages has reached us and the renewal of the world has been irrevocably constituted and is being anticipated in this world in a real sense: for already on earth the church is adorned with true though imperfect holiness. However, until the arrival of the new heavens and the new earth in which justice dwells, the pilgrim church in its sacraments and institutions, which belong to this age, carries the figure of this world which is passing and it dwells among creatures who groan and till now are in the pains of childbirth and await the revelation of the children of God (*LG* 48).

This emphasis on the eschatological character of the Church had been notably absent in Roman Catholic ecclesiology before Vatican II. It is, after all, difficult to maintain that the Church is a perfect society and then say that it is "always in need of purification"!

Beyond this eschatological dimension, the "people of God" metaphor also stresses the commonality of the baptized, clergy and lay. Through baptism we are all constituted as God's people. One of the more significant changes to take place in the movement from the second to the third draft of the schema on the Church concerned the division and ordering of chapters. In the second draft of the constitution there was a single chapter on the people of God and the laity. Cardinal Leo Suenens proposed dividing this into two chapters. He then suggested placing the separate chapter on the people of God in front of the respective chapters on the hierarchy and the laity. This rearrangement of chapters suggested that our commonalities as the community of the baptized are more fundamental than that which distinguishes us by ordination. The council would insist, for example, that both the laity and the clergy participate, each in their proper way, in the priestly, prophetic, and kingly offices of Christ. The Church still possesses an institutional structure, but this structure, in the texts of Vatican II, is no longer conceived strictly as a descending ladder of ecclesiastical ranks and states. There is a greater appreciation for diversity in the various roles and ministries exercised within the one Church.

By complementing the image of the Church as the body of Christ with the images of the Church as people of God and pilgrim people, the council was able to affirm both the historical and transcendent dimensions of the Church. It was able to insist that Jesus Christ continues to be sacramentally present to his people through the mediation of the Church, which is Christ's body. At the same time the council recognized that Christ's Church was a human Church, ever in need of renewal, existing in history, and still awaiting its eschatological fulfillment.

The Church as the Temple of the Holy Spirit

One of the welcome emphases of the first chapter of *Lumen gentium* was the stress on the role of the Holy Spirit. For much of the history of Western ecclesiology, the role of the Holy Spirit has been eclipsed by a certain Christo-monism, a tendency to focus exclusively on the saving work of Christ. This has long been the objection of Orthodox theologians[28] and it was made time and again by French Dominican ecclesiologist Yves Congar.[29] This Christo-monism locates the origin of the Church in the Last Supper where, it was commonly held, Christ instituted the sacraments of Eucharist and holy orders. In this view the Church was instituted whole and entire at the Last Supper. The difficulty with this approach lies in the nature of institution. As the Orthodox theologian John Zizioulas has noted, "institution is something presented to us as a fact, more or less a *fait accompli*."[30] The result is a static conception of the Church that has little place for change or development. When one considers not only the Church's institution by Christ but its constitution by the Spirit, there can be a greater appreciation for the Church's historicity. "Constitution is something that involves us in its very being, something we accept freely, because we take part in its very emergence."[31] In the Spirit's constitution of the Church we must admit an ongoing, dynamic presence of the Spirit, continuing to mold and shape the Church through the exercise of human freedom. The Church is seen not only as a stable institution but as a dynamic entity open to the future.

[28]See Nikos Nissiotis, "The Main Ecclesiological Problem of the Second Vatican Council," *Journal of Ecumenical Studies* 2 (Winter 1965) 31–62; idem, "Pneumatological Christology as a Presupposition of Ecclesiology," in *Oecumenica: An Annual Symposium of Ecumenical Research 1967* (Minneapolis: Augsburg, 1967) 235–52; John D. Zizioulas, "The Pneumatological Dimensions of the Church," *Communio* 1 (1974) 142–58; Dumitru Staniloe, *Theology and the Church* (Crestwood: St. Vladimir's Seminary Press, 1984).

[29]Yves Congar, "Pneumatologie ou 'Christomonisme' dans la traditione latine," in *Ecclesia a Spiritu Sancto edocta,* festschrift for Gérard Philips (Louvain: Duculot, 1970) 41–63.

[30]Zizioulas, *Being as Communion,* 140.

[31]Ibid.

The documents of Vatican II reflect a greater appreciation for this pneumatological approach:

> The Spirit dwells in the Church and in the hearts of the faithful as in a temple, and he prays in them and bears witness to their adoption as children. He leads the church into all truth, and he makes it one in fellowship and ministry, instructing and directing it through a diversity of gifts both hierarchical and charismatic, and he adorns it with his fruits. (*LG* 4).

Viewing the Church as the temple of the Holy Spirit reminds us that the life of the Church is not merely the result of human accomplishment; the Church is a social organization, but it is not only a social organization. The life of the Church is a spiritual gift. It is the Spirit that binds together the people of God.

This pneumatological approach to the Church also represented a rejection of the centuries-old opposition between charism and office in which Protestants stressed the primacy of charism and Catholics the primacy of office. The council acknowledged that Church office cannot exist unless it is animated by the Holy Spirit and charisms cannot survive unless they submit to an ordering that seeks the good of the whole Church. Without dissolving the distinction between hierarchic and charismatic gifts, the flourishing of lay ministries in the years since the council suggests a movement away from the ministry of the few to the ministry of the many. The community of believers is characterized by a multiplicity of relationships, each contributing to the constitution of the Church in that place.

Later, in article 12, *Lumen gentium* again affirms the role of the Holy Spirit in apportioning spiritual gifts "among the faithful of every rank" in order to render all of the faithful "fit and ready to undertake the various tasks and offices which help the renewal and the building up of the church." In the Decree on the Apostolate of the Laity the council explicitly drew attention to this plurality of ministries:

> In the church there is diversity in ministry but unity in mission. The office and power of teaching in the name of Christ, of sanctifying and ruling, were conferred by him on the apostles and their successors. Laypeople, sharing in the priestly, prophetic and kingly offices of Christ, play their part in the mission of the whole people of God in the church and in the world. . . . To help in the exercise of this apostolate, the Holy Spirit, who works the sanctification of God's people through ministry and sacrament, also gives special gifts to the faithful,

"apportioning to each one individually as he wills." Thus, "as all use whatever gifts they have received in service to one another," they may be "good stewards dispensing the grace of God in its varied forms," towards the building up of the whole body in love. Through receiving these gifts of grace, however unspectacular, everyone of the faithful has the right and duty to exercise them in the church and in the world for the good of humanity and for the building up of the church. They do this in the freedom of the Spirit who "blows where he wills" and, at the same time, in communion with the fellowship in Christ, especially with his pastors, whose part it is to judge about their true nature and ordered use, not indeed so as to extinguish the Spirit but in order to test everything and to hold on to what is good (*AA* 2, 3).

This passage situates ordained ministry not above but within the Christian community. The ministry of the ordained does not exhaust the activity of the Church. Ordained ministry is a ministry of leadership, a ministry of order. The ordained minister is responsible for the discernment and coordination of the charisms and ministries of all the baptized. Yet by baptism and confirmation/chrismation all the faithful are empowered by the Spirit to participate in the life and ministry of the Church.

The Church and the Reign of God

The biblical metaphor "the reign of God," so important to understanding the preaching and ministry of Jesus Christ, was included in the council's treatment of the Church at the request of several Latin American bishops. It had become common in Catholic theology over the past century to identify the reign of God with the Church. Vatican II, both in *Lumen gentium* and in the Pastoral Constitution on the Church in the Modern World, *Gaudium et spes*, moved away from equating these two realities. Important passages in these documents suggested instead that the reign of God was a reality that transcended the boundaries of the Church. Indeed, in a basic sense, the Church was to be a servant of God's reign. In *Lumen gentium* the council writes:

When, therefore, the church . . . receives the mission of announcing the kingdom of Christ and of God and of inaugurating it among all peoples, it has formed the seed and the beginning of the kingdom on earth. Meanwhile as it gradually grows, it aspires after the completion of the kingdom, and hopes and desires with all its strength to be joined with its king in glory. (*LG* 5).

We noted earlier that chapter 1 of *Lumen gentium* described the Church as a sacrament of communion with God and the unity of humankind. In *Gaudium et spes* this notion of the Church as a sacrament is employed once again, but here that which is manifested sacramentally is the kingdom of God, "the mystery of God's love for humanity":

> While it helps the world and receives much from the world, the church has only one goal, namely the coming of God's kingdom and the accomplishment of salvation for the whole human race. Whatever good God's people can contribute to the human family, in the period of its earthly pilgrimage, derives from the church's being "the universal sacrament of salvation," which shows forth and at the same time brings into effect the mystery of God's love for humanity (*GS* 45).

The relationship between the Church and the reign of God suggested in the council documents reflects the council's more positive view of the relationship between Church and world. Since Church and the reign of God were not coterminus, hints of that reign could be found outside of the Church. And while the reign of God could certainly not be equated with earthly progress, with the accomplishments of humankind, neither were the two unrelated (cf. *GS* 39). It is part of the mission of the Church to illuminate those anticipations of God's reign that occur daily in our world.

The Contributions of Vatican II Toward an Understanding of Authority in the Church

This brief review of some of the ecclesiological themes developed at the council leads us to an appreciation of the range and depth of reflection on the Church engaged in by the council members. But what are the implications of the council's ecclesiological vision for a theology of doctrinal teaching authority?

The Authority of the Church Depends on the Authority of God

When the Church teaches, it does not do so because it believes itself to be a body of extraordinarily wise sages whose skills of reasoning and vast knowledge deserve respect. The Church teaches because it believes that the message it proclaims is not its own; it is the word of God. The authority of the Church is dependent on the authority of God's word. In recalling the divine origins of its message the Church can more fearlessly proclaim the good news of Jesus Christ, "in and out of season." Vatican II's recovery of the Church's Trinitarian and sacramental foundations challenges today's Church to be ever mindful of its transcendent ground. There is always the danger of forgetting this relationship of dependence on God. The authority the Church exercises is not its own but depends on the Church's openness to the Spirit of God alive in its midst. As a pilgrim people, the Church is not perfect; it can err apart from its infallible teaching, as the council admitted in its Decree on Ecumenism. The authority the Church possesses is then not a self-validating authority but an authority conditioned by the Church's openness to God's Spirit.

Ecclesial Authority Is Exercised within and not above the Church

Many of the ecclesiological developments of Vatican II involved moving away from a pyramidical view in which the Church is made up of a descending ladder of ecclesiastical ranks to one in which the fundamental Christian identity is grounded in baptism. The pyramidical and institutional conceptions of the Church that became dominant between Trent and Vatican II were virtually absent in both the canonical and noncanonical texts of the first three centuries and, for the most part, throughout the whole first millennium. Of course the transition from an ecclesiology of communion to a more pyramidical and juridical ecclesiology did not occur overnight. This view of the Church has its own complicated history, a review of which would take us beyond the scope of this work. Such a history, however, would have to include consideration of some of the following factors: (1) the gradual assimilation of the Greco-Roman world's class structure configured around a plurality of social and political orders (e.g., the *ordo senatorius*); (2) the increasing influence of Neoplatonism on Christian thought forms, which viewed the cosmos as a descending hierarchy of being, culminating in the tremendously influential sixth-century writings of Pseudo-Dionysius; (3) medieval theologians' application of the ontological hierarchy of Pseudo-Dionysius to the

Church, leading to what Congar called a "hierocratic" ecclesiology;[32] (4) the legitimization of the hierarchical structure of the Church by baroque Catholic apologists like Bellarmine against the attacks of the reformers; (5) the transformation of the laity from subjects who actively participate in the "traditioning" process of the Church to passive objects who docilely receive God's word from the clergy; (6) the assimilation of a monarchical view of civil governance into the Church's theology of the papacy in the nineteenth century.

Vatican II did much to dismantle this pyramidical vision of the Church. First, it affirmed that all share *by baptism* in the priestly, prophetic, and kingly offices of Christ. Second, it considered the Church as the people of God before considering its institutional structure, incorporating the ecclesiological principle that we begin our consideration of the Church with what we share by baptism before considering our different roles in the life of the Church. Third, it acknowledged a diversity of "hierarchical and charismatic gifts" to be exercised by the whole people of God. And fourth, it portrayed priests and bishops not as rulers who exercise authority over the Church but as pastoral leaders who gather their people around the table of the Lord.

Yet in many ways the postconciliar Church has yet to integrate this theme fully into its self-understanding and practice. The following passage from an encyclical of Pope Pius X continues to reflect the attitude of some in the Church today:

> It follows that the Church is essentially an unequal society, that is, a society comprising two categories of persons, the Pastors and the flock, those who occupy a rank in the different degrees of the hierarchy and the multitude of the faithful. So distinct are these categories that with the pastoral body only rests the necessary right and authority for promoting the end of the society and directing all its members towards that end; the one duty of the multitude is to allow themselves to be led, and, like a docile flock, to follow the Pastors.[33]

While few today would speak of the Church as an "unequal society," many ecclesiastical structures, Church policies, significant elements

---

[32]Yves Congar, *L'Église de Saint Augustin à l'époque moderne* (Paris: Cerf, 1970) 226ff. Congar's magisterial study explores in considerable detail virtually all of the factors that can only be listed in this section.

[33]Pius X, *Vehementor nos*, no. 8. The English translation is from *The Papal Encyclicals*, ed. Claudia Carlen (New York: McGrath, 1981) 3:47–48.

of the current Code of Canon Law, and even our continued usage of the language of "laity" and "clergy" often perpetuate this essentially preconciliar view of the Church as a society consisting of two different ranks of Christians. For some ordination is seen less as a specification of our baptismal ordination within the Christian community than a promotion to a new ecclesiastical rank. If we are to see a real renewal in the Church's exercise of its doctrinal teaching authority, it will demand more than a new theological vision; it will demand the implementation of this vision in the Church's policies and structures.

An ecclesiology of communion views the Church as a fundamentally relational reality. The structures and concrete exercise of ecclesial authority must reflect this life of communion. An authority exercised *within* the Church is an authority that acknowledges the dignity, the rights, and the responsibilities of every member of the Church. It is an authority that recognizes that God's Spirit communicates to the Church not only through ecclesiastical office but through the lives of all believers. One would expect that such an authority would then be inclusive, consultative, and responsive in its manner of exercise.

There Are Different Kinds of Authority Exercised within the Church

After the Protestant Reformation there was a certain polarization of Protestant and Catholic conceptions of ecclesial authority. Protestantism tended to stress the charismatic foundations of authority, while Catholicism emphasized the institutional offices of authority. Ironically, while the ecumenical movement has done much to moderate this polarization, one can find evidence of it continuing within Roman Catholicism itself. In the years immediately following Vatican II there were some theological voices arguing for the "democratization" of the Church in ways that now seem somewhat naive and uncritical.[34] Others have clung to the identification of Church authority with hierarchical office.[35] At Vatican II, however, one can recognize the begin-

[34]One might mention, for example, Patrick Granfield's early work, *Ecclesial Cybernetics: A Study of Democracy in the Church* (New York: Macmillan, 1973).

[35]See, for example, James Hitchcock, *Catholicism and Modernity: Confrontation or Capitulation?* (New York: Seabury, 1979); George Kelly, *The Battle for the American Church* (Garden City: Doubleday, 1979).

nings of a way beyond this polemical impasse. The council clearly reaffirmed the legitimacy of the episcopate and the papacy as essential structures of ecclesial authority. At the same time it recognized that ecclesiastical office and charism need not be in opposition. Many different gifts, "both charismatic and hierarchical," may be exercised cooperatively for the good of the Church. The recovery of a pneumatological vision of the Church was crucial for ecclesial renewal as it allows us to see Church office and charism as complementary manifestations of the work of the one Spirit animating the Church.

Although it did not consider the nature of ecclesial authority in a systematic fashion, Vatican II seemed to recognize different kinds of authority exercised within the Church. Avery Dulles has referred to this as a "pluralistic" model of authority.[36] This is reflected in many of the ecclesial images and metaphors employed by the council—people of God, body of Christ, temple of the Holy Spirit—all of which stressed the organic, dynamic, and interactive aspects of the Church. The council continued to affirm the authority of the Bible as a privileged medium of God's word. It also reasserted the particular authority of the magisterium to proclaim Church teaching normatively in service of that word. At the same time, however, the council acknowledged the authority of the whole Church as a body of believers who possess an instinct or sense of the faith that allows the people of God to recognize and respond to God's word (cf. *LG* 12; *DV* 8, 10). The council's pastoral constitution, *Gaudium et spes,* recognized the carefully circumscribed competencies of the Church's pastors and affirmed the authority and expertise of the laity to apply the gospel to the complex questions that arise in the world today (cf. *GS* 43). The council also insisted that one's individual conscience itself possesses an inviolable authority (cf. *GS* 16; *DH* 3). Finally, scholars and theologians are recognized for the authority that is theirs in virtue of their expertise (cf. *GS* 62, 44; *AG* 22).

This pluralistic model presumes a vision of the Church that is interactive and organic. The Spirit animates the whole Church, clergy and laity, and cooperates with the gifts and expertise of each believer. While a pluralistic model of authority certainly acknowledges the special authority of the ecclesiastical magisterium, it refuses to limit the Spirit's activity to the exercise of Church office. The life of the

[36]Avery Dulles, *The Resilient Church* (Garden City: Doubleday, 1977) 93–112.

Church should be characterized by a Spirit-inspired harmony among these various loci of authority.

In summary, we can say that with the ecclesiological renewal at Vatican II we find a recontextualization of doctrinal teaching authority. First, those who exercise doctrinal teaching authority must always be cognizant of that authority's transcendent ground. The Church does not possess an authority in its own right but only in radical dependence on God's word borne in the Church by the power of the Holy Spirit. The authority of the ecclesiastical magisterium can only be asserted in the context of an understanding of the Church, whole and entire, as the recipient of God's word. In other words, we must be able to speak of the whole people of God as both a teaching Church and a learning Church. Only then can we inquire after the specific role played by the formal doctrinal teaching authority in the Church, the college of bishops.

In the remaining chapters I will return to consider these themes in greater detail. In this chapter it has sufficed to sketch out in broad strokes ecclesiological themes present in the documents of Vatican II that support a renewed theology of doctrinal teaching authority in the Church. In the next chapter I will turn directly to the ecclesial structures responsible for the normative exercise of doctrinal authority, the episcopate and the papacy.

For Further Reading

Classic Texts Influencing
Contemporary Roman Catholic Ecclesiology

Bouyer, Louis. *The Church of God: Body of Christ and Temple of the Holy Spirit.* Chicago: Franciscan Herald, 1982.

Congar, Yves. *The Mystery of the Church.* Rev. ed. Baltimore: Helicon, 1965.

_____. *The Mystery of the Temple.* Westminster: Newman, 1967.

Fries, Heinrich. *Aspects of the Church.* Westminster: Newman, 1966.

Küng, Hans. *The Church.* Garden City: Doubleday, 1967.

Le Guillou, Marie-Joseph. *Christ and Church: A Theology of the Mystery.* New York: Desclée, 1966.

Lubac, Henri de. *The Splendour of the Church.* London: Sheed & Ward, 1979.

Rahner, Karl. *The Church and the Sacraments.* New York: Crossroad, 1963.

Survey Articles and Basic Texts on Contemporary Roman Catholic Ecclesiology

Dulles, Avery. "A Half Century of Ecclesiology." *Theological Studies* 50 (1989) 419–42.

_____. *Models of the Church.* Garden City: Doubleday, 1974.

Fahey, Michael. "Church." In *Systematic Theology: Catholic Perspectives.* Vol. 2, 1–74. Minneapolis: Fortress, 1991.

Garijo-Guembe, Miguel M. *Communion of the Saints: Foundation, Nature, and Structure of the Church.* Collegeville: The Liturgical Press, 1994.

Sanks, T. Howland. *Salt, Leaven, and Light: The Community Called Church.* New York: Crossroad, 1992.

Sullivan, Francis A. *The Church We Believe In.* New York: Paulist, 1988.

Ecclesiology of Communion

Congregation for the Doctrine of the Faith. "Some Aspects of the Church Understood as Communion." *Origins* 22 (June 25, 1992) 108–12.

Hamer, Jérôme. *The Church Is a Communion.* New York: Sheed & Ward, 1964.

Hertling, Ludwig. *Communio: Church and Papacy in Early Christianity.* Chicago: Loyola, 1972.

Lawler, Michael, and Thomas Shanahan. *The Church: A Spirited Communion.* Collegeville: The Liturgical Press, 1995.

Provost, James H., ed. *The Church as Communion.* Washington: Canon Law Society of America, 1984.

Tillard, J.-M. R. *Church of Churches: The Ecclesiology of Communion.* Collegeville: The Liturgical Press (A Michael Glazier Book) 1992.

Zizioulas, John D. *Being as Communion.* Crestwood: St. Vladimir's Seminary Press, 1985.

Vatican II

Alberigo, Giuseppe, Jean-Pierre Jossua, and Joseph A. Komonchak, eds. *The Reception of Vatican II*. Washington: Catholic University of America Press, 1987.

Butler, Christopher. *The Theology of Vatican II*. Rev. ed. Westminster: Christian Classics, 1981.

Hastings, Adrian, ed. *Modern Catholicism: Vatican II and After.* New York: Oxford Univ. Press, 1991.

Kloppenburg, Bonaventure. *The Ecclesiology of Vatican II*. Chicago: Franciscan Herald, 1970.

Latourelle, Réne, ed. *Vatican II: Assessment and Perspectives*. 3 Vols. New York: Paulist, 1988.

Miller, John H., ed. *Vatican II: An Interfaith Appraisal*. Notre Dame: Univ. of Notre Dame Press, 1966.

Nissiotis, Nikos. "The Main Ecclesiological Problem of the Second Vatican Council." *Journal of Ecumenical Studies* 2 (Winter 1965) 31–62.

Rahner, Karl. "Basic Theological Interpretation of the Second Vatican Council." In *Theological Investigations*. Vol. 20, 77–89. New York: Crossroad, 1981.

_____. "The Abiding Significance of the Second Vatican Council." In *Theological Investigations*. Vol. 20, 90–102. New York: Crossroad, 1981.

Vorgrimler, Herbert, ed. *Commentary on the Documents of Vatican II*. 5 Vols. New York: Crossroad, 1989.

2

The Teaching Office of the Church

In the Roman Catholic Church the bishops have the principal responsibility for authoritatively teaching Catholic doctrine.[1] On the eve of Vatican II there were sufficient questions about the nature of the episcopal office that the council devoted almost all of the third chapter of the Dogmatic Constitution on the Church, *Lumen gentium,* to the episcopate. This was accompanied by a separate decree on the ministry of the bishop. Neither the papacy nor the other orders of priest-presbyter and deacon received as much attention. While it is obvious that a theology of doctrinal teaching authority will have to attend to the role of the bishop, there are important ecumenical reasons as well for careful consideration of the topic.

The last three decades have seen remarkable advances in ecumenical dialogue regarding such previously contentious issues as justification, baptism, Eucharist, and the relationship between Scripture and tradition. It has been the conviction of many in the ecumenical movement that questions regarding authority and leadership now provide the biggest challenge to ecumenical conversation. Even in this area considerable work has been done. Largely gone are the polemical attempts of both Protestants and Catholics to oppose charism and

[1]The key qualifier here is the word "authoritative." By that I mean that they are the "official teachers" of the Catholic faith who alone are empowered to present a teaching of the Church as, in at least some sense, normative for the faith life of believers. All the baptized, of course, carry the obligation of passing on the Christian faith. I will consider the meaning of "normative" in chapter 4.

office. Certainly the Anglican and Orthodox traditions have always maintained the important role of Church office and the office of the episcopate in particular. Beyond those traditions, however, we find a growing convergence among other Christian communions regarding the value of episcopal ministry in the Church. The well-known 1982 Lima Document, *Baptism, Eucharist, and Ministry* (BEM), at several points affirms the importance of episcopal ministry and calls for those Churches without an episcopal ministry to reconsider their position on this ecclesiological question.[2] Significant progress is particularly evident in the national and international Lutheran-Catholic dialogues.[3] Even the more controversial question of papal primacy has been treated with unprecedented openness outside of Roman Catholicism.[4] However, these studies, while articulating important ecumenical convergences on matters related to the episcopate and papal

---

[2]*Baptism, Eucharist, and Ministry,* Faith and Order Paper no. 111 (Geneva, WCC, 1982), see especially nos. 19–38. For the official response of the Vatican to this statement see "Baptism, Eucharist, and Ministry: An Appraisal," *Origins* 17 (November 19, 1987) 401–16. For a collection of theological responses commissioned by the CTSA see Michael A. Fahey, ed., *Catholic Perspectives on Baptism, Eucharist, and Ministry* (New York: Univ. Press of America, 1986).

[3]See, for example, "The Ministry in the Church," a document produced in 1981 by a joint commission appointed by the then Secretariat for Promoting Christian Unity and the Executive Committee of the Lutheran World Federation, in Harding Meyer and Lukas Vischer, eds., *Growth in Agreement* (New York: Paulist, 1984) 248–75.

[4]See Paul C. Empie and T. Austin Murphy, eds., *Papal Primacy and the Universal Church,* Lutherans and Catholics in Dialogue 5 (Minneapolis: Augsburg, 1974). For consideration of papal primacy in the dialogues of the Anglican–Roman Catholic International Commission (ARCIC) see the Venice (1976) and Windsor (1981) statements, "Authority in the Church," in Meyer and Vischer, *Growth in Agreement,* 88–118. One should also consult the important study by noted Protestant ecumenist, Jean Jacques von Allmen, *La primauté de Pierre et Paul: Remarques d'un Protestant* (Fribourg: Editions universitaires, 1977). For the Orthodox view of the problems associated with papal primacy see the agreed statement of the U.S. Orthodox–Roman Catholic Consultation, "Conciliarity and Primacy in the Church," *The Greek Orthodox Theological Review* 35 (Autumn 1990) 217–20. Important early essays on papal primacy from an Orthodox perspective can be found John Meyendorff, ed., *The Primacy of Peter* (rev. ed., Crestwood: St. Vladimir's Seminary Press, 1992).

primacy, have also raised a host of questions to which contemporary Catholic ecclesiology must respond.

A central concern of Orthodox theologians is directed toward the relationship between the college of bishops (and therefore the bishop of Rome) and the whole people of God. They challenge what they see as Roman Catholicism's opposition of hierarchy and Church, with the bishops exercising an autonomous authority *over* the Church. Particularly since the Slavophile reform movement of the nineteenth century, Russian Orthodox theologians have emphasized the notion of *sobornost,* the organic unity of the whole Church—a unity that applies in particular to the relationship between bishops and the whole Church.[5] For the Orthodox the ministry of the bishop, as presider of a local Eucharistic community, is only intelligible in relation to the Church he serves. Authority is always exercised *within* rather than *above* the Church.[6]

In a similar vein, some Protestant theologians have been more willing to grant an authority to Church office that is more than the mere delegation of the authority of all believers. The 1972 Malta Report of the Lutheran–Roman Catholic dialogue states that both Lutherans and Catholics "agree that the office of the ministry stands over against the community as well as within the community. Further they agree that the ministerial office represents Christ and his over-againstness to the community only insofar as it gives expression to the gospel."[7] Nevertheless, Lutheran theologians would still insist on the mutual reciprocity of office and community and the sovereignty of the gospel itself over all Church offices.[8] They question whether this reciprocity and the subordination of office to gospel is adequately preserved in Catholic doctrine and practice.

[5]This concept, largely associated with nineteenth century Russian philosopher and theologian Alexei S. Khomiakov, and its influence on Orthodox ecclesiology, is summarized in Joost van Rossum, "A. S. Khomiakov and Orthodox Ecclesiology," *St. Vladimir's Theological Quarterly* 35 (1991) 67–82.

[6]See Paul Evdokimov, *L'Orthodoxie* (Neuchâtel: Delachaux & Niestlé, 1959) 160ff.; John D. Zizioulas, *Being as Communion* (Crestwood: St. Vladimir's Seminary Press, 1985) 171–208.

[7]Meyer and Vischer, *Growth in Agreement,* 180.

[8]Paul Althaus, *Die christliche Wahrheit* (Gütersloh: Mohn, 1966) 510. For a survey of Protestant positions see Heinz Schütte, *Amt, Ordination, Sukzession* (Düsseldorf, 1974) chs. 6–8.

The bishops at Vatican II were certainly aware of at least some of these criticisms. The council's teachings, while not offering a coherent and systematic response to these questions, offered considerable advances toward an understanding of Church office that is responsive to non-Catholic Christian concerns.

Toward a Contemporary Catholic Theology of the Episcopate

When Vatican II began consideration of the ministry of the bishop, the principal debates centered around the notion of collegiality, that is, the relationship of all the bishops to one another and to the bishop of Rome. The second draft of the constitution explicitly taught that the whole college of bishops shared with the bishop of Rome supreme pastoral authority over the whole Church. At the same time the council reemphasized the bishop's role of pastoral leadership in his own diocese. The considerable attention given to the episcopate was the result of a perceived imbalance in preconciliar teaching, an imbalance that could be traced back to the First Vatican Council.

At the First Vatican Council the bishops had intended to promulgate a comprehensive constitution on the Church. Because of difficulties with the original draft on the Church all but the chapter on the papacy were returned to committee for revision. Unfortunately Vatican I was suspended when the Italian troops entered Rome during the Franco-Prussian War, and the rest of the constitution was never considered. Only the material on the papacy would be promulgated, in expanded form, as *Pastor aeternus.* Some ninety years later, many bishops at Vatican II were determined to address this serious lacuna.

Vatican II's principal treatment of the bishop is found in the third chapter of *Lumen gentium* and in the Decree on the Pastoral Office of Bishops in the Church, *Christus Dominus.* Unlike Vatican I's *Pastor aeternus,* which treated the episcopacy in the context of the papacy, Vatican II, *began* with consideration of the episcopate. Though the council's treatment of the ministry of the bishop was uneven, it had the merit of turning for inspiration at several points to the theology and practice of the early Church. Consequently, a full appreciation of this retrieval demands a brief review of some of the more significant characteristics of the ministry of the bishop as it developed in the early centuries of Christianity.

The Ministry of the Bishop in the Early Church

What we think of as the episcopal office did not emerge as a universal leadership structure in the Church until the mid to late second century.[9] After the death of the founding apostles, the early Churches adopted a number of different leadership structures. Some Churches relied more on the ministry of prophets and others on a college of elders, or *presbyteroi*. However, we do know that by the end of the second century the emergence of a monarchical or presidential episcopate (one leader for each local Eucharistic community) had become the norm. In spite of considerable regional diversity, this emerging episcopal ministry consisted of two fundamental elements: (1) the ministry of Eucharistic presidency/pastoral leadership and (2) the ministry of apostolic witness to the Christian *kerygma*.

It is common today to distinguish between the bishop's ministry of sanctification (priestly office), governance (kingly office), and teaching (prophetic office). However, in the early Church all were closely interrelated. The bishop functioned as both the pastoral leader of the local Church and the principal if not exclusive presider at the community's Eucharistic celebration, the sacrament of ecclesial communion. The ministry of pastoral leadership and that of Eucharistic presidency mutually conditioned each other. It is true that the bishop generally was the president of the Eucharist *because* he was already the pastoral leader of the local community. At the same time, his Eucharistic presidency provided the essential context for understanding his pastoral leadership. The letters of St. Ignatius of Antioch, the first witness of the emergence of the presidential episcopate, emphasize

---

[9]For a consideration of the many complicated scholarly questions concerning the historical transition from a plurality of leadership structures to the tripartite structure of bishop-presbyter-deacon, see Edward Schillebeeckx, *The Church with a Human Face* (New York: Crossroad, 1985); Raymond E. Brown, *The Churches the Apostles Left Behind* (New York: Paulist, 1984); Hermann von Lipps, *Glaube, Gemeinde, Amt: Zum Verständnis der Ordination in den Pastoralbriefen* (Göttingen: Vandenhoeck & Ruprecht, 1979); James D. G. Dunn, *Unity and Diversity in the New Testament* (Philadelphia: Westminster, 1977); André Lemaire, *Les ministères aux origines de l'Église—Naissance de la triple hierarchie: évêques, presbytres, diacres* (Paris: Cerf, 1971); Hans Campenhausen, *Ecclesiastical Authority and Spiritual Power in the Church of the First Three Centuries* (Stanford: Stanford Univ., 1969).

the Eucharistic foundations of early episcopal ministry. In gathering the faithful around the table of the Lord the bishop functioned as an icon of Christ, who forms the Church as his body. The bishop was the principle of unity in the Church, and it was as the guarantor of the Church's unity that he presided over the Eucharist, the sacrament of unity.[10] His ministry was defined by a dual relation to Christ as sacramental icon and to the Eucharistic community as the principle and servant of its unity.

One major characteristic of this Eucharistic perspective was the location of the bishop *within* the community as its liturgical center. St. Ignatius of Antioch certainly stressed the authority of the bishop and the importance of the people showing obedience, reverence, and respect to the bishop. At the same time, Ignatius did not see the bishop as an external authority over the community. The bishop ministered *to* the community as a member *of* the community. This was a commonly held view in the early Church. In a third-century letter of St. Cyprian, bishop of Carthage, we find this oft quoted passage: "[T]he Church consists of the people who remain united with their bishop, it is the flock that stays by its shepherd. By that you ought to realize that the bishop is in the Church and the Church is in the bishop, and whoever is not with the bishop is not in the Church."[11] This passage reflects Cyprian's deep commitment to the authority and unity of the episcopate, but it also demonstrates the way in which Cyprian situated the episcopate within and not above the Church itself. Ludwig Hertling tells us:

> On the one hand, there is no doubt that the bishop was the absolute and sole master of the house, on whom everything depended and through whose hands everything passed, even to details about the care of the poor. On the other hand, at the bishop's side we find the clergy, whom he addresses as his brothers, copresbyters, and codeacons, and without whom he decides nothing. Also the people themselves are expected to

---

[10] John S. Romanides, "The Ecclesiology of St. Ignatius of Antioch," *The Greek Orthodox Theological Review* 7 (1961–62) 70. This emphasis on the relationship between the bishop and the Eucharist is in striking contrast to the relatively little attention, if any, given in the Second Testament texts on the question of who presides at the Eucharist. For a consideration of this question see Hervé-Marie Legrand, "The Presidency of the Eucharist According to Ancient Tradition," *Worship* 53 (1979) 367–91.

[11] *Epistle* 66, 8.

express their opinion on almost every question, even on the appointment of a lector.[12]

This relationship of interdependence between bishop and community was dictated by the bishop's liturgical ministry. Yves Congar writes: "The ancient liturgy has no 'I' distinct from the 'we' of the whole community. The celebrant, that is, the president of the assembly and the head of the community, speaks in the name of all, for he is one with all its members."[13] Although the bishop was the authoritative leader of the community, the character of the bishop's Eucharistic presidency precluded any conception of pastoral leadership that viewed the bishop as an autonomous locus of power and authority exercised *over* the Church.

The relationship of bishop to Church was further reflected in the participation of the people, and in particular the local clergy, in the election of their bishop. Cyprian writes: "Moreover, we can see that divine authority is also the source for the practice whereby bishops are chosen in the presence of the laity and before the eyes of all, and they are judged as being suitable and worthy after public scrutiny and testimony."[14] There is further testimony from the early third century in Hippolytus' *Apostolic Tradition:*

> Let the bishop be ordained after he has been chosen by all the people; when he has been named and shall please all, let him, with the presbytery and such bishops as may be present, assemble with the people on Sunday. While all give their consent, the bishops shall lay hands upon him.[15]

This mandate for local election reappears in the fourth-century compilation of ancient ecclesiastical law, *Apostolic Constitutions.*[16] Admittedly one must be cautious in characterizing the precise form of the faithful's participation in the election of bishops. It is not always clear in patristic texts whether it is an election strictly speaking that is recounted or merely a public acclamation of a candidate.

[12]Ludwig Hertling, *Communio: Church and Papacy in Early Christianity* (Chicago: Loyola Univ. Press, 1972) 43.

[13]Yves Congar, *Power and Poverty in the Church* (London: Chapman, 1964) 42.

[14]*Epistle* 67, 4.

[15]*Apostolic Tradition* 1, 2, 3.

[16]*Apostolic Constitutions* 8, 4, 2.

Nevertheless there is ample evidence for a real participation of the whole community, whatever form it might take.

It should not surprise us that an episcopal ministry so configured by Eucharistic presidency would also preclude any practice of absolute ordinations, the conferral of sacramental power on the ordinand apart from a pastoral charge to a local Christian community. The ordination of a bishop without reference to a particular community would violate the Eucharistic foundations of episcopal ministry. Sacramental power could not be separated from service to a particular Church. Ordination was not concerned with the transfer of a set of sacramental powers but with the reconfiguration of one's relationship with God and the community. Consequently, ordination without community was unintelligible. Evidence of this concern could still be found in the fifth-century Council of Chalcedon, which expressly prohibited the practice of absolute ordination.[17]

Closely related to the bishop's ministry of pastoral leadership and Eucharistic presidency was the ministry of apostolic witness to the Christian *kerygma*. The bishop's ministry was to be apostolic inasmuch as he served as the authoritative guardian of the apostolic faith. As pastoral and liturgical leaders of their local Churches, the bishops were called to discern that which was and was not in conformity with the apostolic tradition in the life of their communities. They did this, however, as leaders of Churches that were themselves bearers of apostolicity. The bishop did not impart a secret knowledge with which his flock was unfamiliar. The bishop proclaimed the apostolic faith with authority, but in so doing he functioned as a custodian of the faith given to the whole Church. In apostolic service to their communities, the bishops received, verified, validated, and proclaimed the truths of the faith that were prayed and lived in their communities.

In both the ministry of Eucharistic presidency/pastoral leadership and the ministry of apostolic teaching, there was a consistent emphasis on both the authority of the bishop *and* the bishops's immersion

---

[17]"No one, whether presbyter or deacon or anyone at all who belongs to the ecclesiastical order, is to be ordained without title, unless the one ordained is specially assigned to a city or village church or to a martyr's shrine or a monastery. The sacred synod has decreed that the ordination of those ordained without title is null, and that they cannot operate anywhere, because of the presumption of the one who ordained them." Canon 6 of the Council of Chalcedon in Norman Tanner, ed., *Decrees of the Ecumenical Councils,* (Washington: Georgetown Univ. Press, 1990) 1:90.

in the Christian community. As Ignatius insisted in his letters, there can be no community without a bishop. But it is equally clear that neither could there be a bishop without a community that shared the apostolic faith.

The bishop, primary sacramental minister and pastoral leader of the local Church, begins to be displaced by the ministry of the priest only after the sixth century. The numerous historical and ecclesiological factors involved in this shift of roles cannot be considered here. Suffice it to say that from the sixth century on, and particularly after the tenth century, the bishop would be understood more in terms of his administrative function than that of cult and/or leadership.[18] This marginalization of the ministry of the bishop in the life of the local Church would encourage theological debates regarding whether episcopal consecration was, properly speaking, sacramental. This situation would not be substantively changed until the Second Vatican Council.

Vatican II's Consideration of the Ministry of the Bishop

Vatican II restored much of the early Church's theology of the episcopate. First, in article 21 of *Lumen gentium* the council explicitly affirmed the sacramental character of episcopal consecration. The episcopate was not just the "highest degree" of the priesthood but the fullness of the sacrament of holy orders. Following ancient practice, it is now the bishop rather than the priest who is the principal minister of the local Church. Article 21 also states that the offices or functions of sanctifying, teaching, and governing were conferred on the bishop at episcopal consecration itself. The episcopal power *(potestas)* associated with the fulfillment of these three offices or functions is not delegated but is proper to each bishop and is exercised by that bishop ordinarily and immediately even if it is subject to the regulation of the bishop of Rome (cf. *LG* 27). This last development was more significant than it may at first seem.

---

[18]For a history of the theology of the episcopate see Seamus Ryan, "Episcopal Consecration: The Fullness of the Sacrament of Order," *Irish Theological Quarterly* 32 (1965) 295–324; idem, "Episcopal Consecration: The Legacy of the Schoolmen," *Irish Theological Quarterly* 33 (1966) 3–38; idem, "Episcopal Consecration: Trent to Vatican II," *Irish Theological Quarterly* 33 (1966) 133–50; idem "Vatican II: The Re-Discovery of the Episcopate," *Irish Theological Quarterly* 33 (1966) 208–41; Yves Congar and B.-D. Dupuy, eds., *L'épiscopat et l'Église universelle* (Paris: Cerf, 1962); Jean Colson, *L'évêque dans les communautés primitives* (Paris: Cerf, 1951).

In the four centuries prior to Vatican II the episcopal functions of teaching and governing generally were tied to the power of jurisdiction, and there was some disagreement among bishops and theologians as to whether the power of jurisdiction came from episcopal consecration itself or was delegated by the pope. Vatican II did recognize the right of the pope to *regulate* episcopal jurisdiction;[19] however, by grounding the power to teach and govern in episcopal consecration itself, the council aimed at restoring the integrity of episcopal ministry. The bishop was more than a vicar of the pope. Article 27 states that every bishop could rightly be called a "vicar of Christ." Regarding the nature of the bishop's pastoral responsibilities, the council writes:

> The pastoral office, that is to say the habitual and daily care of their sheep, is completely entrusted to the bishops and they are not to be considered vicars of the Roman pontiffs, because they exercise a power that is proper to themselves and most truly are said to be presidents of the people they govern (*LG* 27).

The distinctive ministry of the bishop does not consist in a particular set of cultic powers unique to bishops (e.g., the power to confirm or ordain) but in his being *consecrated* as shepherd of a Church.[20] It is as shepherd of a flock that the bishop exercises his ministries of teaching, sanctifying, and governing. Among his many responsibilities two important aspects of the pastoral ministry of the bishop are particularly highlighted in the council documents: Eucharistic presidency and the proclamation of the gospel.

The Eucharistic Presidency of the Bishop

Recalling the understanding and practice of the early Church, Vatican II taught that it is the bishop rather than the priest who is the principal Eucharistic presider in the local Church. The priest's Eucharistic presidency is dependent on that of the bishop; the priest assists the bishop in the fulfillment of the bishop's liturgical responsibilities. This is stated most clearly in the Constitution on the Sacred Liturgy, *Sacrosanctum concilium:*

---

[19]See preliminary explanatory note, no. 2, which was attached to the constitution in order to clarify this technical matter.

[20]Ryan, "Vatican II: Re-Discovery," 215–16.

The bishop should be thought of as the high priest of his flock; the life of his people in Christ in some way derives from him and depends on him. Therefore, everyone should regard the liturgical life of the diocese centering on the bishop, above all in the cathedral church, as of the highest importance. They should be convinced that the church is displayed with special clarity when the holy people of God, all of them, are actively and fully sharing in the same liturgical celebrations—especially when it is the same eucharist—sharing one prayer at one altar, at which the bishop is presiding, surrounded by his presbyterate and his ministers (SC 41).

This liturgical ministry creates a relationship between the bishop and the community characterized by reciprocity and interdependence. This liturgical relationship has been fruitfully explored in the context of postconciliar dialogues with the Churches of the East. For example, in a recent ecumenical document, "The Church, the Eucharist, and the Trinity," we find the following passage:

The function of the bishop is closely bound to the eucharistic assembly over which he presides. The eucharistic unity of the local church implies communion between him who presides and the people to whom he delivers the word of salvation and the eucharistic gifts. Further, the minister is also the one who "receives" from his church, which is faithful to tradition, the word he transmits.[21]

This text suggests that the reciprocal relationship established between people and bishop in the Eucharistic synaxis also extends to the bishop's ministry of the proclamation of the word of God.

The Bishop's Ministry of the Proclamation of the Word of God

Vatican II states that "among the principal tasks of bishops, the preaching of the gospel is pre-eminent" (*LG* 25, cf. *CD* 12; *AG* 20). Too little attention has been given to the Eucharistic context for understanding the proclamation of the gospel. Just as in the Eucharist there is a reciprocal relationship between the presider and the assembly, the proclamation of the gospel has its own dialogical rhythm in the life of the local Church. Indeed, this dual focus on Eucharistic presidency

---

[21]The Joint International Commission for Theological Dialogue Between the Roman Catholic Church and the Orthodox Church, "The Church, the Eucharist, and the Trinity," *Origins* 12 (1982–83) 159.

and the proclamation of the gospel are both in keeping with the council's more fully developed theology of the local Church.[22]

This theology holds that the local Church is not a mere subdivision of the universal Church but the locus of the universal Church's realization. God's word is not first proclaimed from the pope as from the pinnacle of an ecclesiastical pyramid and then passed down to the local bishops. It is not the pope who is the principal minister of the gospel but the local bishop. There can be no ecclesiastical trickledown theory at work here.

> For the bishops are the heralds of the faith who bring new disciples to Christ. They are the authentic teachers, that is, teachers endowed with the authority of Christ, who preach to the people entrusted to them the faith to be believed and put into practice; they illustrate this faith in the light of the holy Spirit, drawing out of the treasury of revelation things new and old, they make it bear fruit and they vigilantly ward off errors that are threatening their flock (*LG* 25).

Furthermore, this guardianship of the apostolic faith cannot be separated from the apostolic community over which the bishop presides. The Dogmatic Constitution on Divine Revelation, *Dei verbum,* confirms this:

> This tradition which comes from the apostles progresses in the church under the assistance of the holy Spirit. There is a growth in understanding of what is handed on, both the words and the realities they signify. This comes about through contemplation and study by believers, who "ponder these things in their hearts"; through the intimate understanding of spiritual things which they experience; and through the preaching of those who, on succeeding to the office of bishop, receive the sure charism of truth (*DV* 8).

The apostolic faith is passed on through the preaching of the bishops but also through the "contemplation and study of believers" and through their "intimate understanding" of what they experience in their spiritual lives. In fact, the preaching of the bishops is only mentioned *after* the consideration of the role of all believers. These are not so much two distinct media for the transmission of the faith as they are two poles in one dynamic "traditioning" process.

[22]For a masterful treatment of the theology of the local Church see Hervé-Marie Legrand, "Nature de l'Église particulière et rôle de l'évêque dans l'Église," in *La charge pastorale des évêques,* ed. W. Onclin, R. Bézac, and others (Paris: Cerf, 1969) 103–76.

Because the gospel the bishop proclaims is not a secret gospel but is the authoritative proclamation of that apostolic tradition that continues to progress within the whole community, the bishop must be an effective listener if he is to be an effective teacher. This is affirmed in the chapter on the laity in *Lumen gentium*:

> The laity have the right, as do all the faithful, to receive abundant help from the sacred pastors out of the spiritual goods of the church, especially the help provided by the word of God and the sacraments; and they should make known to these pastors their needs and desires with that freedom and confidence which befits children of God and sisters and brothers in Christ. *In accordance with the knowledge, competence or authority that they possess, they have the right and indeed sometimes the duty to make known their opinion on matters which concern the good of the church. . . . [T]he sacred pastors are to acknowledge and promote the dignity and the responsibility of the laity in the church; they should willingly make use of their prudent counsel* (*LG* 37, my emphasis).

Of course, just as the bishop is not simply a mouthpiece for the pope, neither is he a mouthpiece for the opinions of his flock as reflected in the latest poll. The "special charism of truth" is given to him, and it is his responsibility and his alone to exercise faithfully that charism. While the bishop serves as a *testis fidei,* a witness to that faith professed by those in his community, he is also the authoritative teacher and judge *(iudex fidei)* responsible for safeguarding that faith from the distortion and error that is always possible within any individual community.

Episcopal Collegiality and the *Communio Ecclesiarum*

The ministry of the individual bishop is not exhausted by his relationship to his local Church. Through episcopal consecration the bishop is inserted into the college of bishops (*LG* 22.1). By connecting membership in the college with episcopal consecration the council reinforced the conviction that the college of bishops was not an incidental ecclesiastical institution but rather possessed a sacramental foundation.[23] *Lumen gentium* also reaffirmed traditional Church teaching that the whole college of bishops succeeds in the authority of the college of apostles (*LG* 18). What was new was the council's

[23]Ryan, "Vatican II: Re-Discovery," 219–20.

extended reflection on the nature of the collegial relationship among the bishops, including the bishop of Rome. Of course, the concept of collegiality, if not the term itself, was not new. A sense of the collegial relationship of the bishops could be traced back to the early Church.

In patristic ecclesiology[24] the collegial relationship of the bishops was an expression of the communion that existed among the Churches. The bishop, in his relationship with other bishops, was the agent of that ecclesial communion. Thus collegial acts among bishops manifested the ecclesial communion among the Churches. As Walter Kasper puts it, "[c]ollegiality is . . . the official, outward aspect . . . of the sacramental unity in communion."[25] It followed then that any legitimate authority exercised together by the bishops emerged out of their relationships to their respective Churches.

The Orthodox refer to this ancient conviction as the principle of *synodality*. Ecclesial authority must emerge out of the communion of Churches and not as an external principle exercised *over* the Churches. Congar has something similar in mind when he speaks of the principle of *conciliarity*. He sees regional synods, ecumenical councils, and other institutional expressions of ecclesial authority as concrete manifestations of the Church's fundamental nature as a communion:

> Councils, while creations of the church, are an expression of the conciliarity which derives from the very nature of the Church, which is to be a communion, *koinonia*. . . . A council seeks to express the community of views, the unanimity of the Church on the basis of the local or particular churches . . . whether this unanimity exists implicitly and has to be elicited and made explicit, or has to be sought in order to be expressed.[26]

[24]For an in-depth historical analysis of the notion of collegiality in patristic ecclesiology see Joseph Ratzinger, *Das neue Volk Gottes: Entwürfe zur Ekklesiologie* (Düsseldorf: Patmos, 1969) 121–224.

[25]Walter Kasper, *Theology and Church* (New York: Crossroad, 1989) 157.

[26]Yves Congar, "The Conciliar Structure or Regime of the Church," *Concilium* 167 (1983) 3–4. See also Congar's "Konzil als Versammlung und gründsätzliche Konziliarität der Kirche," in *Gott in Welt* (festschrift for Karl Rahner), ed. Herbert Vorgrimler (Freiburg: Herder, 1964) 2:135-65; John D. Zizioulas, "The Development of Conciliar Structure to the Time of the First Ecumenical Council," in *Councils and the Ecumenical Movement* (Geneva: WCC, 1968) 34–51.

It is this ecclesiological conviction that is often overlooked in contemporary understandings of synods and councils. The deliberations of bishops in synod or council were not for the early Church, and should not be today, understood as the exercise of a kind of governing board placed over the Church. Rather, synodal and conciliar deliberations are concentrated expressions of the mind of the Churches.[27]

Vatican II drew from this ancient tradition in its description of the relationship between the college of bishops and the communion of Churches:

> The individual bishops . . . are the visible principle and foundation of unity in their own particular churches, formed in the likeness of the universal church; in and from these particular churches there exists the one unique catholic church. For this reason *individual bishops represent their own church, while all of them together with the pope represent the whole church* in the bond of peace, love and unity (*LG* 23, emphasis mine).

When understood in the context of the communion of Churches, episcopal collegiality can be appreciated as a properly theological and ecclesiological principle for understanding Church leadership.

Unfortunately the relationship between the college of bishops and the communion of Churches was not consistently presented in the conciliar

---

[27]"The capacity of the bishops to reflect the mind of the Church universal conditions and is conditioned by their capacity to reflect the mind of the local churches. The conciliar structure of the church is short-circuited when the bishops cannot or do not act as the corporate voices of their churches. . . . The Church as the Spirit-inspired communion of local communities, reflecting the communion of Christians one with another and grounded in participation in the self-gift of God, authoritatively expresses its common life, its tradition, through the episcopal college." Michael J. Himes, "The Ecclesiological Significance of the Reception of Doctrine," *Heythrop Journal* 33 (1992) 154. Needless to say, this stress on the bishop's relationship to his local Church challenges the wisdom if not the validity of formal ordination to the episcopate, the practice of ordaining a bishop without giving that bishop a responsibility for a local Church. That the Church recognizes the importance of this connection, even if it is only affirmed in the most trivial way, is reflected in the practice of granting a titular see (an ancient Church that no longer exists) to bishops not given a true pastoral charge, for example, apostolic nuncios, and auxiliaries. I will consider further the ecclesiological difficulties embedded in this practice in the conclusion of this volume.

documents.[28] For example, some theologians have lamented the council's decision to separate membership in the college of bishops from the assignment of a pastoral charge to a local Church (cf. *LG* 21). Vatican II taught that a bishop became a member of the episcopal college immediately upon episcopal consecration. There is no mention of the need for a pastoral charge. However, if a bishop can be a member of the college of bishops without any relationship to a local Church, then the relationship between the episcopal college and the communion of Churches, central to the understanding of the early Church, is seriously weakened. Furthermore, from this position it is only a small step to viewing the authority of the college as essentially independent of and external to the communion of Churches.[29] Collegiality, a theological and ecclesiological principle of leadership for the early Church, risks becoming, as it was before Vatican II, a mere juridical principle of leadership.

In spite of this inconsistency, the integral relationship of the college of bishops to the communion of Churches was clearly asserted by the council. Still to be considered, however, is the relationship of the college of bishops to the bishop of Rome, its head.

Collegiality and Papal Primacy

In 1967 Pope Paul VI himself admitted, "The pope—as we all know—is undoubtedly the gravest obstacle in the path of ecumen-

---

[28]Cf. Joseph Famerée, "Collégialité et communion dans l'Église," *Revue théologique de Louvain* 25 (June 1994) 199–203; Hervé-Marie Legrand, "Collégialité des évêques et communion des Églises dans la réception de Vatican II," *Revue des sciences philosophiques et théologiques* 75 (1991) 545–68.

[29]This difficulty is reflected in the view of Karl Rahner: "As a college it is not simply the union of *local* bishops as such, but a collegial governing board in the Church which cannot as such derive its authority from the locally limited authority of its members as local bishops." Rahner's intent, apparently, was to justify the membership in the college of auxiliary and titular bishops. Karl Rahner, "The Episcopal Office," in *Theological Investigations* (New York: Crossroad, 1982) 6:323. Rahner's position is challenged in the following studies: Hervé-Marie Legrand, "Nature de L'Église particulière et rôle de l'évêque dans l'Église," in *La charge pastoral des évêques: Décret "Christus Dominus,"* ed. P. Veuillot and Yves Congar (Paris: Cerf, 1969) 118f.; Yves Congar, *Ministères et communion ecclésiale* (Paris: Cerf, 1971) 123–40; and T. Strotmann, "Primauté et céphalisation: A propos d'une étude du P. Karl Rahner," *Irénikon* 37 (1964) 186–97.

ism."[30] In his encyclical on ecumenism, *Ut unum sint,* Pope John Paul II repeated what he had already stated in a 1984 address to the World Council of Churches, namely that the ministry of the bishop of Rome "constitutes a difficulty for most other Christians, whose memory is marked by certain painful recollections" (*UU* 88). In that same encyclical the Pope extended a remarkable invitation to other Church leaders and theologians

> to engage with me in a patient and fraternal dialogue on this subject, a dialogue in which, leaving useless controversies behind, we could listen to one another, keeping before us only the will of Christ for his church and allowing ourselves to be deeply moved by his plea "that they may all be one . . . so that the world may believe that you have sent me" (*UU* 96).

The Pope is certainly correct in his judgment that further ecumenical progress will require honestly addressing the questions regarding papal primacy posed by the Catholic Church's ecumenical conversation partners. Many of these questions concern the relationship of the bishop of Rome to his brother bishops. For example, the Orthodox contend that Roman Catholicism's traditional account of papal primacy, with its strong emphasis on the universal jurisdiction of the papacy, violates the Eucharistic foundations of the Church. Since each Eucharistic community under the leadership of the bishop is wholly the body of Christ, these communities and their bishops are fundamentally equal and may not be subordinated one to another. Historically, Orthodoxy calls attention to the significant role played by the five ancient patriarchates (Rome, Constantinople, Alexandria, Antioch, and Jerusalem), within which, they generally admit, Rome played a preeminent role. However, they challenge traditional Roman Catholic understandings of the role of the patriarch of Rome. In the theology of the pentarchy, which developed in the East, the authority of the patriarchs was an expression of synodality and therefore was inextricably bound to the communion of Churches.[31] Orthodoxy, then,

[30]Quoted in Peter Hebblethwaite, *Paul VI: The First Modern Pope* (New York: Paulist, 1993) 9.

[31]It is important to note, however, that Orthodox theologians are not themselves in complete agreement regarding the concrete expressions of this relationship between the bishops and the Churches. The great nineteenth-century Russian theologian Alexei Khomiakov insisted that the validity of councils depended on the reception of their decisions by the whole people of God. See

generally has rejected any notion of primacy by which Rome assumes a supra-episcopal authority, and consequently it has rejected any primacy understood as a power *over* other local bishops and their Churches.[32] On the contrary, "the first and the essential form of primacy" for Orthodoxy lies in the synod of bishops, as there and only there does one find a primacy rooted in the episcopacy itself.[33]

Out of the Anglican–Roman Catholic dialogues there has emerged a significant convergence regarding the value of a ministry of universal primacy. This dialogue explicitly envisions this primacy as a service to the *koinonia* of Churches and not as an autonomous authority exercised over the Churches. Important questions have been raised by Anglicans, however, regarding the meaning of Roman Catholicism's assertion that the universal primacy of the bishop of Rome exists by "divine right" and its assertion that the pope possesses universal, ordinary, and immediate jurisdiction over the whole Church. Anglicanism sees the danger, verified by numerous historical examples, of the bishop of Rome usurping the responsibilities of the local bishop.[34] Finally, the Malta Report from the Roman Catholic–Lutheran dialogues also admits the value of a ministry of primacy as a service to the unity of the Church but insists on applying to any ministry of primacy the principle that all Church office is subordinate to the gospel.[35] Any rethinking of papal primacy must take into account these ecumenical concerns.

It was observed earlier that in the third chapter of *Lumen gentium* Vatican II drew on a more ancient vision of Church authority and, while reaffirming papal authority, claimed that the bishops "together with their head, the Supreme Pontiff, and never apart from him" also "have supreme and full authority over the universal church" (*LG* 22). In other words, the whole college of bishops shares, with the pope, in the pastorate of the universal Church. To some bishops this teaching

---

Alexei S. Khomiakov, *The Church Is One* (New York: Archdiocese of Eastern Orthodox Church of America, 1953). This thesis, however, has not been universally accepted within Orthodoxy.

[32] For a presentation of this view see the essays in Meyendorff, *The Primacy of Peter,* particularly those by Afanassieff and Schmemann.

[33] Alexander Schmemann, "The Idea of Primacy in Orthodox Ecclesiology," in Myendorff, *The Primacy of Peter,* 158.

[34] For the treatment of this issue in ARCIC I see Meyer and Vischer, *Growth in Agreement,* 88–118.

[35] "The Malta Report," in Meyer and Vischer, *Growth in Agreement,* 184.

stood in clear contradiction to the teaching of Vatican I's *Pastor aeternus* that supreme authority over the Church resided in the Roman pontiff. Yet *Lumen gentium,* far from denying the teaching of Vatican I, had affirmed Vatican I's definitions on papal primacy and infallibility. How could two groups have such differing understandings of collegiality?

The Historical Origins of the Controversy over Collegiality and Primacy

The source of the disagreement can be traced at least back to the dominance of canonical considerations of the Church in the Middle Ages. Yves Congar has frequently noted the influence of concepts from Roman law for medieval teaching on the Church. From this body of legal theory it became common to consider the Church as a universal corporation under the authority of its head, the pope.[36] Canon lawyers were often engaged in questions regarding the nature and limits of papal authority. These concerns came to a head in the Western schism of the fourteenth and fifteenth centuries in which the Church relied on the authority of a council (Constance, 1414–18) to resolve a situation in which there were first two and then three claimants to the Holy See. Some took this extraordinary situation as an opportunity to propose that councils possessed an authority intrinsically superior to that of the pope.[37] This view was rejected by Pope Eugenius IV and the Council of Florence, which strongly reaffirmed the primacy of pope over council. Out of that controversy came the enduring suspicion of any increase in the authority of the bishops as a return of conciliarism. Unfortunately the theological, canonical, and political presuppositions underlying this conflict had little reference to an ecclesiology of communion, that is, to a view of the Church universal as a communion of Churches. As Patrick Burns has observed:

> Not *communio* but juridical concepts like *plenitudo potestatis* constituted the central concern of the canonists, papal and anti-papal, who

[36]Yves Congar, *L'Eglise de saint Augustin à l'époque moderne* (Paris: Cerf, 1970) 149–50.

[37]For a consideration of this topic, the best work probably remains Brian Tierney's *Foundations of Conciliar Theory: The Contributions of the Medieval Canonists from Gratian to the Great Schism* (Cambridge: Cambridge Univ., 1955).

now became so influential in the concrete life of the church. Not only the question of papal primacy but the basic context for all ecclesiological reflection was dominated by a universalist perspective that tended to reduce the individual local churches to mere units in an administrative whole.[38]

What seemed common to all sides of the conciliarist controversy, papalist and anti-papalist, was a kind of zero-sum ecclesiology in which the papacy and the bishops represented two distinct claimants to power and authority—the increase in the power and authority of one necessarily entailing the diminishment in the other.

This opposition of episcopate and papacy would only be exacerbated in the centuries following the Protestant Reformation. The reformers were not reluctant to attack the authority and very ecclesial foundations of the papacy. Even within the Church the Jansenist controversy and the challenges to papal authority associated with both Gallicanism and Febronianism led the papacy to be suspicious of any rival claims to ecclesiastical authority. By the nineteenth century the papacy was involved in bitter Church-state disputes over the civil prerogatives of the Church in matters related to education, marriage, and the family. The rise of Italian nationalism led to calls for an end to the Church's temporal authority over the Papal States. On the intellectual front the emergence of new philosophical schools of thought and important developments in Church history were influencing theologians to break out of accepted scholastic approaches to Catholic theology. In 1864 Pope Pius IX felt compelled to issue the famous *Syllabus of Errors,* condemning numerous propositions related to philosophy, theology, history, biblical studies, science, and Church-state relations. The result of all of these developments was something of a siege mentality among the ecclesiastical leadership in Rome.

Vatican I's Pastor Aeternus *on Papal Primacy*

Vatican I's constitution, *Pastor aeternus,* was the culmination of a centuries-long historical trajectory toward a view of the Church that was pyramidical, juridical, and to some extent reactionary.[39] The first

---

[38]Patrick J. Burns, "Communion, Councils, and Collegiality: Some Catholic Reflections," in *Papal Primacy and the Universal Church,* ed. Paul C. Empie and T. Austin Murphy (Minneapolis: Augsburg, 1974) 155.

[39]My analysis of *Pastor aeternus* is drawn from the study on the papacy by J.-M. R. Tillard, *The Bishop of Rome* (Wilmington: Glazier, 1983).

draft of the constitution was distributed to the bishops at the beginning of the council. The bishops were fairly critical of the draft, and sent it back to committee for revision. The second draft was never distributed to the bishops. Instead another draft was proposed to the bishops that included a new introduction, the earlier draft's chapter on papal primacy, plus material on papal infallibility that had been prepared independently by some ultramontanist theologians. It was this new constitution, comprising an introduction and four chapters, that was eventually voted upon and approved.

Pastor aeternus begins with a brief introduction on the institution and foundation of the Church and of the papacy. Significantly, the introduction of the constitution defines papal ministry in terms of service to the Church:

> In order, then, that the episcopal office should be one and undivided and that, by the union of the clergy, the whole multitude of believers should be held together in the unity of faith and communion, he [Christ] set blessed Peter over the rest of the apostles and instituted in him the permanent principle of both unities and their visible foundation.[40]

In this brief statement, which received little further development in the constitution, lies the kernel of a contemporary theology of papal primacy. The papacy does not exist for its own sake but as a ministry of service to the Church. Its fundamental purpose is the preservation of the "unity of faith and communion."

The first chapter affirms the divine institution of papal primacy over the whole Church. It maintains that this primacy was given to Peter and to all of his successors. The chapter also condemns those (presumably the Eastern Orthodox) who would grant to the papacy nothing more than a primacy of honor. Rather, the constitution insists upon a juridical primacy, that is, a primacy exercised under the force of law. Indeed, this chapter reflects the document's general preference for juridical rather than theological approaches to questions of ecclesiology. As we shall see, this juridical preoccupation is one of the more serious limitations of the document.

The second chapter continues the constitution's consideration of papal primacy, now focusing on the permanence of the Petrine ministry. One important and often overlooked feature of this chapter is the way in which the argument for papal primacy begins with quotations

[40]Tanner, *Decrees of Ecumenical Councils,* 2:812.

from both St. Irenaeus and St. Ambrose, which speak not of the primacy of the *bishop* of Rome but rather of the *Church* of Rome. This represents an important if largely undeveloped return to the origins of papal ministry in the early Church.

Long before the authority of the bishop of Rome was connected explicitly with St. Peter, the authority of the Roman bishop was derived from the prestige of the Roman Church itself. That prestige, in turn, was largely due to (1) the political significance of Rome and (2) the association of both Peter and Paul with the Church of Rome where they were said to have been martyred.[41] It is this connection with Peter and Paul that helps explain the early establishment of Rome as the preeminent Church of apostolic witness. For example, St. Irenaeus writes:

> But since it would be extremely long in a book such as this to give the succession lists for all the churches (we shall take just one), the greatest and most ancient church, known to all, founded at Rome by the two most glorious apostles, Peter and Paul. We shall show that its tradition, which it has from the Apostles and the faith preached to [all], comes down to us through the succession of bishops. . . . For every church, i.e. the faithful who are in all parts of the world, should agree with this church because of its superior foundation. In this church the tradition from the Apostles has been preserved by those who are from all parts of the world.[42]

[41] The ecumenical potential of the authority of Rome being rooted in the reputation and prestige of both Peter *and* Paul has been explored in William R. Farmer and Roch Kereszty, *Peter and Paul in the Church of Rome* (New York: Paulist, 1990).

[42] *Adversus haereses* 3, 3, 2. The translation of the key phrase, "ad hanc enim ecclesiam propter potiorem principalitatem necesse est omnem convenire ecclesiam," is much disputed. Matters are of course not helped by the fact that we cannot know the identity of the original Greek phrase that "potiorem principalitatem" is translating. I am here following the translation of Robert Eno in his *Teaching Authority in the Early Church* (Wilmington: Glazier, 1984) 45. For more on this text and its ecclesiological implications see J.-M. R. Tillard, *Church of Churches: The Ecclesiology of Communion* (Collegeville: The Liturgical Press [A Michael Glazier Book], 1992) 284ff.; Emmanuel Lanne, "L'Église de Rome, a gloriossimis duobus apostolis Petro et Paulo Romae fundatae et constitutae Ecclesia," *Irénikon* 49 (1976) 275–322. For an accessible study of the origins of papal primacy see Robert Eno, *The Rise of the Papacy* (Wilmington: Glazier, 1990).

As we shall see later, this emphasis on the local Church of Rome will be vital for developing a theology of papal primacy.

The third chapter of the constitution formally defines papal primacy, citing the teaching of the Council of Florence. Once again, however, the council speaks first not of the primacy of the pontiff but of the Roman Church. In the following passage the nature and extent of papal primacy is explicitly developed:

> Wherefore we teach and declare that, by divine ordinance, *the Roman church possesses a pre-eminence of ordinary power over every other church, and that this jurisdictional power of the Roman pontiff is both episcopal and immediate.* Both clergy and faithful, of whatever rite and dignity, both singly and collectively, *are bound to submit to this power by the duty of hierarchical subordination and true obedience,* and this not only in matters concerning faith and morals, but also in those which regard the discipline and government of the church throughout the world. In this way, by unity with the Roman pontiff in communion and in profession of the same faith, *the church of Christ becomes one flock under one supreme shepherd.* This is the teaching of the catholic truth; and no one can depart from it without endangering his faith and salvation (my emphasis).[43]

Several elements in this passage deserve comment. Again, the constitution considers the ministry of the papacy primarily in a canonical or juridical rather than a theological mode. From its emphasis on obedience to its description of papal ministry in terms of jurisdiction we see a substantially legal consideration of the structures of the Church. While one cannot ignore the juridical aspects of the Church, the almost complete exclusion of a more theological treatment of the papacy is a serious shortcoming. For example, one might imagine this document receiving a rather different reception from the Orthodox and Anglican communions if the ministry of the pope were described in the language of universal pastoral concern and solicitude rather than that of obedience and jurisdiction.

Second, the text is strikingly lacking any theology of the local Church. According to the constitution the pope possesses a universal primacy over the whole Church that is described as "one flock under one supreme shepherd." The pope's jurisdiction is everywhere ordinary and immediate. This passage reflects the intent of the council to offer a firm foundation to the legitimate universal pastoral ministry of

[43]Tanner, *Decrees of Ecumenical Councils,* 2:814.

the pope. However, the language gives the impression that each diocese is but a subdivision of the universal Church. It was difficult for many bishops at Vatican I to reconcile this ordinary papal jurisdiction with any real jurisdiction for the local bishop. In response to this difficulty the council inserted into the constitution the following passage:

> This power of the supreme pontiff by no means detracts from that ordinary and immediate power of episcopal jurisdiction, by which the bishops, who have succeeded to the place of the apostles by appointment of the Holy Spirit, tend and govern individually the particular flocks which have been assigned to them. On the contrary, this power of theirs is asserted, supported and defended by the supreme and universal pastor; for St. Gregory the Great says: "My honour is the honour of the whole church. My honour is the steadfast strength of my brethren. Then do I receive true honor, when it is denied to none of those to whom honour is due."[44]

This important text confirms that it was not the intent of the bishops at Vatican I to place papal jurisdiction in competition with the jurisdiction of the local bishop.[45] Papal primacy should not undermine but rather support and strengthen the ordinary jurisdiction of the local bishop.

Nevertheless, many were confused by the wording of *Pastor aeternus*. Otto von Bismarck, the chancellor of Germany, for example, had read the constitution to mean that the pope could assume episcopal rights over every diocese, that episcopal jurisdiction was absorbed by papal jurisdiction, and therefore that the bishops were mere instruments of the pope. After the council the German bishops felt compelled to respond formally to the chancellor:

> According to [the] teaching of the Catholic church, the pope is bishop of Rome but not bishop of another diocese or another town. . . . But as bishop of Rome he is at the same time pope, that is, the pastor and supreme head of the universal Church, head of all the bishops and the faithful and his papal power should be respected and listened to everywhere and always, not only in particular and exceptional cases. In this position the pope has to watch over each bishop in the fulfillment of the whole range of his episcopal charge. If a bishop is prevented, or if some need has made itself felt, the pope has the right and the duty, in

[44]Ibid.

[45]Gustave Thils, "Potestas ordinaria," in *L'Épiscopat et l'Église universelle*, ed. Yves Congar and B.-D. Dupuy (Paris: Cerf, 1962) 689–708.

his capacity as pope and not as bishop of the diocese, to order whatever is necessary for the administration of that diocese. . . . The decisions of the Vatican Council do not offer the shadow of a pretext to claim that the pope has by them become an absolute sovereign and, in virtue of his infallibility, a sovereign more perfectly absolute than any absolute monarch in the world.[46]

In March of 1875 Pope Pius IX gave formal approval of the German bishops' declaration.[47] Some twenty years later Pope Leo XIII would again insist that the bishops "are not to be looked upon as vicars of the Roman Pontiffs; because they exercise a power really their own, and are most truly called the ordinary pastors of the people over whom they rule."[48] Clearly, in the mind of the bishops at Vatican I the jurisdiction of the individual bishop over his local Church had to differ in some way from the pope's jurisdiction over the universal Church. However, neither Vatican I nor subsequent popes were able to explain *how* the two ordinary jurisdictions of the pope and the local bishop could be reconciled.

Part of the difficulty can be traced to the technical meaning attached to the juridical language being employed. That the pope's jurisdiction over the whole Church is described as *ordinary* means simply that it is proper to the bishop of Rome; it is not a *delegated* jurisdiction.[49] The pope is not the "first bishop" of each local Church. He is *bishop* of only one local Church, the Church of Rome. As such, he has a pastoral concern and responsibility over the universal Church which is ordinary, immediate, and universal inasmuch as it properly belongs to him and involves a constant attitude of vigilant concern for the "unity of faith and communion of the whole Church."

The so-called minority bishops at Vatican I, bishops who expressed varied reservations regarding the more extreme claims for papal authority, all sought to tie the exercise of papal authority to the ministry of the whole college of bishops. Their concerns were expressed most

---

[46] An English translation of this text can be found in Hans Küng, *The Council and Reunion* (London: Sheed & Ward, 1961) 283–95.

[47] Cf. DS 3112–17.

[48] *Satis cognitum, ASS* 28 (June 29, 1896) 732.

[49] This was reiterated by Vatican I relator Bishop Zinelli in J. D. Mansi, ed., *Sacrorum conciliorum nova et amplissima collectio* (Graz: Akademische Druck, 1961) 52:1105 (hereafter cited as Mansi, followed by the volume and column numbers). See also Thils, "Potestas Ordinaria," 691.

insistently with respect to the constitution's definition on papal infallibility, a topic I will discuss in chapter 7. After the close of the council the minority was able to accept the council's teaching on papal primacy, largely because they interpreted it in the light of the more moderate, authoritative commentaries offered by the council's official spokespersons, Bishops Zinelli and Gasser. However, their more moderate interpretation of the council decrees would be overshadowed by a more "maximalist" reading of the council. After Vatican I many of the Latin seminary manuals would propose a vision of the Church that highlighted papal prerogatives and the centralization of authority in the papacy. One ecclesiology manual for example, written in 1891 by Domenico Palmieri, bore the title *Tractatus de Romano pontifice cum prolegomena de Ecclesia* (Tract on the Roman pontiff with an introduction on the Church). As the title of this manual indicates, within the manual tradition at least considerations of the Church were often dominated by the papacy. There were manualists who took a more moderate course, and important new ecclesiological studies emerged in the early twentieth century that set the stage for Vatican II. Nevertheless, for much of the ninety years between Vatican I and Vatican II the dominant reading of the teachings of Vatican I would suffer, if not from any fundamental defect, then certainly from a pronounced imbalance.

Vatican II's Renewed Theology of Papal Primacy

At Vatican II there was a new group of minority bishops. This group was fiercely loyal to the teachings of Vatican I and saw the teaching on episcopal collegiality as a threat to Vatican I's teaching on papal primacy. The majority of the bishops, however, did not believe that episcopal collegiality undermined papal primacy. It was their intention simply to redress an earlier ecclesiology that appeared to place the authority of the bishops and that of the pope in opposition. In the late nineteenth century the German bishops had insisted, against the view of Bismarck, that the pope was not the bishop of every diocese but *the bishop of Rome*. It logically followed that if the pope is himself a bishop of a local Church, the papacy and the college of bishops cannot be two separate entities. As bishop of a *local* Church the pope is a member among other members of the college of bishops; as bishop of the local Church *of Rome* the pope is also the head of the college of bishops. This relationship, commonly accepted in the early centuries of the Church, had gradually become obscured as Catholic ecclesiology became more juridical, institutional, and universalist in character. The key then, to overcoming what I have referred to as a zero-sum view of ecclesial authority was to ground the papacy in the episcopate—to reinsert the papacy fully into the college of bishops. This approach to papal authority seems to have been the key for Vatican II's reconciliation of papal primacy and episcopal collegiality.

First, the council explicitly reaffirmed Vatican I's teaching on papal primacy. After considering membership in the episcopal college the council stated that:

> the college or body of bishops does not have authority unless this is understood in terms of union with the Roman pontiff, Peter's successor, as its head, and the power of this primacy is maintained intact over all, whether they be shepherds or faithful. For the Roman pontiff has, by virtue of his office as vicar of Christ and shepherd of the whole church, full, supreme and universal power over the church, a power he is always able to exercise freely (*LG* 22.2).

But immediately following this passage is the insistence that the college of bishops "is also subject of supreme and full power over the universal church, provided that it remains united with its head, the Roman pontiff, and never without its head." By joining papal authority with the authority of the college of bishops and recognizing that *they share supreme and full authority over the Church,* the council placed the papacy in a new or, more accurately, a more ancient ecclesiological context.

Unlike episcopal consecration, the election of the pope has never been regarded as sacramental. When a pope resigns, he ceases to be pope. Under the revised guidelines established by Pope Paul VI,[50] if upon election the pope is not a bishop he is to be ordained immediately after election and *before* he is honored by the college of cardinals and presented to the people. The prerogatives of the papacy are conditioned on the pope being bishop/pastor of the local Church of Rome. If the pope has primacy over the universal Church it is because he is first bishop of a local Church, Rome. Vatican II's acknowledgment of the bishop's dual relationship to local Church and episcopal college made it possible to restore the pope to his proper place with the college of bishops as its head.

[50]*Romano pontifici eligendo, AAS* 67 (November 30, 1975) 609–45.

But does not this emphasis on the pope as bishop of a local Church reduce the pope to simply the "first among equals" *(primus inter pares)*? After all, while Orthodox theologians have generally been willing to grant this title to the pope, Roman Catholicism has insisted that this title falls short of full Roman Catholic teaching on papal primacy. First, the pope is the first among equals inasmuch as he too belongs to the college of bishops and is one with his fellow bishops in the episcopal *ordo*. However, he is not *merely* the first among equals in that he still possesses authority over other Churches.

Here lies the confusion that Vatican I had been unable to clear up. How can the pope's immediate, ordinary, episcopal, and universal jurisdiction be reconciled with the jurisdiction of the local bishop? Does not this universal jurisdiction turn the pope into a superbishop altogether different from other bishops? This issue has important ecumenical ramifications. Recent ecumenical dialogues suggest an increased willingness to accept some kind of universal Petrine ministry, but few if any are willing to accept a pope characterized as a "superbishop." One of the more helpful attempts to address this issue is that undertaken by Dominican theologian J.-M. R. Tillard.

Tillard contends that the universal jurisdiction of the pope does not exceed the bounds of episcopal ministry. He proposes as a basic ecclesiological principle that the power *(potestas)* associated with all episcopal authority only exists in relation to a bishop's particular pastoral charge *(officium)*. Ministry is always ordered to service. The Holy Spirit will assist the bishop in ways appropriate to that bishop's particular ministry. Yet the pastoral charges of bishops may differ considerably. Some minister to very small rural dioceses, others are the pastors of huge urban archdioceses. The bishop of Rome too possesses a unique pastoral charge. His charge is to the local Church of *Rome*. But this particular local Church has since ancient times held a privileged position among the Churches. It has been looked to for guidance and inspiration over the centuries because of its consistent fidelity to the gospel. In time this primacy developed juridical "teeth," as it were, so that the local Church of Rome could guard and preserve the unity of the Church universal more effectively. It is to *this* local Church that the bishop of Rome possesses a pastoral charge. Therefore, we should expect that the bishop of Rome would be given the power and assistance appropriate to this particular pastoral charge. The pastoral responsibility of the bishop of Rome is unique inasmuch as it involves, in addition to a pastoral concern for the local Church of Rome, a pastoral concern for the communion of Churches.[51] Thus the pastoral responsibility of the bishop of Rome demands a power and authority that while not duplicated by that of other bishops is nevertheless episcopal in form. In this view the universal pastorate of the pope makes him more than "first among equals," yet without compromising his identity as a bishop among bishops.

This understanding of papal primacy recalls the ancient title for the pope employed by St. Gregory the Great, the servant of the servants of God *(servus servorum Dei)*. By viewing the pope as a bishop among bishops who is head of the college because he is first a member of the college, we can better understand his ministry as a service to the ministry of the other bishops, who share with him a pastoral concern for the Church universal. As Tillard notes, the unique authority of the bishop of Rome is not exercised as a *dominium* but a *ministerium,* a service offered in support of the ministry of the other bishops.[52] Here we find an ecclesial application of the principle of subsidiarity central to Catholic social teaching. Pastoral concerns should be addressed by the Church authority closest to the locus of the pastoral issue.[53] The "normal" ministry of the bishop of Rome

[51]Tillard, *Bishop of Rome,* 40–41. See also Tillard, *Church of Churches,* ch. 4.

[52]Tillard, *Church of Churches,* 272–73.

[53]The principle of subsidiarity was originally developed within Roman Catholicism's developing social justice tradition and was explicitly treated in Pius XI's 1931 encyclical *Quadragesimo anno.* The general principle is that no higher organization or association should undertake a task that can better and more effectively be handled by a more proximate organization or association. Its first ecclesiological application came in an address by Pius XII to newly created cardinals on February 20, 1946. Making reference to Pius XI's social application of the term, Pius XII said: "Our predecessor of happy memory, Pius XI, in his Encyclical *Quadragesimo Anno* on social order, drew a practical conclusion . . . when he announced a principle of general application, viz.: that what individual beings can do by themselves and by their own forces, should not be taken from them and assigned to the community. It is a principle that also holds good for smaller communities and those of lower rank in relation to those which are larger and in a position of superiority. For—as the wise Pontiff said, developing his thought—every social activity is of its nature subsidiary *(subsidiaria);* it must serve as a support to members of the social body and never destroy or absorb them. These are surely enlightened words, valid for social life in all its grades and *also for the*

would be one of encouragement and support for the pastoral ministry of the local bishops. As the bishop among bishops called to a special ministry of universal pastoral concern, one can imagine pastoral situations that would demand the direct intervention of the bishop of Rome because the unity of faith and communion of the whole Church demanded it. While such exercises of papal authority would be ordinary in the canonical sense that the authority to intervene is proper to the bishop of Rome and not delegated, they generally would be extraordinary in frequency.[54]

Against this view of the ministry of the bishop of Rome one might argue that both Vatican I and II affirmed unequivocally that the papal exercise of supreme and universal power over the whole Church does not require the delegation of authority or even the consent of the episcopal college. The pope may exercise this power "on his own." Does not the ability of the pope to act apart from the college render his relationship to his fellow bishops superfluous?

There are now a growing number of theologians[55] who find the insistence of Vatican I and Vatican II that the pope can "act alone" somewhat misleading. They would contend that even when the pope exercises his papal authority "alone," his ministry is nevertheless collegial in character. These theologians hold that there cannot be two "inadequately distinct subjects" of supreme authority, pope and college, as many of the neo-Scholastic manuals put it. Rather, from an ontological point of view there is only one subject of supreme authority in the Church, and that subject is the college of bishops. It is this college, which of course is only a college when under the headship of the bishop of Rome, that possesses the supreme teaching authority of the Church. That supreme authority is then exercised either in an explicit collegial act of the whole college, as with a council, or in an implicit collegial act exercised through the head of that college,

---

life of the Church without prejudice to its hierarchical structure." AAS 38 (1946) 144–45 (my emphasis).

[54]This conviction was affirmed in the *relatio* of Bishop Zinelli at Vatican I. Cf. Mansi 52, 1105.

[55]Cf. Tillard, *Bishop of Rome,* 157ff.; Yves Congar, *Fifty Years of Catholic Theology: Conversations with Yves Congar,* ed. Bernard Lauret (Philadelphia: Fortress, 1988) 51; Karl Rahner, "On the Relationship Between the Pope and the College of Bishops," in *Theological Investigations* (New York: Seabury, 1977) 10:50–70.

the bishop of Rome. That is, since the pope is always head of the episcopal college, every papal exercise of universal pastoral concern, every action on behalf of "the unity of faith and communion" of the whole Church, is an exercise of the college itself. Juridically one can distinguish between a papal exercise of supreme authority and an exercise of that supreme authority by the episcopal college, but ecclesiologically they are the same.

It follows, then, that although the pope need not explicitly "consult" his fellow bishops in every exercise of his universal pastoral ministry, he must maintain a real and substantial communion with them. This communion among pope and bishops, of course, is a spiritual reality and therefore cannot be *reduced* to some set of institutional structures. At the same time, since the Church is a sacramental reality this spiritual communion, if it is real, will normally be manifested in concrete structures and sets of recognizable social relations. If this communion among the bishops is not to be trivialized, there must be a habitual consultation and conversation in which the pope not only instructs but listens to his fellow bishops. It should be noted that both Pius IX and Pius XII consulted the bishops prior to their respective definitions of the dogmas of the immaculate conception and the bodily assumption of Mary. While their potential has yet to be fully realized, the role of regional episcopal conferences and the world synod of bishops offer concrete examples of the way in which the principle of collegiality could be concretely exercised.

In summary, let me try to describe a view of papal primacy within this ecclesiology of communion. Vatican I itself taught that the papacy was to serve the unity of faith and communion of the multitude of believers by serving the unity of the bishops and clergy. This is why Roman Catholic theologians generally insist that the principle of synodality, so central to the Eastern Orthodox tradition and in need of retrieval by the Western tradition, must be complemented by the Petrine principle in which the papal ministry functions as a ministry of unity. Patrick Burns writes:

> In Catholic tradition the local church of Rome constitutes a true center of the ecumenical Christian communion, and the bishop of Rome is a true head of the universal episcopal college. His office is one of maintaining peace, unity, and purity of faith in the church universal, *as* head of the college of bishops and *in communion with* the world-wide *communio* of local and regional churches. Papal actions which violate this basic arrangement do not contribute to the good of the universal

church and inevitably provoke prophetic protest with the Christian communion and the universal episcopal college.[56]

The pope must be able to exercise that power and authority, no more and no less, that is necessary for the preservation of the Church in faith and communion. Tillard writes of the bishop of Rome:

> This is a bishop among other bishops who is commissioned, on the basis of the shared grace of episcopacy, to gather his brother bishops into a college of which he is the *centrum unitatis*. He is a bishop within the college who must by the Lord's expressed will extend the *sollicitudo* of all the churches which is shared throughout the body of bishops to the point where it becomes a personal "watch" over whatever in these churches affects the apostolic faith and the communion in the *catholica*.[57]

Finally, hints of this view of papal ministry can be found in John Paul II's encyclical on ecumenism:

> In the beautiful expression of Pope St. Gregory the Great, my ministry is that of *servus servorum Dei*. This designation is the best possible safeguard against the risk of separating power (and in particular the primacy) from ministry. Such a separation would contradict the very meaning of power according to the Gospel: "I am among you as one who serves." . . . As the heir to the mission of Peter in the church . . . the bishop of Rome exercises a ministry originating in the manifold mercy of God. . . . The authority proper to this ministry is completely at the service of God's merciful plan, and it must always be seen in this perspective. Its power is explained from this perspective. . . . This service of unity, rooted in the action of divine mercy, *is entrusted within the college of bishops* to one among those who have received from the Spirit the task, not of exercising power over the people—as the rulers of the gentiles and their great men do—but of leading them toward peaceful pastures. . . . *[T]he mission of the bishop of Rome within the college of all pastors consists precisely in "keeping watch" (episkopein), like a sentinel,* so that through the efforts of the pastors the true voice of Christ the shepherd may be heard in all the particular churches. . . . With the power and the authority without which such an office would be illusory, the bishop of Rome must ensure the communion of all the churches. For this reason, he is the first servant of unity. . . . *All this, however, must always be done*

---

[56]Burns, "Communion, Councils, and Collegiality," 170.
[57]Tillard, *Bishop of Rome,* 157.

in communion. When the Catholic Church affirms that the office of the bishop of Rome corresponds to the will of Christ, *she does not separate this office from the mission entrusted to the whole body of bishops,* who are also "vicars and ambassadors of Christ." . . . I am convinced that I have a particular responsibility in this regard, above all in acknowledging the ecumenical aspirations of the majority of the Christian communities and in heeding the request made to me to find a way of exercising the primacy, which, while in no way renouncing what is essential to its mission, is nonetheless open to a new situation (*UU* 88, 92, 94–95, my emphasis).

This remarkable vision of papal ministry has tremendous potential for reinvigorating the ecumenical movement, but only to the extent that it becomes concretely realized in visible institutional structures and in the actual exercise of authority in the Church. Today many of our ecumenical dialogue partners pay less attention to ecclesiastical pronouncements and more attention to the concrete structures, policies, and ecclesiastical actions that reflect Catholicism's *operative* ecclesiology.

Conclusion

This chapter has considered the principal structures of ecclesial authority, the college of bishops, and the papacy. Of particular importance was the way in which Vatican II offered the beginnings of an account of ecclesial authority grounded in an ecclesiology of communion. With respect to ecclesial authority this communion exists at two levels: (1) the communion that exists between the college of bishops and the communion of Churches and (2) the communion that exists among the bishop of Rome and the other bishops of the episcopal college. This twofold communion will serve as the foundation for our consideration of doctrinal teaching authority in the Church.

This ecclesiology of communion also represents an important attempt to respond to many of the questions raised by Orthodox, Anglican, and Protestant theologians cited throughout this chapter. It is an ecclesiology that agrees with many non-Catholic theologians regarding the necessity of situating the college of bishops *within* the communion of Churches. Episcopal authority is only intelligible in terms of its relationship to the Church. At the same time this *communio* ecclesiology suggests that papal primacy need not be viewed as an independent, external authority over the bishops. Rather, papal primacy is best understood in terms of the papacy's relationship to the college of bishops as both member and head. The next two chapters will consider the particular concern of Protestantism regarding the teaching office of the Church's relationship to the gospel itself.

An essential aspect of the ministry of the pope and college is the preservation of the apostolic faith of the Church in all its integrity. The pope and the other members of the college together function as the formal subject of doctrinal teaching authority in the Church. To them is entrusted the responsibility of preserving the apostolic faith of the Church by authoritatively proclaiming that faith in Church doctrine. But what is it, precisely, that the pope and bishops teach? What do we mean by the "apostolic faith"? How is their teaching related to the word of God as it is mediated through Scripture and tradition? Part 2 of this volume will shift from the subject of doctrinal teaching authority to its object, the divinely revealed word of God.

For Further Reading

The Ministry of the Bishop and Episcopal Collegiality

Congar, Yves. "The Conciliar Structure or Regime of the Church." In *The Ecumenical Council. (Concilium* 167). Ed. Peter Huizing and Knut Walt, 3–9. Edinburgh: T & T Clark, 1983.

Legrand, Hervé-Marie. "Theology and the Election of Bishops in the Early Church." In *Election and Consensus in the Church. (Concilium* 77). Ed. Giuseppe Alberigo and Anton Weiler, 31–42. New York: Herder, 1972.

Rahner, Karl, and Joseph Ratzinger. *Episcopate and Primacy.* New York: Herder & Herder, 1962.

Ryan, Seamus. "Episcopal Consecration: Fullness of Order." *Irish Theological Quarterly* 32 (1965) 295–304.

Tierney, Brian. *Foundations of Conciliar Theory: The Contributions of the Medieval Canonists from Gratian to the Great Schism.* Cambridge: Cambridge Univ., 1955.

Wood, Susan. "The Sacramentality of Episcopal Consecration." *Theological Studies* 51 (1990) 479–96.

Zizioulas, John D. "The Development of Conciliar Structure to the Time of the First Ecumenical Council." In *Councils and the Ecumenical Movement*, 34–51. Geneva: WCC, 1968.

The Papacy

Brown, Raymond E., Karl P. Donfried, and John Reumann, eds. *Peter in the New Testament.* New York: Paulist, 1973.

Dionne, J. Robert. *The Papacy and the Church: A Study of Praxis and Reception in Ecumenical Perspective.* New York: Philosophical Library, 1987.

Empie, Paul C., and T. Austin Murphy, eds. *Papal Primacy and the Universal Church.* Lutherans and Catholics in Dialogue V. Minneapolis: Augsburg, 1974.

Eno, Robert. *The Rise of the Papacy.* Wilmington: Glazier, 1990.

Farmer, William R., and Roch Kereszty. *Peter and Paul in the Church of Rome.* New York: Paulist, 1990.

Granfield, Patrick. *The Limits of the Papacy.* New York: Crossroad, 1987.

_____. *The Papacy in Transition.* New York: Doubleday, 1980.

McCord, Peter J., ed. *A Pope for All Christians?* New York: Paulist, 1976.

Meyendorff, John, ed. *The Primacy of Peter.* Crestwood: St. Vladimir's Seminary Press, 1992.

Tillard, Jean M.-R. *The Bishop of Rome.* Wilmington: Glazier, 1983.

Part Two

The Object of Doctrinal
Teaching Authority

3

What the Church Teaches: In Service of the Word of God

Vatican II's consideration of divine revelation is one of the more overlooked contributions of the council. The theological developments in the Dogmatic Constitution on Divine Revelation, *Dei verbum*, were less obvious than the changes in the liturgy and less dramatic than the seismic shift that occurred in the treatment of the Church in both *Lumen gentium* and the Pastoral Constitution on the Church in the Modern World, *Gaudium et spes*. Nevertheless, *Dei verbum* laid the foundations for a profoundly reconceived theology of revelation. In this chapter I will briefly summarize some of the more significant features of this theology as they relate to a theology of doctrinal teaching authority in the Church.

The Dominance of a Propositional View of Revelation on the Eve of Vatican II

There is no definitive listing of Catholic Church teachings. There are, of course, many creeds, catechisms, and ecclesiastical documents of various sorts, but nowhere is there a definitive list of every Catholic teaching. Given the importance that Catholicism places on the authoritative teaching of doctrine, this may seem surprising. Just thirty years ago it was common for someone desiring admission into the Roman Catholic Church to receive "instructions" from the parish priest. In these instructions Catholicism was often presented as a collection of discrete propositional truths. The assumption was that assent to these truths was equivalent to assent to the Catholic faith. If the inquirer could assent to these teachings he or she could be admitted into the Church. This understanding of the Catholic faith followed from a propositional view of divine revelation the origins of which can be traced back to the late Middle Ages. It is a view or "model" of revelation that became dominant in Catholic thought in the centuries following the Council of Trent.[1]

This propositional model of revelation presented divine revelation as the communication of fundamental truths about God.[2] In this view supernatural revelation was concerned primarily with the transmission of conceptual knowledge and was conceived on the analogy of human speech.[3] Consequently, dogmatic propositions often took on the authority of "divine utterances." Since not all of the dogmatic propositions proposed by the Church as divinely revealed could be found in Scripture this view of revelation led some to assert the existence of two distinct sources of divine revelation, Scripture and tradition. While certain propositional truths were explicitly articulated in Scripture, others could only be found in tradition. This view reflects a revelational positivism in which revelation itself is identified with its historical mediations.[4] It is this propositional and positivistic view of revelation with its attendant two-source theory that was ultimately challenged by the bishops at Vatican II.

During the first session of Vatican II the bishops were presented with a draft document on divine revelation that presupposed much of this propositional model.[5] This draft presented a theology of revelation

[1] Avery Dulles considers this approach to revelation as one of several different "models of revelation." In this context a given model suggests "a possible and consistent way of thinking about a certain set of problems." *Models of Revelation* (Garden City: Doubleday, 1983) 31–32. Dulles refers to what I have called the "propositional model" as "revelation as doctrine." For his initial treatment of this model see 36–52.

[2] For examples of this model of revelation see Christian Pesch, *Praelectiones dogmaticae,* 5th ed. (Freiburg: Herder, 1915) and Reginald Garrigou-Lagrange, *De Revelatione per Ecclesiam catholicam proposita,* 4th ed. (Rome: Ferrari, 1945).

[3] Cf. Pesch, *Praelectiones dogmaticae,* 1:116.

[4] Joseph Ratzinger, "The Dogmatic Constitution on Divine Revelation," in *Commentary on the Documents of Vatican II,* ed. Herbert Vorgrimler (New York: Crossroad, 1989) 3:190–91.

[5] Joseph Ratzinger, "Dogmatic Constitution on Divine Revelation, Origin and Background," in *Commentary on the Documents of Vatican II,* 3:155–67. For further background on the Dogmatic Constitution on Divine Revelation,

in cognitive terms as a collection of propositional statements or doctrines. It assumed problematic understandings of the inspiration of the biblical authors and the nature of the assistance of the Holy Spirit given to the Church hierarchy. In considerations of biblical authorship, for example, the text downplayed the human element and considered the biblical authors as little more than passive conduits of divine truth.

During the first session of the council several bishops were emboldened by Pope John XXIII's opening address and arose in opposition to this draft when it was introduced for debate. Cardinal Achille Liénart of Lille, France, drew particular attention to the first chapter of the schema, entitled "Two Sources of Revelation." He contended that this conception of revelation was foreign to Scripture, the writings of the early Church, and even St. Thomas Aquinas. Liénart insisted that there was but one font of divine revelation, the word of God, transmitted in both Scripture and tradition. He further noted the disastrous consequences of such a formulation for ecumenical relations, sustaining as it did the mistaken notion that the Catholic hierarchy was empowered to "add" to divine revelation. Other bishops joined in opposition to the schema, with many calling for its complete withdrawal in favor of a new document. In what would be a major turning point in the council, John XXIII ultimately demanded the removal of the schema and established a new commission to draft a shorter alternative.

Important Developments in Vatican II's Dogmatic Constitution on Divine Revelation

The Dogmatic Constitution on Divine Revelation, *Dei verbum,* would go through many revisions.[6] Probably more than the other

---

Dei verbum, see L. Alonso Schökel, ed., *Concilio Vaticano II: Comentarios a la Constitución Dei Verbum* (Madrid: BAC, 1969); B.-D. Dupuy, ed., *La Révélation divine* (Paris: Cerf, 1968); René Latourelle, *Theology of Revelation* (Staten Island: Alba, 1966). Brief but helpful summary analyses of the document include Robert Murray, "Revelation," in *Modern Catholicism: Vatican II and After,* ed. Adrian Hastings (New York: Oxford Univ. Press, 1991) 74–83; Donald Senior, "Dogmatic Constitution on Divine Revelation," in *Vatican II and Its Documents: An American Reappraisal,* ed. Timothy E. O'Connell (Wilmington: Glazier, 1986) 122–40.

[6]A helpful introductory text on a theology of revelation would be Dermot Lane, *The Experience of God: An Invitation to Do Theology* (New York:

three constitutions promulgated by the council, *Dei verbum* was a compromise document. Often new formulations of a theology of revelation were juxtaposed with those more reflective of the propositional view.[7] Nevertheless, the constitution made significant advances. In the three decades since the council a number of these themes have received further development. While it is not possible to give any kind of comprehensive consideration to the constitution, a review of these themes and their potential for contemporary theological reflection on our topic will be valuable.

The Primacy of the Word of God

The opening sentence of *Dei verbum* begins by describing the task of the council: "Hearing the Word of God with reverence, and proclaiming it with faith . . ." (*DV* 1).[8] This remarkable opening passage introduces a theology of revelation closely related to the emerging ecclesiology of the council. The Church cannot be reduced to a self-contained institution that has divine truth as its private possession. The Church transcends itself in an attitude of openness and receptivity to a word it receives as servant rather than as master. This introduces a major theme of the constitution, namely the primacy of the living word of God, spoken from the beginning of creation, incarnate in Jesus of Nazareth, and proclaimed in the life of the Church.

The stress on the primacy of the word of God is further explored in the first chapter of the constitution, which sketches out a more personalist and Trinitarian theology of divine revelation:

> By this revelation, then, the invisible God, from the fullness of divine love, addresses men and women as friends, and moves among them, in

Paulist, 1981). Gerald O'Collins' writings are also helpful. Cf. *Fundamental Theology* (New York: Paulist, 1981); *Retrieving Fundamental Theology* (New York: Paulist, 1993). A more ambitious, scholarly treatment would be Roger Haight, *Dynamics of Theology* (New York: Paulist, 1990), which, in varying degrees, draws on the fundamental theologies of Karl Rahner and Paul Tillich.

[7] For more on this method of juxtaposition at Vatican II see Hermann J. Pottmeyer, "A New Phase in the Reception of Vatican II: Twenty Years of Interpretation of the Council," in *The Reception of Vatican II,* ed. Giuseppe Alberigo, Jean-Pierre Jossua, and Joseph A. Komonchak (Washington: Catholic Univ. of America Press, 1987) 27–43.

[8] Translation from Austin Flannery, ed., *Vatican II: The Conciliar and Post Conciliar Documents,* study ed. (Grand Rapids: Eerdmans, 1987).

order to invite and receive them into his own company. This economy of revelation is realized by deeds and words, which are intrinsically bound together. As a result, the works performed by God in the history of salvation show forth and bear out the doctrine and realities signified by the words; the words, for their part, proclaim the works, and bring to light the mystery they contain. The most intimate truth which this revelation gives us about God and the salvation of humanity shines forth in Christ, who is himself both the mediator and the sum total of revelation (*DV* 2).[9]

Perhaps no conciliar passage better illustrates the shift in revelational theology effected at the council. In his commentary on this text Joseph Ratzinger observes:

> The Council's intention in this matter was a simple one. . . . The fathers were merely concerned with overcoming neo-scholastic intellectualism, for which revelation chiefly meant a store of mysterious supernatural teachings, which automatically reduces faith very much to an acceptance of these supernatural insights. As opposed to this, the Council desired to express again the character of revelation as a totality, in which word and event make up one whole, a true dialogue which touches man in his totality, not only challenging his reason, but, as dialogue, addressing him as a partner, indeed giving him his true nature for the first time.[10]

This "economy of revelation realized in deeds and words" takes the form of a relationship in which God addresses us as friends. Therefore any account of that divine truth communicated in revelation must have as its starting point a view of revealed truth understood not so much as a body of information communicated in a set of propositional statements but truth communicated in the form of a relationship—in a word, communion. In divine revelation what we encounter is God's very being in personal relationship. It is in this sense that we might properly speak not of divine words about God but of a divine "Word"—the perfect self-expression of God. God's Word, God's personal self-disclosure, comes to us in history in the form of an address. As addressed to humanity, it is fully realized, it becomes fully "word," only when it is received. God's revelation is itself, then, an event of communion and of transformation; it demands a dialogue

---

[9]This is my adaptation of the English translation in Flannery, *Vatican II.*
[10]Ratzinger, "Dogmatic Constitution," 172.

between God and humankind. It is a Word offered to us in love by a God whose very being is love and it is by the power of God's Spirit that we are able to respond to that Word. Commenting further on *Dei verbum's* theology of revelation, Ratzinger writes:

> We can see again here how little intellectualism and doctrinalism are able to comprehend the nature of revelation, which is not concerned with talking *about* something that is quite external to the person, but with the realization of the existence of man, with the relation of the human "I" to the divine "thou," so that the purpose of this dialogue is ultimately not information, but unity and transformation.[11]

We might reflect for a moment on the many ways in which this divine self-communication is manifested. We discover echoes of God's Word in the first instance in creation itself, which bears the imprint of its Creator. It is effective in the innumerable experiences of human transcendence in which the human person finds himself with a longing and desire that cannot be satisfied. God is revealed to us in the human questions that elude answers, in those human experiences that confront us with the limits of our existence and yet lead us to ask if there is indeed something more, something ultimate. We can affirm the revelatory character of the explicitly religious dimensions of human existence even when this religious dimension is actualized outside the Judeo-Christian tradition (cf. *NA* 2). According to the Christian faith, this divine self-communication in love finds a privileged form in God's covenantal relationship with Israel. In that relationship, recounted in the First Testament of the Bible, we find a rich testimony to God's self-communication in word and deed.

Finally, Christianity contends that this divine Word, spoken throughout all of history, has come to us unsurpassably in Jesus Christ. Christ is the definitive self-communication of God. For Christians, Jesus Christ functions as the perfect mediation, the norm and fulfillment of divine revelation. This Christocentric view of revelation reminds us that the culmination of God's self-communication comes to us not in a set of propositions but in a person, Jesus of Nazareth.

One of the great dangers of the propositional model of revelation was that by virtually identifying divine revelation with propositional statements or doctrines it risked reducing God to some body of knowledge available for our cognitive mastery. Overlooked was the essen-

---

[11]Ibid., 175.

tial distinction between ordinary knowledge and that knowledge of God given to us in divine revelation. Ordinary knowledge is concerned with the ability to intellectually grasp, comprehend, or master some reality. Yet God is not a reality who can be grasped or comprehended; God can only be embraced in love.

The unique character of that knowledge of God given us in divine revelation demands that we avoid two extremes. On the one hand, to reject completely any cognitive content to divine revelation as communicated in Church doctrine is to deny the fundamental significance of the incarnation of the word of God in Jesus Christ. In the doctrine of the incarnation Christians hold that God's saving word has become visible and intelligible in human history. The intelligibility of that revelation in Jesus Christ means that it must be possible for revelation to receive some conceptual form. There must be some recognizable "content." Consequently we must grant that propositional statements provide a legitimate means for giving expression to that revelatory content. We will return to this in our treatment of Church dogma. On the other hand, revelation is not primarily a didactic explication of the being of God—it is an invitation to divine communion with the Father, through Christ, in the Spirit. We can speak analogously of a "knowledge" of God given in divine revelation, but it is that kind of knowledge that "inhabits" a relationship and cannot be easily extracted from it. The language of love is only fully intelligible to those who abide in the loving relationship. The same applies to the language of faith. This is what the Church means when it claims that Scripture and tradition must be received "in faith." For it is only in Christ through the power of the Spirit that one can receive the saving knowledge of God. Doctrine does communicate divine truth, but only within the life of faith and in a manner consonant with a relationship with the God who is incomprehensible, holy mystery. Our understanding of the role of dogma in communicating divine revelation must acknowledge the primacy of this more participative view of revelation.

Let me conclude with a helpful summary of this important shift at Vatican II in the Catholic understanding of revelation offered by Dermot Lane:

> Revelation no longer appears simply as a body of supernatural truths contained in Scripture and taught by the Church. There is a clear movement in *Dei Verbum* away from revelation as simply *revelata* (truths disclosed) to *revelatio* (personal disclosure). The basic emphasis

is now placed on the personal self-communication of God to humanity in Christ. This does not neglect or diminish the new knowledge expressed in doctrine that results from this personal disclosure. . . . It does imply, however, that this new knowledge is something consequent to the more important emphasis on the personal self-communication of God in Christ.[12]

A Theology of Tradition

While Jesus Christ was God's definitive self-expression, the Word incarnate to which there is nothing left to be added, nevertheless that Word is received by humanity in history; it is kept alive in the living memory of the Church. As a dynamic, living Word, it speaks anew to each generation of believers. Therefore, God's Word must continue to take new forms as it takes root in the hearts of believers and in the life of the Church. This is the understanding of tradition in its most dynamic sense, as God's Word actualized in the life of the Church.

> The expression "what has been handed down from the apostles" includes everything that helps the people of God to live a holy life and to grow in faith. In this way the church, in its teaching, life and worship, perpetuates and hands on to every generation all that it is and all that it believes.
>
> This tradition which comes from the apostles progresses in the church under the assistance of the holy Spirit. There is a growth in understanding of what is handed on, both the words and the realities they signify. This comes about through contemplation and study by believers, who "ponder these things in their hearts"; through the intimate understanding of spiritual things which they experience; and through the preaching of those who, on succeeding to the office of bishop, receive the sure charism of truth. Thus, as the centuries advance, the church constantly holds its course towards the fullness of God's truth, until the day when the words of God reach their fulfillment in the church (*DV* 8).

This text was most likely authored by Yves Congar, and it reflects the considerable influence of the Tübingen school's theology of tradition, which was itself informed by German Romanticism.[13] The text portrays tradition as dynamic and progressive. It is neither reduced to a

[12]Dermot Lane, *Experience of God,* 56–57.
[13]Cf. Yves Congar, *Tradition and Traditions: An Historical and a Theological Essay* (New York: Macmillan, 1967).

collection of Church doctrine, nor is it identified with the magisterium, but rather is presented as the very sum of the Church's identity. Tradition is the living gospel in all of its various historical embodiments in the life of the Church. This view of tradition, referred to in the singular, clearly dominates the council's theology. It represents a remarkable departure from the more common tendency to identify tradition with a collection of doctrinal statements and ecclesiastical customs and practices or with the magisterium itself.

Not developed in this passage is the necessary distinction between *tradition* as the ongoing life of the Church testifying to the gospel of Jesus Christ and *ecclesiastical traditions* as constituent components of the Church's life which vary significantly in the degree to which they transmit in a permanent and enduring manner the one gospel of Jesus Christ. During the council debates Cardinal Meyer of Chicago had in fact complained about this omission. He insisted that the language of this text did not sufficiently encourage a critical stance toward various Church traditions. The Church must freely admit that among the many legitimate components in the Church's tradition there were also serious deficiencies and distortions that must be forthrightly addressed.[14] Indeed, implicit in Cardinal Meyer's concern is the much larger question of whether the language of "development," "evolution," or "progress" is even helpful when applied to tradition viewed diachronically. Can one not speak as well of occasional periods of regression and impoverishment in Church tradition?[15] This shortcoming notwithstanding, the theology of tradition developed in the constitution contained several significant features that have far-reaching implications for fundamental theology and that therefore deserve further comment.

The Pneumatological Character of Divine Revelation

I noted earlier the Christocentric view of divine revelation reflected in *Dei verbum* 2. However, in article 8 the council also considered the

---

[14]*Acta synodalia* III/3, 150–151.

[15]I cannot discuss here the important question regarding the adequacy of a "developmental" or "evolutionary" view of doctrinal change. These approaches originated in the nineteenth century with both the Tübingen school and John Henry Newman and were very influential at Vatican II. For an analysis of the adequacy of developmental theories see Nicholas Lash, *Change in Focus: A Study of Doctrinal Change and Continuity* (London: Sheed & Ward, 1973).

pneumatological dimension of divine revelation as it comes to us in Church tradition. It is in the Spirit that the Church comes to *recognize* divine truth: "The holy Spirit, too, is active, making the living voice of the gospel ring out in the church, and through it in the world, leading those who believe into the whole truth, and making the message of Christ dwell in them in all its richness." The word of God takes root in the people of God through the work of the Holy Spirit. It is in the Spirit that the community is able to recognize and respond to God's word in faith. In *Lumen gentium* this ability to recognize and respond to God's word was called a supernatural sense of the faith, a gift given by the Spirit to all baptized believers:

> Through this sense of faith which is aroused and sustained by the Spirit of truth, the people of God, under the guidance of the sacred magisterium to which it is faithfully obedient, receives no longer the words of human beings but truly the word of God; it adheres indefectibly to "the faith which was once for all delivered to the saints"; it penetrates more deeply into that same faith through right judgment and applies it more fully to life (*LG* 12).

This pneumatological perspective when properly understood negates any attempt to conceive of God's word as the unique possession of any one group within the Church, including the bishops. God's word continues to abide in the whole Church through the Holy Spirit. In fact, in the council's listing of the ways in which the Church grows in the truth, the preaching of the bishops is preceded by the role of the faithful. Mary, who pondered Christ's words in her heart, serves as a model for the role of the faithful. This represents an important expansion of the "traditioning" process of the Church. While some post-Tridentine theologies of tradition stressed the role of the bishops in passing on the faith through apostolic succession,[16] the council members at Vatican II affirmed that this process of passing on the faith is the work of the whole Church. It occurs whenever a parent catechizes his or her child, whenever the liturgy is celebrated and the gospel proclaimed, whenever the values of the gospel are testified to in the work habits and attitudes of Christians in the marketplace. We shall develop the implications of the pneumatological understanding of revelation in chapter 5.

[16]Though important exceptions can be found in the writings of such nineteenth-century theologians as Johann Baptist Franzelin and Matthias Scheeben.

The Eschatological Character of Divine Revelation

The second significant feature of *DV* 8 is its eschatological treatment of divine revelation. The fullness of truth has been given to the Church in the person of Jesus Christ. Yet at the same time the Church looks to the *plenitude* of that truth as something that awaits the Church in its final eschatological consummation. There is a sense in which the truth revealed in Christ is not something that the Church can possess; rather it is the truth that possesses the Church.[17] For this truth, given to the Church in Jesus Christ, transcends all attempts at human mastery. And so, while living in truth, the pilgrim Church continually progresses toward the "plenitude of truth," which it will acquire only in the eschaton. This eschatological conception of divine truth that eludes cognitive mastery and is encountered primarily by an ecclesial "abiding" has profound implications, as we shall see, for an understanding of dogma.

Conclusion: Anamnesis *as a Way of Viewing*
Christian Tradition

In postconciliar theology, one helpful way of developing this more dynamic view of tradition has been through the analogy of memory. Memory can illuminate the category of tradition both in its active sense as a process of handing on the apostolic faith and in its objective sense as the actual content of that faith. "Memory" is not here meant in its everyday meaning in which it refers to a mere recalling things from the past but in its ancient biblical and liturgical usage in which the transformative power of past events is brought to bear on present realities.

The biblical view of memory is reflected in the First Testament usage of the Hebrew verb *zkr*, in which, according to Xavier

---

[17]"In matters of faith, no [one], not even the Pope or the bishops, *possesses* the truth. . . . This divine truth *possesses us.* . . . Truth takes possession of us. But we must go a step further. It does not take possession of us individually, for this truth is *entrusted* before all to *the Church*. Similarly, at the level of the Church as a whole, we cannot strictly say: 'The Church is in possession of the truth, of the true faith.' Yet the true faith is unfailingly entrusted to the Church, the Body of Christ and the Bride of the Lord. It is entrusted to her as a sacred heritage which never becomes her own property. In other words, the sum total of her teaching will never exhaust all its wealth." Piet Fransen, "The Authority of Councils," in *Problems of Authority*, ed. John M. Todd (Baltimore: Helicon, 1962) 45.

Léon-Dufour, "memory and action are intrinsically connected."[18] For the Hebrew people, what was to be "remembered" above all was the covenant made between God and the people of Israel. To "remember" this covenant was to allow the covenant to lay claim on their present reality. "Memory and action are thus the two sides—the internal and the external—of the relationship between God and human beings. God saves human beings—which is certainly a "memorable" action; when they remember this action, they renew their fidelity to the covenant."[19] Remembrance meant becoming aware of present obligations to remain faithful to God. Not surprisingly, Léon-Dufour notes, this active sense of memory naturally led to cultic expression. In the complex system of ritual sacrifices and the developing calendar of liturgical feasts, the unifying principle was an active remembering that constituted the unique identity of the Jewish people. Liturgical feasts ritually enacted this process of remembering. This ritual memory is at the heart of the Passover ritual with its rich narrative of God's past deeds recalled precisely to invoke and celebrate God's present liberating and salvific activity in the life of Israel.

This Hebrew understanding of memory is taken up in the Second Testament use of the Greek word *anamnesis,* particularly as it was used in connection with the Christian Eucharist. Christ's mandate at the Last Supper, "do this in memory of me" (cf. Luke 22:19; 1 Cor 11:23-26), according to Léon-Dufour, involved much more than a command to engage in later "memorials"; it called for the performance of a ritual action that would have both cultic and prophetic dimensions. As cult, Eucharistic *anamnesis* ("making remembrance") means remembering in the celebration of the Eucharist the past event of Christ's own passover from death into new life in such a way that the celebrating community is drawn up into the paschal mystery. As prophetic, the celebration of the Eucharist calls forth eschatological realities; the Eucharistic community "remembers" a future that is not yet fully in its possession.[20] The Church's memory impels it toward

---

[18]Xavier Léon-Dufour, *Sharing the Eucharistic Bread* (New York: Paulist, 1987) 102. This brief treatment of biblical memory depends substantially on Léon-Dufour.

[19]Ibid., 105.

[20]Ibid., 111. Léon-Dufour's treatment of the biblical "institution narratives" assumes a great deal regarding their historicity which would not be granted by many biblical scholars. I do not believe, however, that the question of the historicity of these texts negates his elucidation of the notion of *anamnesis.*

the future. It is on the basis of our ecclesial memory of who God has been for us that we are engaged in meaningful human projects that draw us into the future. Liturgical scholar Mary Collins offers a wonderful reflection on this particular understanding of corporate memory:

> *Anamnesis* is biblical language which was long ago taken up by the Church and recently recovered as liturgical language. . . . We can perhaps best understand anamnesis by considering it indirectly. Anamnesis speaks about a distinctive kind of human remembering. In common speech we are more likely to talk about its opposite, amnesia. We are familiar with the disorder of clinical amnesia, a diagnosis given to name a memory lapse of a crucial kind. The amnesiac is not the person who has misplaced her glasses one time too many. She is the person who has forgotten who she is. She has lost her conscious awareness of the basic relationships that give her her identity. . . . "Anamnesis" and "amnesia" come from a common Greek root. The biblical and liturgical use of the word "anamnesis" rises from a perception that there is a disorder analogous to clinical amnesia that plagues the human community. To be human is to be threatened with spiritual amnesia. At the level of our spiritual identity we do not remember for long who we really are. Those ultimate relationships that give us our spiritual identity slip from consciousness all too easily, and we lapse into noncomprehension about our deepest identity.[21]

I believe that this biblical and liturgical sense of memory can enrich our understanding of tradition. Tradition can be viewed as the "memory" of God's word residing in the corporate consciousness of the Church. J.-M. R. Tillard has fruitfully employed this biblical understanding of corporate memory in his reflection on tradition:

> Memory in the biblical sense of the term is not simply storage of the sediment of the past. It is also the humus from which life never stops borrowing. As the memory of the Church, Tradition represents the permanence of a Word which is always alive, always enriched, and yet radically always the same, where the Church never ceases to nourish its faith.[22]

[21]Mary Collins, *Contemplative Participation* (Collegeville: The Liturgical Press, 1990) 55.

[22]J.-M. R. Tillard, *Church of Churches: The Ecclesiology of Communion* (Collegeville: The Liturgical Press, 1992) 141. Nicholas Lash contends that the notion of *anamnesis* may prove helpful for addressing the core problematic for any theology of tradition, namely, how to address the historical structure of Christian truth. Cf. Lash, *Change in Focus,* 71–72, 168–82.

To Tillard's application of *anamnesis* to a theology of tradition must be added the eschatological aspect of memory evident in Scripture and fruitfully developed by political and liberation theologians. Advocates of these related theological movements insist that far from being mere nostalgia, God's word as a living memory is also a "dangerous" memory precisely because it calls us to conversion.[23] Furthermore, this conversion cannot be understood in a merely private and pious sense. The dangerous memories of the Christian faith subvert any complacent acceptance of the social and political status quo, any reduction of the Christian faith to mere bourgeois religion.[24] According to German theologian Johann Baptist Metz, this is what is meant by *eschatological* memory:

> What is meant here is . . . not the memory that sees the past in a transfiguring light, nor the memory that sets a seal on the past by being reconciled with all that is dangerous and challenging in that past. It is also not the memory in which past happiness and salvation are applied merely individually. What is meant in this context is that dangerous memory that threatens the present and calls it into question because it remembers a future that is still outstanding.
>
> This memory breaks though the grip of the prevailing consciousness. It claims unresolved conflicts that have been thrust into the background and unfulfilled hopes. It maintains earlier experiences in contrast to the prevailing insights and in this way makes the present unsafe.[25]

While critics of political and liberation theologies legitimately warn of a reduction of God's saving word to the realm of socioeconomic and political realities, we cannot ignore the concrete political implications of God's word. The word of God is not proclaimed on some suprahistorical plane; it addresses us precisely in our concrete histories. If it is to be a truly effective word, its implications will be evident in all the particularities of human history. To immerse oneself in the life of the Church is to allow oneself to be shaped by this ecclesial memory. The identity a Christian assumes as a follower of Jesus will always have a countercultural element, a sense of worldly dis-

---

[23]For this notion of "dangerous memories," see the political theology of Johann Baptist Metz, *Faith in History and Society: Towards a Practical Fundamental Theology* (New York: Crossroad, 1980) 184–218.

[24]See Johann Baptist Metz, "Messianic or Bourgeois Religion," in *The Emergent Church* (New York: Crossroad, 1981) 1–16.

[25]Metz, *Faith in History and Society,* 200.

orientation. In some ways it is this experience of disorientation in the world, a realization that all is not as it should be, that confirms that the tradition in which we abide is truly a living and dynamic tradition that has preserved an alternative way of living. This alternative way, remembered within the community, places demands on our present; it challenges the various projects that occupy our time and asks us to evaluate them in the light of the gospel.[26]

The Word of God Is the One Font of Divine Revelation

Against the two-source theory that dominated Catholic theology over the past several centuries, Vatican II stressed the organic unity of the one word of God expressed in both Scripture and tradition:

> Hence, sacred tradition and sacred Scripture are bound together in a close and reciprocal relationship. They both flow from the same divine wellspring, merge together to some extent, and are on course towards the same end. Scripture is the utterance of God as it is set down in writing under the guidance of God's Spirit; tradition preserves the word of God as it was entrusted to the apostles by Christ our lord and the holy Spirit. . . . Tradition and Scripture together form a single sacred deposit of the word of God, entrusted to the church (*DV* 9–10).

This text represents an obvious departure from those post-Tridentine theologies that viewed tradition as a distinct, additional source of revelation apart from Scripture.[27] Vatican II viewed Scripture and

---

[26]Don Saliers has offered an important caution regarding what he calls the notion of "canonized memories." The corporate, Christian memory, he warns, is precisely what many Christian feminists have experienced as patriarchal and oppressive. Don E. Saliers, *Worship as Theology* (Nashville: Abingdon, 1994) 236–37 n. 1. Feminist theologians like Elisabeth Schüssler Fiorenza and Marjorie Procter-Smith, drawing on critical theory, have demonstrated the way Church tradition can be reduced to ideology and can oppress or marginalize whole groups of people (particularly women) by suppressing certain "memories" at the expense of others. Cf. Elisabeth Schüssler Fiorenza, *In Memory of Her: A Feminist Theological Reconstruction of Christian Origins* (New York: Crossroad, 1983); Marjorie Procter-Smith, *In Her Own Rite: Constructing Feminist Liturgical Tradition* (Nashville: Abingdon, 1990).

[27]One of the more technical aspects of the conciliar debate concerned whether it was possible to speak of the *material* sufficiency of Scripture, the belief that there were no teachings found in tradition that could not at least

tradition as representing distinct but interrelated modalities of God's one self-communication in "Christ our lord, in whom the whole revelation of God is summed up" (*DV* 7). This was due to the abandonment of a quantitative approach to revelation that sought to break down the deposit of faith into its constitutive components, determining which could be found in Scripture and which could not. When we accept that God's revelation comes to us primarily as a person, Jesus Christ, making present a saving offer, this kind of quantitative approach can no longer serve.

The good news of Jesus Christ, the fullness of divine revelation, was proclaimed by the whole Christian community under the leadership of the apostles. The apostolic witness would be preserved both in the canonical Scriptures and in the ongoing *paradosis* or handing on of the apostolic faith in the Christian community. The unity of Scripture and tradition is grounded then in the one word whose presence in human history comes to its unsurpassable actualization in Jesus Christ. Scripture and tradition must be viewed as interrelated witnesses to that word. Furthermore, neither Scripture nor tradition can be separated from the Church. The unity of Scripture, tradition, and the living communion of the Church itself is fundamental.[28] To follow our reflections on the analogy of memory, we might say that Scripture and tradition are distinct but interconnected cells of the Church's memory. This explains why Catholicism has resisted an easy enumeration of Church dogma; a focus on a set number of dogmatic statements would obscure the fundamental unity of all dogma in the saving work of Jesus Christ.

The Magisterium Teaches in Service of the Word of God

From the very first sentence of this constitution we have encountered the Church's dual task of listening to and proclaiming God's word. This dual role establishes a basic framework for evaluating the teaching ministry of the bishops—they teach only what they hear. This suggests that the great attention that the Roman Catholic tradition has given to the *teaching* acts of the bishops needs to be matched

---

implicitly be found in Scripture. In spite of the impression given by the addition to article 9 made at the request of Paul VI, this question was left open.

[28]"Therefore Holy Scripture, tradition and the communion of the Church are not entities isolated from one another; they form an inner unity." ITC, "On the Interpretation of Dogmas," *Origins* 20 (May 17, 1990) 11.

by equal attention to the *listening* process of the bishops. If the bishops are the authoritative *teachers* of the apostolic faith, it is only because they are first *hearers*. Their teaching is not a *determinatio fidei,* an independent determination of the faith of the Church, but a *testificatio fidei,* a witness to that which they have received, to that which they have heard. In this regard the council writes:

> This Magisterium is not superior to the Word of God, but is its servant. It teaches only what has been handed on to it. At the divine command and with the help of the Holy Spirit, it listens to this devotedly, guards it with dedication and expounds it faithfully. All that it proposes for belief as being divinely revealed is drawn from this single deposit of faith (*DV* 10).[29]

This passage must be understood in conjunction with article 8, which affirmed the role of the whole people of God in transmitting the faith. For if the authoritative teachers of the faith are to first listen to the word before they can teach it, where do they turn to hear God's word? This word does not drop down from heaven. Does it not reverberate in the life and worship of the Christian community itself? We must dismiss any supernaturalist notion of divine assistance that bypasses human processes or imagines that at episcopal ordination a bishop receives a supernaturally infused "microchip" containing the totality of divine revelation!

How then do the bishops "hear" God's word? Without being exhaustive, at least four different means for hearing God's word come to mind: (1) through a prayerful study of Scripture, the writings of the early Church, and the *doctores*; (2) through a devout celebration of the Church's liturgy, which gives rise to a prayerful contemplation on the liturgy as a privileged medium of God's Word; (3) through an open consultation with theologians representing diverse views and perspectives; (4) through an attentiveness to the insight and life witness of the faithful. These will be developed in later chapters.

As for the bishops' authoritative proclamation of God's word, this proclamation must not be reduced to simply one in a chorus of voices. Catholic teaching insists that the teaching of the ecclesiastical magisterium, the college of bishops, functions normatively within the Catholic Christian communion. But it is still left for us to consider concretely how it is that the word of God is appropriated by the whole

---

[29]Translation from Flannery, *Vatican II.*

Christian community and articulated normatively by the bishops in doctrinal form. How does this doctrine, articulated in propositional formulae, relate to the one word of God that lives within the Christian community? In other words, how do we move from the word of God, a divine self-communication given unsurpassable expression in the Christ event, to propositional doctrine? What is gained and what is lost in this transformation? These questions were not directly considered at Vatican II, but any contemporary understanding of doctrinal teaching authority in the Church will have to attend to them.

From Word to Doctrine

Christians believe that God's word was definitively given to us in Jesus Christ. The good news of Jesus Christ, accepted and proclaimed by the apostolic communities, was preserved in Scripture and continues to be passed on in the Christian community through the writings of the early Church, through other great theological texts, through religious symbols, rituals, disciplinary practices, through the simple testimony of the daily lives of believers, through the authoritative teaching of bishops—in sum, through Church tradition, broadly conceived. This "traditioning" process, as we saw above, is inseparable from the whole life of the Church. The International Theological Commission, in its statement on the interpretation of dogmas, writes:

> The church is the sacrament: that is, the locus, the sign and the instrument of the *paradosis*. It announces the Gospel of God's saving deeds *(martyria);* it transmits the confession of faith to those to be baptized (Rom 6:17); it professes its faith in the breaking of bread and in prayer (Acts 2:42) *(leitourgia);* and it serves Jesus Christ in the poor, the persecuted, the imprisoned, the sick and the dying (Matt 25) *(diaconia).*[30]

When we look to the origins of the Christian faith then, we find a plurality of media by which the faith was passed on: story and hymnody, ritual and moral code. Within this diversity of media for passing on the faith, creedal statements have played an important role. Understanding the role of basic creedal statements, particularly in the life of the early Church, may provide insight for an adequate rendering of the various functions of doctrine as it relates to divine revelation.

---

[30]ITC, "Interpretation of Dogmas," 11.

The Functions of Creedal Statements in the Early Church

During the first five centuries of the Church it is possible to identify at least four distinct but interrelated functions of creedal statements: (1) confessional, (2) doxological, (3) catechetical, and (4) regulative.[31]

Confessional

While there are no formal creeds found in the Second Testament literature, one can find brief confessional formulas like that referred to in 1 Corinthians 12:3, "Jesus is lord!" or that of the Ethiopian eunuch in Acts: "I believe that Jesus Christ is the Son of God (Acts 8:37)."[32] In the early postbiblical period these brief creedal statements developed further, often taking on an interrogatory form that reflected their predominantly confessional character.[33] This early interrogatory form suggests that these were formulations intended to elicit a response of faith. As part of the sacrament of initiation the person to be baptized would respond to certain questions with "I believe!" Incorporation into the Christian community through baptism involved a profession of faith, a formal response to that word addressed to the believer. Consequently, the language of these creedal statements was more "performative" in nature. That is, the utterance of such an "I believe" was not primarily an affirmation of some objective state of affairs. Rather, the profession itself brought the one making the profession into a particular relationship with God. Nicholas Ayo, in his extended meditation on the role of creeds in the life of the Church, writes:

> Thus the creed was the confession of faith, the profession of hope, the protestation of a personal love. One bore witness to faith in the mystery

---

[31]For general studies of the history of creeds see Frances Young, *The Making of the Creeds* (Philadelphia: Trinity, 1991); J.N.D. Kelly, *Early Christian Creeds,* 3rd ed. (Essex: Longman, 1972).

[32]This confession, however, is not found in the earliest manuscripts of Acts. For a consideration of creedal formulas in the Second Testament, see James D. G. Dunn, *Unity and Diversity in the New Testament,* 2nd ed. (Philadelphia: Trinity, 1990) 33–59.

[33]The classic study is that of the Lutheran ecumenical theologian Edmund Schlink, "Die Struktur der dogmatischen Aussage als ökumenisches Problem," *Kerygma und Dogma* 3 (1957) 251–306.

of God who is beyond all formulations in this simple and public recitation of the rule or standard of faith that comprises the creed.[34]

This ancient understanding of creedal statements offers us an important horizon for understanding the role of dogma in the early Church. There was little sense that early creeds were seen as exhaustive representations of the deposit of faith. For example, the creedal statement "I believe in one God" was not strictly a descriptive statement about some objective reality, though it surely included this, but was an expression and enactment of one's personal faith commitment.

Doxological

While formal creeds did not find their way into the Eucharistic liturgy until the fifth century, this may have been only because the Eucharistic prayers were themselves viewed as professions of faith.[35] The eventual inclusion of formal creeds into the liturgy has sometimes been viewed by liturgiologists as a violation of the nature of liturgy, an intrusion of a foreign catechetical or regulative element into the rhythm of the liturgy. This view anachronistically presupposes the primacy of the catechetical and regulative functions (which we will consider below) of creeds. However, a study of the various uses and understandings of these creeds reveals their thoroughly doxological character. The trinitarian structure that dominated virtually all of the early creeds suggests that this profession of faith was also an act of worship, an offering of praise and thanksgiving to the one who has effected our salvation in Christ by the power of the Spirit. The profession of the creed served to give both narrative and propositional "shape" to the offering of praise by recapitulating the substance of baptismal faith. Catherine Mowry LaCugna writes:

> Although we cannot name God, we can pray the name of God given to us, thereby activating relationship with the God who names Godself. Soteriology culminates in doxology. . . . Praise is never directed to God in an abstract way, as if one could offer praise to God on the basis of speculative attributes such as immutability. Praise is always rendered in response to God's goodness to Israel, or God's majesty in creation, or God's faithfulness to the covenant, or God's peacemaking in the heart of

---

[34]Nicholas Ayo, *Creed as Symbol* (Notre Dame: Univ. of Notre Dame Press, 1989) 2.

[35]Jean-Pierre Jossua, "Signification des Confessions de Foi," *Istina* 17 (1972) 48–56.

the sinner, or God's face seen in Christ. Praise is offered because in the concrete aspects of God's life with us we experience God's steadfast love, God's gracious and everlasting presence among us.[36]

Creeds function as doxology precisely because they give the concrete shape to our praise, reminding us of who the object of our praise really is. The recitation of the creed is a doxological act that flows out of the experience of the saving work of God in Christ by the power of the Spirit.[37] It is no coincidence that early creeds and Christian hymns were so close in form and content—the latter being, in essence, "a sung confession of faith."[38] It is the trinitarian pattern of God's saving work that is the focus of the creeds and the motive for their use in communal worship.

Catechetical

One important transition in the history of creeds involved the gradual shift from the interrogatory form to the declarative form. By the fourth century the latter form had become dominant. This shift reflected the growing use of creeds as catechetical tools, concise summaries of the Christian faith.[39] The role of creeds in the actual celebration of the sacrament of initiation led to their use in the catechetical preparation for this sacrament. This catechetical usage is reflected in one of the names given to early Christian creeds, *symbolum,* the "symbol" or summary of the Christian faith. Early Christian creeds were helpful catechetical tools in the formation of Christian identity. Two early commentators on the creed, Rufinus of Aquileia and St. Augustine, both offer reflections on the use of the *symbolum* by relating it to the *symbola distincta* that military commanders conferred on their soldiers to serve as passwords, enabling the soldiers to identify one another as friend or foe.[40] To study the creed was to study

[36]Catherine Mowry LaCugna, *God For Us: The Trinity and Christian Life* (San Francisco: HarperCollins, 1991) 335, 337.

[37]Lash, *Change in Focus,* 48. For a development of this way of interpreting the creeds of the Church see Nicholas Lash, *Believing Three Ways in One God* (Notre Dame: Univ. of Notre Dame Press, 1992).

[38]Geoffrey Wainwright, *Doxology: The Praise of God in Worship, Doctrine, and Life* (New York: Oxford Univ. Press, 1980) 182–217 at 183.

[39]Kelly, *Early Christian Creeds,* 51.

[40]Berard Marthaler, *The Creed: The Apostolic Faith in Contemporary Theology* (Mystic: Twenty-Third, 1993) 6.

the meaning of Christian discipleship, the nature of the identity one would assume through initiation into the Church. The catechetical use of creeds drew on the narrative structure, which was particularly evident in the earlier creeds.

> In the context of catechetical instruction the declaratory form of the creed simply tells a story of creation and salvation. . . . [T]he baptismal creed . . . narrates the saving events that are the basis for the faith of the Christian community. The three parts of the Christian story tell of God's action in creation, in Jesus of Nazareth, and in the Spirit who continues to work in the life and history of the church. As with most stories, it has a beginning, middle, and end. The narrative function of the Creed is most evident in the middle part, which tells of Jesus' heavenly origins, his birth, life, death, and resurrection. It recapitulates the main points of the *kerygma* and makes it clear that everything else is interpreted in the light of the events that climaxed his early career.[41]

In conclusion, to say that the early Christian creeds were used catechetically is not to say they were viewed as simple collections of propositional statements, the status of which was determined by the formal authority with which they were proposed. The individual statements, later referred to as "articles of faith," that made up the creed, were included because they were concerned with the story of God's saving work on our behalf and consequently with the concrete shape of Christian identity. One important consequence of this view was that only those statements directly concerned with the economy of salvation could properly be considered creedal or called articles of faith.[42] The proliferation of dogmatic statements by popes and councils from the late Middle Ages on and the tendency to view those statements as "articles of faith" represented a significant departure from this patristic and early medieval view.

Regulative

Very early in the history of Christianity, certainly by the mid-second century, there was a widespread recognition of the need to "regulate" the faith. This regulation of the faith entailed the practice of marking off *authentic* articulations of the received apostolic faith from those viewed as counterfeit. Universally assumed was the exis-

---

[41]Ibid., 6, 8.
[42]Lash, *Change in Focus*, 50–51.

tence of a discernible apostolic testimony, which, in contrast to Gnosticism, was public and available to all. From this conviction grew the notion of a *regula fidei,* a "rule of faith" or "canon of truth," which became prominent in the writings of the late second- and early third-century theologians Tertullian and St. Irenaeus of Lyons. This rule was not a fixed creed but a fluid yet recognizable body of beliefs that constituted the core of the Christian *kerygma.*[43] Only those who could affirm this rule were held to be in rightful possession of the apostolic faith. The rule of faith did not stand in competition with Scripture but reflected the proper interpretation of God's word as it was found in Scripture.[44]

By the fourth century two different trajectories of development, the notion of a *regula fidei* and the development of formal creeds, gradually converged, with the creed itself being viewed as a rule of faith. During this period, in the midst of serious Christological and Trinitarian controversies, creedal statements came to "norm" Christian faith in a particular way by marking off authentic or "orthodox" belief from those articulations of the apostolic faith that were viewed by the Christian communities, for various reasons, as distortions. Walter Kasper has remarked on the significance of this development:

> The development from confession to doctrinal formulation started at an early date. Unlike the Nicene-Constantinopolitan Creed, that of Chalcedon was not incorporated in the liturgy. The dogma then became the correct interpretation of the confession which was taken for granted. It is no longer a matter of opposing faith to unbelief but rather of orthodoxy to heterodoxy, and it now sought to build up the confession

---

[43]Dunn addresses the complicated question of whether one can speak of a core *kerygma,* or a multiplicity of *kerygmata* in the Second Testament. While acknowleging the considerable diversity regarding the content of early Christian proclamation, Dunn does conclude to the existence of "a common element present in these different proclamations." This common element has three components: "First, the proclamation of the risen, exalted Jesus. . . . Second, the call for faith, for acceptance of the proclamation and commitment to the Jesus proclaimed. . . . Third, the promise held out to faith— whether it be put in terms of Spirit, or of its various aspects (forgiveness, salvation, life) or of a continuing relation thus established between exalted Christ and believer (union with Christ, mutual indwelling)." Dunn, *Unity and Diversity in the New Testament,* 29–30.

[44]J.N.D. Kelly, *Early Christian Doctrines,* rev. ed. (San Francisco: Harper & Row, 1978) 29–51.

of faith. Thus the dogma became the rule of faith *(regula fidei, regula veritatis, canon veritatis)*.[45]

Consequently, the focus of later dogmas or creedal statements was less on their confessional, liturgical, or catechetical appropriateness and more on the kind of conceptual clarity essential for a statement to serve as a norm for all present and future expressions of the apostolic faith. Only this kind of clarity could help in the determination of orthodoxy, or "right belief." The wording of the creeds themselves drew less and less on biblical and liturgical sources in favor of a growing lexicon of abstract and speculative terminology employed so as to differentiate the orthodox understanding of the faith from the often subtle shades of heterodoxy. The need for formal regulation in Church belief is difficult to dispute. At the same time, one can lament the way in which this regulative function came to eclipse other uses of Church dogma.

Terminological Clarifications: Creed, Dogma, and Doctrine in Contemporary Usage

At this point, I believe it is necessary to make a distinction between two terms that are often used interchangeably: "dogma" and "doctrine." In biblical Greek the word "dogma" generally referred to a juridical or disciplinary decree (cf. Luke 2:1; Acts 16:4, 17:6-7; Eph 2:14-15; Col 2:14). In the early centuries of the Church the field of meaning broadened. "Dogma" continued to be used with respect to disciplinary decrees but some of the early Church writers also used it to denote the totality of Church doctrine. In any event, it carried nothing of the narrow, technical meaning it possesses today.[46] The closest thing to what we mean by "dogma" today were the early creedal statements I have discussed above. During the medieval period of Church history, the term "dogma" was seldom employed. Late patristic and early medieval writers preferred the term *articulus fidei*.

In the sixteenth century at the Council of Trent, the term "dogma" reappeared, retaining a broad and imprecise field of meaning. "Dogma" certainly included divinely revealed articles of faith, but it also denoted any number of ecclesiastical traditions and customs. It

[45]Walter Kasper, "The Relationship Between Gospel and Dogma: An Historical Approach," in *Man as Maker and Believer,* Concilium 21 (1971) 158.

[46]See Karl Rahner and Karl Lehmann, "Kerygma und Dogma," in *Mysterium Salutis,* ed. Johannes Feiner and Magnus Löhrer (Einsiedeln: Benziger, 1965) 1:622–703, especially 639–60.

was only in the eighteenth century that "dogma" came to be limited to those propositional formulations thought to be divinely revealed. This more strict and technical understanding of dogma has continued up to the present. In its contemporary Roman Catholic usage, then, a "dogma" is any propositional formulation that is (1) divinely revealed and (2) proposed as such by the magisterium, either through a solemn definition of pope or council, or by the universal teaching of the bishops in their ordinary and universal magisterium (we shall deal with these modes of Church teaching authority in chs. 6 and 7).

The word "doctrine" comes from the Latin noun, *doctrina,* and its related verb form, *docere,* meaning "to teach or instruct." While "doctrine" is sometimes employed as a synonym for "dogma," its field of meaning has remained much broader than that of "dogma." "Doctrines" are generally understood today to be any authoritative or normative formulation of a belief of the Church, whether revealed or not. A Church doctrine is intended to articulate a formal and official belief of the Church that it draws in some fashion from its reflection on divine revelation. This is not to say that the belief articulated in a given doctrinal statement is in fact divinely revealed but only to say that all doctrines should bear some authentic relationship to divine revelation. As we shall see in chapter 9, because of the many ways in which a doctrine can be related to divine revelation, the binding character of Church doctrines will differ considerably. It follows that "dogma" should be understood as a much smaller subset of the larger category of Church "doctrine."

The Uses of Dogma and Doctrine in the Church Today

While *Dei verbum* by and large avoided any consideration of the role of doctrine or dogma in the life of the Church, its development of a more personalist and dialogical model of revelation certainly opens the door for a retrieval of the more ancient view of creed and dogma explored above. If divine revelation consists in an invitation to relationship as *Dei verbum* 2 suggested, then dogma must be situated within the dialogical structure of divine revelation. Dogma can no longer be understood as a unidirectional representation or mediation of that which God communicates to us—also constitutive for dogma must be *our* response to that self-communication, *our* confession of faith. This suggests the importance of retrieving the ancient primacy of the confessional and doxological functions of dogmas/creeds that was considered above. This confessional and doxological horizon for interpreting dogmas illuminates the way in which all dogmatic affirmations are taken up into the saving relationship that obtains between God and the believer. Precise conceptual distinctions inevitably recede into the background as cognitive mastery of some objective reality gives way to praise and the confession of faith in the triune God.

Of course, within this dialogical relationship revelation does mediate something. The symbolic structure of revelation entails that divine revelation communicate some intelligible *meaning(s)*. German theologian Magnus Löhrer has in mind this symbolic function of dogma, I believe, when he identifies a basic tension between divine revelation in its primary mediation as *kerygma,* the proclamation of the saving gospel of Jesus Christ, and its secondary mediation as *dogma*. Löhrer contends that *dogma* exists solely to mediate *kerygma*.[47] Propositional expressions serve the proclamation of saving realities. Similarly, the International Theological Commission writes: "Dogmas express the same tradition of faith by way of teaching. Because of this, they may not be separated from the context of the Church's life and interpreted as purely conceptual formulations. Their meaning and interpretation are rather soteriological."[48] This represents a welcome return to the early Church's understanding of dogmatic statements as mediations of the central Christian mystery—God's offer of salvation. In this view the dogmatic status of a doctrinal statement was found not in the formal authority of the one proposing the doctrine but in the intrinsic authority of the teaching itself. According to the patristic and medieval understanding, only those doctrinal teachings that directly mediated God's saving offer, regardless of the formal authority by which they had been proposed, could truly qualify as articles of faith, what we now call "dogma."

When revelation is no longer conceived as a collection of truths found in Scripture and tradition but is rather seen as the self-communication of God in Jesus Christ by the power of the Spirit, what qualifies as a dogma will have to be thoroughly reconceived. The positivistic theology of revelation presupposed in many of the

---

[47]Magnus Löhrer, "Träger der Vermittlung," in *Mysterium Salutis,* ed. Johannes Feiner and Magnus Löhrer, (Einsiedeln: Benziger, 1965) 2:545–87, see especially 545–55. See also Kasper, "The Relationship Between Gospel and Dogma," 153–67.

[48]ITC, "Interpretation of Dogmas," 11.

neo-Scholastic manuals contributed to the proliferation of dogmatic statements (teachings proposed as *de fide*). Thus from the presence of angelic beings in numerous biblical passages one could conclude to the existence of angels as a *de fide* teaching or dogma of the Church.[49] This move could be made with little or no reflection on whether the existence of angels played any essential role in the communication of God's saving offer. When we fully attend to the soteriological character of dogma, there is likely to be a significant contraction in the number of formal doctrinal pronouncements considered truly dogmatic.

The ITC document on the interpretation of dogma introduces another function of dogmas not unlike one of the functions of creedal statements in the early Church, namely their regulative or normative function. "[Church dogmas] are to protect the community of the church from errors; heal the wounds of error; and contribute to growth in living faith."[50] In general, a doctrine or dogma can be said to function regulatively or normatively in the sense that it (1) is articulated by the authoritative teachers of the Church, the bishops, and (2) either affirms or rejects the legitimacy of a particular theological formulation of a belief of the Church. Positively, when a doctrine articulates a belief of the Church it is affirming the legitimacy of that articulation. Negatively, a doctrinal statement may also reject a particular theological interpretation or formulation as a corruption of a particular belief of the Church.

Even when functioning regulatively a doctrinal formulation does not offer the *only* legitimate interpretation or understanding of Christian belief. However, when the orthodoxy of some alternative theological formulation is called into question, the burden of proof lies with the proponents of the alternative formulation to demonstrate the congruity of their formulation with that expressed in the doctrinal statement. In this sense the doctrine serves as a kind of benchmark or reference point for further theological interpretation. The recognition of this congruity is no easy task, and it would be a mistake to assume that this determination falls upon the magisterium alone. While certainly empowered to make binding judgments on these matters, the recognition that a new theological formulation is

---

[49]Cf. Ludwig Ott, *Fundamentals of Catholic Dogma,* 4th ed. (St. Louis: Herder, 1960) 114.
[50]ITC, "Interpretation of Dogmas," 11.

congruent with a formal doctrinal statement involves protracted study by the theological community and discernment of the way such an alternative formulation "cashes out" in the life of worship and the Christian behaviors it engenders. This view of doctrinal normativity intentionally allows for a substantial plurality in the area of Church doctrine.

There is an intriguing historical precedent for the possible diversity of doctrinal formulations in the fifteenth-century Council of Florence's treatment of Trinitarian doctrine. That council sought agreement between East and West over the thorny question of the procession of the Holy Spirit. Significantly different theological traditions had developed in the East and West over this matter. The East insisted that the Spirit proceeded from the Father *through the Son (per Filium),* while the West, operating out of a different understanding of divine procession, contended that the Spirit proceeded *from the Father and the Son (Filioque).* At Florence, bishops from both the East and the West recognized the legitimacy of the other's doctrinal formulation. The bull *Laetentur coeli* contains a remarkable text enshrining the legitimacy of this diversity in the formulation of a central dogma of the faith:

> For when Latins and Greeks came together in this holy synod, they all strove that, among other things, the article about the procession of the holy Spirit should be discussed with the utmost care and assiduous investigation. Texts were produced from divine Scriptures and many authorities of eastern and western doctors, some saying the holy Spirit proceeds from the Father and the Son, others saying the procession is from the Father through the Son. *All were aiming at the same meaning in different words* (emphasis mine).[51]

The text goes on to explain the legitimacy of each formulation as interpreted from within the context of the respective traditions. From the Western point of view what was essential was that the East's formulation *was congruent with* the doctrinal teaching of the West. In this sense, we can say that the West's teaching on the *Filioque* remained normative without precluding alternative formulations. While this historic attempt at reunion between East and West ultimately failed, the Roman Catho-

[51]*Laetentur coeli,* in Norman Tanner, ed., *Decrees of the Ecumenical Councils* (Washington: Georgetown Univ. Press, 1990) 525. I will consider the question of the relationship between doctrinal formulation and doctrinal meaning in the treatment of the irreformability of dogma in chapter 4.

lic Church has never repudiated the teaching of *Laetentur coeli* and its admission of a legitimate diversity in dogmatic formulation.[52] This regulative dimension has important implications for the contemporary interpretation of dogmatic statements. As the ITC suggests, one of the functions of Church dogma has been to protect the Christian community from error. As the regulative function of dogma grew in Church history, formal dogmatic statements frequently emerged as an ecclesial response to certain issues or crises. Since historically the primary forms for communicating the Christian faith were oriented much more toward Christian liturgy and praxis, the formal articulation of the faith in the form of doctrinal determinations usually came only in the face of some challenge or controversy relating to the apostolic faith. Consequently the proper interpretation of dogmatic statements, when employed regulatively or normatively, must attend to their historical "particularity." Nicholas Lash writes

> In other words, any credal formula is "particular," not only in the sense that it was produced in one cultural and linguistic context rather than in another, but also in the sense that it always more or less deliberately represented a *reaction* by the church against theological tendencies which were felt to threaten the apostolic faith. There is an element of reactive interpretation in any creed.[53]

The implications of the historical particularity of Church doctrine was affirmed in the CDF's 1973 declaration, "In Defense of Catholic Doctrine," a response to some of the positions of the Swiss theologian Hans Küng.

> [W]hen the Church makes new pronouncements she intends to confirm or clarify what is in some way contained in Sacred Scripture or in previous expressions of Tradition; but at the same time she usually has the intention of solving certain questions or removing certain errors. All these things have to be taken into account in order that these pronouncements may be properly interpreted.[54]

---

[52]Cf. Georges Dejaifve, "Diversité dogmatique et unité de la Revelation," in *Una Sancta et Confessiones chrétiennes* (Rome: Pontifical Oriental Institute, 1977) 195–204.

[53]Lash, *Change in Focus,* 50.

[54]CDF, "In Defense of Catholic Doctrine" *(Mysterium Ecclesiae), Origins* 3 (July 19, 1973) 110-111. This point is affirmed in a more sophisticated fashion in the ITC's "Interpretation of Dogmas."

For example, the central Trinitarian doctrine regarding the consubstantiality of the first and second persons of the Trinity emerged in response to the challenges of Arius at a time when Trinitarian reflection was in its earliest, more fluid stages. Similarly, doctrinal determinations of the Church's belief regarding the Eucharistic real presence have their origin in ninth-century controversies over the relationship between the Eucharistic body of Christ, the ecclesial body of Christ, and the resurrected body of Christ. The history of Christian doctrine tells us that the origin of most doctrinal statements can be found in controversies that demanded a formal and normative articulation in order to resolve the dispute. This means that if these doctrinal formulations are to continue to have value and fulfill their regulative function, they must be interpreted in the context of the historical crises and issues they were intended to address. This kind of interpretive analysis may also involve a frank recognition of the many contemporary issues that a dogmatic statement was never intended to address.

The particularity of a doctrinal statement is not limited to its historical context. All doctrinal formulations, while possessing a privileged status, are conditioned by the philosophical, theological, cultural, and linguistic forms in which the doctrine is articulated. To return to the example offered above regarding Eucharistic doctrine, the Council of Trent's teaching on transubstantiation while clearly possessing a normative status is still indebted to a particular philosophical system, namely Scholasticism.[55]

The widespread neglect of the ways in which doctrinal statements are particular and contextual is yet another example of the consequences of revelational positivism. While the foundations for a critique of this positivism can be found in Vatican II's *Dei verbum*, it is regrettable that the council was not able to challenge this approach to Church doctrine in a more explicit and systematic manner. As a result we still find contemporary ecclesiastical documents that, while claiming to be in accord with Vatican II, betray an alarming lack of hermeneutical sophistication regarding the interpretation of the Church's doctrinal tradition.

In conclusion, to speak of the normative character of doctrine is not to suggest that Church doctrines serve as a kind of punctuation mark

---

[55]See ch. 4 of Trent's "Decree on the Eucharist," in which the council speaks of its understanding of the real Eucharistic presence, which "has *suitably and properly been called* . . . transubstantiation." Tanner, *Decrees of the Ecumenical Councils*, 695.

ending discussion or reflection on the particular belief in question. In fact, a doctrinal statement's often terse, conceptual character virtually demands more developed theological formulations.[56] In some sense theological reflection will always be more comprehensive than doctrine. Since the formulation of doctrine usually occurs in response to some challenge, it specifies or clarifies a fairly specific aspect of Christian belief. Those who think that theological reflection or, for that matter, Christian catechesis is limited to the presentation of Christian doctrine seriously misunderstand the function of doctrine. In its regulative usage, a doctrine does not tend toward comprehensiveness or faith exploration but toward clarity. A doctrine can norm Christian belief, but it does not and cannot exhaust it.

In this chapter I have reviewed the important shift that took place at Vatican II regarding a theology of divine revelation. Vatican II moved, if only tentatively, from a propositional and positivistic view of revelation understood as a collection of discrete propositional truths to revelation as God's personal self-disclosure in Jesus Christ. Divine revelation was presented as a living word addressed to humanity, incarnate in Jesus Christ and preserved by the Spirit in the life of the Church. I have also considered the relationship of the word of God, alive in the Christian community, to the formal articulation of that word in Church doctrine. I have intentionally employed the term "doctrine" to include all normative expressions of beliefs that have emerged out of the Church's reflection on divine revelation. However, as was noted above, not every doctrinal teaching of the Church is related to divine revelation in the same way. In the next chapter I will explore some categories offered in recent ecclesiastical documents that can be of assistance in sorting out the relative centrality, authority, and binding status of various Church doctrines.

For Further Reading

Congar, Yves. *Tradition and Traditions.* New York: MacMillan, 1967.
Congregation for the Doctrine of the Faith. "In Defense of Catholic Doctrine" *(Mysterium ecclesiae). Origins* 3 (July 19, 1973) 97–112.

---

[56]This was the important point made by Karl Rahner in his discussion of the teaching of the Council of Chalcedon as both an end and a beginning for Christological reflection. Cf. Karl Rahner, "Current Problems in Christology," in *Theological Investigations* (Baltimore: Helicon, 1961) 1:149–200.

Dulles, Avery. *The Craft of Theology: From Symbol to System.* New York: Crossroad, 1992.

_____. *Models of Revelation.* Garden City: Doubleday, 1983.

_____. *Revelation Theology: A History.* New York: Crossroad, 1969.

_____. *The Survival of Dogma.* New York: Crossroad, 1982.

Haight, Roger. *Dynamics of Theology.* New York: Paulist, 1990.

International Theological Commission. "On the Interpretation of Dogmas." *Origins* 20 (May 17, 1990) 1–14.

Lane, Dermot. *The Experience of God: An Invitation to Do Theology.* New York: Paulist, 1981.

Lash, Nicholas. *Change in Focus: A Study of Doctrinal Change and Continuity.* London: Sheed & Ward, 1981.

Latourelle, René. *Theology of Revelation.* Staten Island: Alba, 1966.

Marthaler, Berard. *The Creed: The Apostolic Faith in Contemporary Theology.* Rev. ed. Mystic: Twenty-Third, 1993.

O'Collins, Gerald. *Fundamental Theology.* New York: Paulist, 1981.

_____. *Retrieving Fundamental Theology.* New York: Paulist, 1993.

Ommen, Thomas. *The Hermeneutic of Dogma.* Missoula, Mont.: Scholars Press, 1975.

Rahner, Karl. "Considerations on the Development of Dogma." In *Theological Investigations.* Vol. 4, 3–35. Baltimore: Helicon, 1966.

Ratzinger, Joseph. "Dogmatic Constitution on Divine Revelation, Origin and Background." In *Commentary on the Documents of Vatican II.* Vol. 3, ed. Herbert Vorgrimler, 155–67. New York: Crossroad, 1989.

Schillebeeckx, Edward, ed. *Man as Man and Believer* Concilium 21. New York: Herder & Herder, 1967.

4

What the Church Teaches: Gradations of Church Doctrine

The unity of Church doctrine lies in its reference to God's saving word. Whenever the Church proclaims a teaching authoritatively it does so in dependence on God's word, even when what it teaches may not specifically and directly proceed from that word.[1] Church doctrine can relate to the word of God in different ways. The distinctions between these various relationships are critical and require careful consideration. Recent ecclesiastical documents presuppose four basic categories of teaching (fig. 1).[2] The rest of this chapter will consist of an exploration of these categories.

[1] This statement is prescriptive rather than descriptive in character. An honest admission of the real humanity and sinfulness of the Church means acknowledging the instances in Church history when Church teaching was not formulated in dependence on God's word but was shaped more by ideology and human bias. Consequently Roman Catholicism holds that only those most central affirmations about God's saving offer to humanity are preserved from fundamental error.

[2] These categories are developed in two recent ecclesiastical documents: "Profession of Faith and Oath of Fidelity," *Origins* 18 (March 16, 1989) 661, 663, and the CDF instruction, "The Ecclesial Vocation of the Theologian," *Origins* 20 (July 5, 1990) 118–26. My interpretation of these documents has been guided by the following analyses. Regarding the Oath of Fidelity see Ladislas Örsy, *The Profession of Faith and the Oath of Fidelity: A Theological and Canonical Analysis* (Wilmington: Glazier, 1990), and *Report of the Catholic Theological Society of America Committee on the Profession of*

101

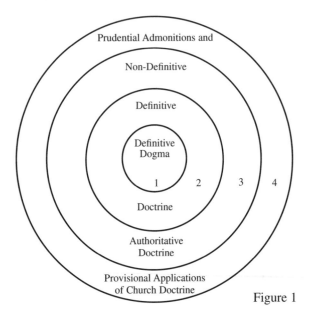

Figure 1

Definitive Dogma

Roman Catholic teaching holds that the Holy Spirit's fidelity to the Church enables the Church itself faithfully to proclaim the gospel of Jesus Christ. It is this saving gospel, the *kerygma* of the Christian faith, that is the substance of divine revelation. When it is a matter of proclaiming this divinely revealed Christian *kerygma,* Roman Catholicism teaches that the Church cannot fall into fundamental error. These doctrinal teachings that directly mediate divine revelation are called "dogmas" (see no. 1 in fig. 1). One can mention the Council of Nicaea's teaching that the Son is one in being with the Father or the

---

Faith and the Oath of Fidelity (Washington: CTSA, 1990). Regarding the CDF instruction see William Spohn, "The Magisterium and Morality," *Theological Studies* 54 (1993) 95–111; Francis A. Sullivan, "The Theologian's Ecclesial Vocation and the 1990 CDF Instruction," *Theological Studies* 52 (1991) 51–68; Joseph Komonchak, "The Magisterium and Theologians," *Chicago Studies* 29 (November 1990) 307–29; Ladislas Örsy, "Magisterium and Theologians: A Vatican Document," *America* 163 (July 21, 1990) 30–32; Peter Knauer, "Das kirchliche Lehramt und der Beistand des Heiligen Geistes," *Stimmen der Zeit* 208 (October 1990) 661–75.

Council of Chalcedon's teaching that in the one person of Jesus Christ there is a union of two natures, divine and human. In a 1991 statement on the teaching ministry of the bishops, the American bishops offered the resurrection of Jesus as an example of a church dogma.[3] To say that these teachings are dogmas is to say that they are reliable mediations of the one divine self-communication of God in Jesus Christ offered to us for our salvation.

According to Catholic teaching, dogmas are taught by the Church in one of three ways: (1) by the solemn definition of the pope when he teaches *ex cathedra* or from the chair of Peter, (2) by the solemn definition of an ecumenical council, and (3) by the teaching of the college of bishops when, while dispersed throughout the world, they are in agreement that a teaching is to be held as definitive.[4]

In a book on the magisterium, it will be impossible to address the many significant theological issues related to Church dogma. A brief

[3] "The Teaching Ministry of the Diocesan Bishop: A Pastoral Reflection," *Origins* 21 (January 2, 1991) 491 n. 14.

[4] These three modes of exercising doctrinal teaching authority with the charism of infallibility will be considered in chapters 6 and 7. There is some question as to whether teachings proposed by the ordinary and universal magisterium ought to be referred to as dogmas, since, while taught with the charism of infallibility by the bishops when dispersed throughout the world, they do not result in a solemn definition but represent simply the common teaching of the bishops regarding central and undisputed matters of faith. Karl Rahner and Karl Lehmann, for example, believe the term "dogma" ought to be limited to teachings proposed by solemn definition, since such teachings possess a higher degree of certitude *(Gewissheitsgrad)* regarding their dogmatic status. Karl Rahner and Karl Lehmann, "Kerygma und Dogma," in *Mysterium salutis,* ed. Johannes Feiner and Magnus Löhrer (Einsiedeln: Benziger, 1965) 1:655. The caution expressed by these theologians proceeds from the fact that in Catholic teaching the rejection of a dogma has usually implied heresy. On this count there is good reason to question whether the rejection of a dogma proposed by the ordinary and universal magisterium, without a solemn definition, would involve heresy, properly speaking. While acknowledging these legitimate concerns, I have chosen to refer to the teachings of the ordinary universal magisterium as dogmas, since I believe they fulfill the basic criteria for a dogma: namely, they are teachings the Church infallibly proposes as divinely revealed. For a more detailed consideration of this question see Richard R. Gaillardetz, *Witnesses to the Faith: Community, Infallibility, and the Ordinary Magisterium of Bishops* (New York: Paulist, 1992) 172–75.

consideration of three questions will have to suffice. First, what does it mean to say that Church dogma is "irreformable"? Second, what kinds of moral teachings can be taught as dogma? Third, is there any order to be discerned among the Church's dogmatic teachings?

The Irreformability of Dogma

Both Vatican I and II qualified Church dogma as *irreformable*. However, the different theological contexts associated with each council suggest that the qualifier did not carry precisely the same meaning.[5] Vatican I was operating out of the more propositional model of divine revelation. Consequently, the understanding of irreformability depended on a largely static conception of dogma—"irreformability" meant "immutability." In the fourth chapter of the Dogmatic Constitution on the Catholic Faith, *Dei Filius,* Vatican I stated that

> the doctrine of the faith which God has revealed is put forward not as some philosophical discovery capable of being perfected by human intelligence, but as a divine deposit committed to the spouse of Christ to be faithfully protected and infallibly promulgated. Hence too, that meaning of the sacred dogmas is ever to be maintained which has once been declared by holy mother church, and there must never be any abandonment of this sense under the pretext or in the name of a more profound understanding.[6]

Some forty years after Vatican I the oath against the errors of modernism contained the following statement:

> I sincerely accept the doctrine of the faith which was handed down to us *in the same meaning and always with the same purport* from the apostles through the orthodox Fathers. I therefore entirely reject the heretical theory of the evolution of dogmas, viz., that they change

---

[5]The reader will note that there is an attempt in this chapter to avoid as much as possible referring to dogmas themselves as infallible. Infallibility pertains not to a dogmatic statement itself, the subject of this chapter, but to *the judgment of the Church* that a particular teaching is true. Judgments of the Church are *infallible*; doctrines proposed by infallible judgment are *definitive, irreformable, permanent,* or *irreversible.* It seems more appropriate then, to treat the question of infallibility in part 3, on the *exercise* of ecclesiastical teaching authority.

[6]Norman Tanner, ed., *Decrees of the Ecumenical Council* (Washington: Georgetown Univ. Press, 1990) 1:809.

from one meaning to another, different from the one which the Church previously held (my emphasis).[7]

In spite of this static conception of Church dogma, both passages appear to have focused on the immutable character of a dogma's *meaning*, cautiously leaving open the question of change in a dogma's *propositional formulation.* This distinction between meaning and propositional formulation was made explicit in several passages in the documents of Vatican II. *Gaudium et spes* echoed Pope John XXIII's address at the opening of the council:

> [W]hile respecting the methods and requirements of theological science, theologians are invited continually to look for a more appropriate way of communicating doctrine to the people of their time; since there is a difference between the deposit or truths of faith and the manner in which—with their sense and meaning being preserved—they are expressed (*GS* 62).

The distinction is found again in the Decree on Ecumenism, *Unitatis redintegratio:*

> In its pilgrimage on earth Christ summons the church to continual reformation, of which it is always in need, in so far as it is an institution of human beings here on earth. Thus if, in various times and circumstances, there have been deficiencies in moral conduct or in church discipline, *or even in the way that Church teaching has been formulated—to be carefully distinguished from the deposit of faith itself—* these should be set right in the proper way at the opportune moment (*UR* 6; my emphasis).

The CDF's 1973 declaration already discussed in chapter 3 also reaffirmed this distinction. It is a distinction that can be traced back to St. Thomas, who distinguished between a propositional statement and that reality to which the statement refers.[8] On the one hand, Thomas insisted that all faith statements are concerned with that divine mystery that transcends any human articulation. On the other hand, Thomas also maintained that this divine mystery is encountered through the

---

[7] J. Neuner and J. Dupuis, eds., *The Christian Faith in the Doctrinal Documents of the Catholic Church,* rev. ed., (New York: Alba, 1982) 50.

[8] Thomas Aquinas, *Summa theologiae* 2ª 2ᵃᵉ q. 1, a. 2. ad 2.

medium of history and historical productions.[9] Thus faith statements must be intelligible and possess a substantive revelatory content, but they can never be exhaustive, since the reality toward which they point is divine mystery. The faith statement itself and the reality to which it points must be distinguished but not separated. This rather sophisticated insight was too often lost in later Catholic theology.

Unfortunately, wide acceptance of this distinction has created some confusion about the meaning of irreformability. For when it is possible to assert that an "irreformable" dogma may in fact be reformulated (even if only at the level of propositional formulation), popular confusion is just around the corner! Consequently, I am inclined to agree with those contemporary theologians who prefer to speak of a dogma as "irreversible"[10] or "definitive."[11] Yet even these terms do not completely solve matters.

[9]See Edward Schillebeeckx, "The Problem of the Infallibility of the Church's Office," in *Truth and Certainty,* Concilium 83, ed. Edward Schillebeeckx and Bas van Iersel (New York: Herder, 1973) 90–91.

[10]Francis Sullivan reinterprets irreformability in the following way: "[A] proposition can be said to be irreformable if what is meant is irreversibly true. . . . [T]o say that a proposition is irreformable means that it will remain true even when reformulated. In my opinion, a better expression than 'irreformable' would have been 'irreversible,' or 'irreversibly true.'" Francis A. Sullivan, *Magisterium: Teaching Authority in the Catholic Church* (New York: Paulist, 1983) 81. The ITC also used the term "irreversible" in its statement "On the Interpretation of Dogmas," *Origins* 20 (May 17, 1990) 6. "This irreversibility and irreformability are implied in the Church's infallibility under the guidance of the Holy Spirit and especially in the infallibility of the pope in faith and morals (DS 3020; 3043)."

[11]For quite different reasons Avery Dulles also has expressed reservations regarding the reformability/irreformability terminology and proposes simply characterizing Church dogma as "definitive." Avery Dulles, *The Craft of Theology,* 208 n. 17. See also his consideration of this issue in his earlier work, *The Survival of Dogma* (New York: Crossroad, 1982), especially 171–203. Bernard Lonergan, intent on dismissing certain "classicist" conceptions of the immutability of dogma, prefers to speak of the "permanence" of a dogma. Bernard Lonergan, *Method in Theology* (New York: Crossroad, 1979) 320ff. In a similar vein, Peter Chirico speaks of the "stability of dogma." Peter Chirico, *Infallibility: The Crossroads of Doctrine* (Wilmington: Glazier, 1983) 129–32.

Recent work in more hermeneutical approaches to Church dogma suggests that the distinction between a dogma's propositional formulation and its fundamental meaning, however helpful, is not without its own difficulties. Contemporary linguistic theorists remind us that no concrete symbolic expression, and particularly no linguistic formulation, serves merely as a passive conduit of meaning and reality; all symbols, including linguistic symbols, shape that which they communicate. Theologians who have further explored this insight insist that the relationship between language and meaning is too complex to imagine that a change in the language of a dogmatic formulation will not bring with it a change in meaning. The ITC statement "On the Interpretation of Dogmas," for example, is careful to avoid a too-facile separation of content and mode of expression. The commission states that "no clear-cut separation can be made between the content and form of the statement. The symbolic system of language is not mere external apparel, but to a certain extent the incarnation of a truth."[12] This suggests that any consideration of dogmatic change over time must reckon with the possibility that such change may go beyond mere changes in propositional formulation. As the Church moves through a succession of historical epochs and adopts new philosophical, cultural, and linguistic constructs for communicating its central articles of faith, the discernible "meaning" of those articles cannot be unaffected.

[12]ITC, "On the Interpretation of Dogmas," 12. Unfortunately, the document goes on to conclude to the permanence of certain linguistic formulations of dogmatic teaching. Many hermeneutical theologians would be inclined to go in the opposite direction and conclude not only to the mutability of dogmatic formulations but also to a certain mutability of dogmatic meaning. For a critique of the ITC document's view of dogma in the light of contemporary hermeneutical concerns see Jack Bonsor, "History, Dogma, and Nature: Further Reflections on Postmodernism and Theology," *Theological Studies* 55 (1994) 295–313. I cannot pursue here the admittedly important questions being raised by so-called postmodern or nonfoundational theologies regarding the adequacy of ontological/foundational conceptions of truth. Bonsor, an advocate of a nonfoundationalist perspective, was in fact responding in part to Thomas Guarino's critique of nonfoundational perspectives in his essay, "Between Foundationalism and Nihilism: Is *Phronesis* the *Via Media* for Theology?" *Theological Studies* 54 (1993) 37–54. For a helpful introduction to the philosophical aspects of these questions see John E. Thiel, *Nonfoundationalism* (Minneapolis: Fortress, 1994); idem, "Tradition and Authoritative Reasoning," *Theological Studies* 56 (December 1995) 627–51.

This more hermeneutical approach to the question of dogmatic change does not necessarily require a rejection of any substantive continuity in dogmatic meaning. The dogmatic continuity that perdures in the midst of change and development and that allows us to speak of such dogmas as irreversible or definitive is, I contend, grounded in the soteriological character of Church dogma. Dogmatic statements are teachings judged by the Church to be faithful and trustworthy mediations of God's offer of salvation revealed to us in Christ by the power of the Spirit. Consequently, dogmatic continuity may not reside in some eternal and immutable core of transcendent meaning but in the saving praxis to which a dogma calls us. In this view, the central insight in the Church's claim regarding the irreversibile and definitive nature of dogma would appear to be that *no dogma could so change or develop as to lead us away from the path to salvation.* It is in this sense that all Church dogmas make a claim on the faith of the believer that is enduring and irreversible even as the dogma itself continues to develop, in formulation and content, within the life of the Church.

Dogmatic Statements in Christian Morality

Quite obviously, Church dogma represents the most important category of Church teaching. Dogmas are symbolic mediations that bring us into saving relationship with God. A dogma faithfully communicates or mediates divine revelation. This raises an important question regarding the scope of Church dogma. How, specifically, do we determine which of the Church's teachings can be said to be divinely revealed? When divine revelation was uncritically identified with Scripture the matter was much easier. Then one could presume that any statement found in Scripture could be considered divinely revealed and, consequently, belonged to the deposit of faith. The more personalist model of revelation developed in *Dei verbum* complicates matters because it locates divine revelation primarily in a person, Jesus Christ, not in a text.

In *Lumen gentium* 25 we find repeated reference to the phrase "faith and morals" *(fides et mores)* as one way of describing the parameters of the deposit of faith. It is a phrase with a long and complicated history.[13] In the Middle Ages and at the Council of Trent the

---

[13]For the history of this important phrase see John Mahoney, *The Making of Moral Theology* (Oxford: Clarendon, 1987) 120–74; Piet Fransen, "A

expression was without real precision. For example, regarding *fides,* Piet Fransen writes:

> The "truths of faith" embraced a rather large scale of truths, many of which we would never call "faith" today. "Truths of faith" were to be found first of all in the Creeds, in the teachings of the saints, in the decisions of some important Councils. . . . They also considered as "truths of faith" truths which were related to faith or whose rejection could endanger the faith; truths implied in some fundamental aspects of faith; and finally, some universal laws of the Church. In their language "faith" was still synonymous with "doctrine" and even with "theology," in the old sense that is.[14]

Mores, in turn, suggested not so much formal moral principles as the practical realization of saving truth in the life of the believer. Thus *mores* included not just that which pertained to moral behavior but to Church discipline in general, and thereby included any number of ecclesiastical customs and practices (e.g., pious devotions, fasting regulations, sacramental rituals).

The First Vatican Council followed Trent in its employment of the phrase *fides et mores,* but with an important shift in meaning. At Vatican I the referent of the term *fides* appears to have been restricted to saving truth divinely revealed. This is clearly articulated in the third chapter of *Dei Filius:*

> Wherefore, by divine and catholic faith (*fide divina et catholica*) all those things are to be believed which are contained in the word of God as found in scripture and tradition, and which are proposed by the church as matters to be believed as divinely revealed, whether by her solemn judgment or in her ordinary and universal magisterium.[15]

One can identify a similar restriction in meaning with regard to *mores.* No longer does *mores* appear to include all Church discipline

---

Short History of the Meaning of the Formula '*Fides et Mores,*'" in *Hermeneutics of Councils and Other Studies,* ed. H. E. Mertens and F. de Graeve (Leuven: Leuven Univ. Press, 1985) 287–318; J. Beumer, "*Res fidei et morum:* Die Entwicklung eines theologischen Begriffes in den Dekreten der drei letzten Ökumenischen Konzilien," *Annuarium Historiae Conciliorum* 2 (1979) 112–34; Maurice Bévenot, "Faith and Morals in Vatican I and in the Council of Trent," *Heythrop Journal* 3 (1962) 15–30.

[14]Fransen, "A Short History," 298.

[15]Tanner, *Decrees of the Ecumenical Councils,* 2:807.

and governance. Unfortunately neither the council itself nor the spokesperson for the council's Deputation of the Faith, Bishop Vincenz Gasser, offered any clarification as to the precise meaning of the term *mores* as it appeared in the definition on papal infallibility.

While there is a growing consensus regarding the meaning of *fides*—those teachings directly communicating the substance of God's saving offer—ascertaining the precise meaning and scope of *mores* has proven more difficult. The matter is complicated by the fact that there are no solemnly defined dogmas that pertain to morals. Of course, Vatican I would not have used the term *mores* in its delimitation of the object of a solemn papal definition if it did not believe in the possibility of such a definition. But what kinds of moral teachings would qualify? For example, could the magisterium solemnly define as a divinely revealed dogma the CDF's current prohibition of artificial insemination? For the answer to be yes, one would have to demonstrate how such a teaching could be found in divine revelation. So then the question is, what kinds of moral teachings belong to divine revelation?[16]

The documents of Vatican II do not clearly answer this question, but *Gaudium et spes* does suggest that the council was not convinced *all* moral teaching was divinely revealed:

> The Church, as guardian of the deposit of God's word, draws religious and moral principles from it, but it does not always have a ready answer to particular questions, wishing to combine the light of revelation with universal experience so that illumination can be forthcoming on the direction which humanity has recently begun to take (*GS* 33).

What is the nature of this distinction between moral principles drawn from God's word and answers "to particular problems" that do not necessarily come from divine revelation? The beginnings of an answer may be found in a brief consideration of the Catholic natural law tradition.

[16]For a more in-depth consideration of this topic from the perspective of an ecclesiologist, see Sullivan, *Magisterium,* 133ff. For a treatment from the perspective of moral theology see Josef Fuchs, "Moral Truths—Truths of Salvation?" in *Christian Ethics in a Secular Arena* (Washington: Georgetown Univ. Press, 1984) 48–67, and Bernard Hoose, *Proportionalism: The American Debate and Its European Roots* (Washington: Georgetown Univ. Press, 1987) 41–67. John P. Boyle offers a helpful historical study in "The Natural Law and the Magisterium," in *Church Teaching Authority: Historical and Theological Studies* (Notre Dame: Univ. of Notre Dame Press, 1995) 43–62.

Roman Catholicism has always stressed the importance of human reason in the moral life. Catholicism has insisted that there is an identifiable moral structure to the universe (we can also speak of this as a moral "law" as long as we overlook the rigorist connotations of the word)[17] and that we are capable of discovering it through rational reflection on human experience. Because of human sinfulness, this is not as easy as it might be. For that reason, in addition to the employment of our powers of reason in reflection on our experience, we may also turn to divine revelation. We believe that God's saving word calls us to moral conversion and a life dedicated to the achievement of virtue and goodness. Therefore at least some of what we might discover in the natural law through reasoned reflection on human experience is also confirmed in divine revelation. But does this hold for the entirety of the natural law? From the sixteenth through the nineteenth centuries it was not uncommon for theologians to teach that all of the natural law belonged to divine revelation, including the most specific of moral injunctions.[18] Few theologians would hold this position today.

It may be helpful to distinguish between two integrally related categories of the moral law. The precise character of the first category is based on the conviction that the primary goal of Christian morality is salvation.[19] In the experience of salvation the human person opens herself up to God's offer of divine communion. In this life of communion with God we are addressed by God in love and invited to respond in love. This loving response entails nothing less than a radical conversion, what Lonergan calls a "transformation of horizons." The Scriptures demand that we love God and neighbor, that we forgive without limits, that we refrain from judging others. The transformative power of so many of the gospel narratives and parables lies in the way in which the reader is invited into an alternative "world" that

[17] For a consideration of the ambiguities inherent in speaking of a moral "law" see Mahoney, "The Language of Law," in *The Making of Moral Theology,* 224–58.

[18] For some examples see Francisco Suarez, *Tractatus de legibus,* lib. 10, cap. 2, n. 3, in *Opera Omnia* (Paris: Vives, 1856) 5:554; Joseph Kleutgen, *Die Theologie der Vorzeit,* 2nd ed. (Innsbruck, 1978) 1:146; Johann Baptist Franzelin, *De divina traditione et scriptura* (Rome: Propaganda Fide, 1870) 110, 547–51.

[19] Here I am largely following the line of argument developed by Fuchs in "Moral Truths—Truths of Salvation?"

demands a whole new set of values and attitudes in keeping with the demands of God's reign. So for example, in the Gospel of Luke the story of Zacchaeus is not a moral fable about the dangers of wealth and the benefits of generosity but a story of the personal world of Zacchaeus turned upside down in the encounter with Jesus. The natural tendency of the reader to identify with the older son in the parable of the Prodigal Son constitutes an invitation to conversion in the face of an act of scandalous and wholly unwarranted generosity. These narratives invite conversion; they engender a set of moral claims concerned not with specific behaviors but with our most basic attitudes and intentions. This conversion is realized concretely in our human actions; our love of God manifests itself and is perfected in our love of neighbor.

Morality, then, is concerned with the transformation of human motivations and human intentionality. In the life of communion we desire to "be good" as an end in itself. This moral "goodness," however, pertains primarily to the person; moral goodness resides not in acts themselves, but in human intentions and attitudes *as they relate to* human actions. We might describe these as *universal moral norms* because they are universal in application and are to be followed without exception—they call us to "put on the mind of Christ." St. Paul says, "Do not conform yourself to this age but be transformed by the renewal of your mind, that you may discern what is the will of God, what is good and pleasing and perfect" (Rom 12:2). These norms can be read as nothing more than variations on the fundamental moral law offered by Jesus, the double commandment of love (Mark 12:28-34). The double commandment of love "is no longer just one in a series of requirements demanded by the Torah";[20] it is the central norm for the Christian life and calls for a basic attitude that must guide all concrete action. As variations on the law of love, universal moral norms clearly belong to divine revelation. There is no human action whose intention need not be in conformity with these norms. God's offer of salvation leads us to a radical conversion in the way we "see the world." The first category of the moral law, then, includes *those moral norms concerned with salvation and the call to conversion* precisely because these norms place claims on human intentions, attitudes, and dispositions. They reveal to us the true nature of moral goodness. Since divine revelation is concerned with that which directly pertains

[20]Wolfgang Schrage, *The Ethics of the New Testament* (Philadelphia: Fortress, 1988) 71.

to our salvation, one can imagine, then, a defined moral dogma the content of which is one or another of these universal norms. This leads to a second category of norms. We believe that a morally "good" person will always strive to do what is "right." And yet we also recognize that it is not always easy for good persons to know what doing the "right thing" demands of them in a particular instance. Often the good person is confronted with difficult moral dilemmas in which important values are in conflict. So, for example, the morally good person might legitimately struggle with whether moral goodness translates into actions that involve the direct taking of the life of another, as in the case of self-defense or a soldier's participation in acts of war. Virtuous and well-meaning Christians have, through the centuries, come to different conclusions about such matters. It is here that we are able to look to Scripture and the moral teaching of the Church as a guide for human action. Jesus himself offered, in addition to the law of love, concrete admonitions. The Church too, in its moral teaching offers *concrete moral norms* that are specific in nature and therefore are of great assistance in discovering what is demanded in a particular situation.

There are two observations that must be made about these *specific or concrete moral norms*. First, because they are concrete, they are concerned with changing moral contexts and empirical data. The interpretation of both moral contexts and empirical data is subject to revision (in fact, empirical data itself may be subject to revision in particular instances). For example, concrete moral norms prohibiting the use of nuclear weapons are dependent on empirical data about the destructive capabilities of these weapons. Centuries ago St. Thomas Aquinas was able to assign a different moral status to an abortion before quickening (when a mother first feels the child move within her womb) as opposed to one after quickening because of his erroneous understanding of embryonic development. Concrete moral norms are of great assistance in the moral life, but because they are dependent in part on changing circumstances they can only apply, as St. Thomas recognized, "in the majority of instances" *(ut in pluribus)*.[21] This dependence on changing empirical data presents a strong argument against considering such norms as belonging to divine revelation.

---

[21]See Thomas' treatment of the virtue of *epikeia,* which he sees as the virtue of penetrating to the true meaning of a given law. *Summa theologiae* II–II, q. 120, a.1.

Second, unlike universal moral norms, which are concerned with human salvation, that is, with the conversion of human intentionality, concrete moral norms are concerned with objectively right behavior. Morally right behavior is not, in itself, a matter of salvation. One may do the right thing, giving alms for example, out of a desire to call attention to oneself. Fuchs writes:

> By themselves neither right nor wrong works within this world determine either salvation or perdition. Works do not, by themselves, determine moral goodness and salvation. But someone who is personally morally good and lives within the realm of salvation will try to behave, within this world, in the right way. If someone does not do so, he shows that he (as person) is not morally good and does not live in the realm of salvation. Right behavior within this world, is, by itself, not yet moral goodness and "salvation": rather it is only—*in itself*—an effect and therefore sign of salvation. The corresponding norms are not truths of salvation in the proper sense, but only in an analogous sense.[22]

Concrete moral norms, concerned as they are with guiding one in objectively right behavior, do not pertain directly to salvation and the conversion of human attitudes, intentions, and dispositions. At the same time, these concrete norms often depend on changeable empirical data, making it difficult to attribute to them the kind of continuity in their fundamental meaning that can be attributed to Church dogma. Consequently, it is the conclusion of many theologians that while it is legitimate and necessary for the pastoral teaching office of the Church to propose concrete moral norms for the guidance of the faithful, these concrete moral norms are not divinely revealed and cannot be taught as dogma.[23]

---

[22]Fuchs, "Moral Truths—Truths of Salvation?" 55.

[23]See Boyle, "Natural Law and the Magisterium," 43–62; Richard A. McCormick, *Corrective Vision: Explorations in Moral Theology* (Kansas City: Sheed & Ward, 1994) 86–89; Franz Böckle, "Le magistère de l'Église in matière morale," *Revue théologique de Louvain* 19 (1989) 3–16; Francis A. Sullivan, "Some Observations on the New Formula for the Profession of Faith," *Gregorianum* 70 (1989) 552–54; Sullivan, *Magisterium,* 136–52; André Naud, *Le magistère incertain* (Montreal: Fides, 1987) 77–121; Karl Rahner, "Basic Observations on the Subject of Changeable and Unchangeable Factors in the Church," *Theological Investigations* (New York: Seabury, 1976) 14:3–23. Jacob David goes even further and suggests that the teaching of concrete norms flows from the Church's pastoral authority rather than its

The Hierarchy of Truths

As I noted above, one of the defining characteristics of Church dogma is its mediation of God's offer of salvation. But this is still somewhat ambiguous. Do all Church dogmas possess the same status? Do they all function in the same way? The Second Vatican Council recognized a certain ordering or configuration of Church dogma in its teaching on the "hierarchy of truths."

The notion of the hierarchy of truths was first proposed at the council in November of 1963 by Archbishop Andrea Pangrazio of Italy. It was incorporated into an important written *modus* offered by Cardinal Franz König of Vienna, who stressed that the truths of the faith should not be conceived as adding up quantitatively. Rather, there is a qualitative order among them with respect to their relation to the foundation of the Christian faith. After much debate this important concept was inserted into the final version of *Unitatis redintegratio,* the Decree on Ecumenism:[24]

> Furthermore, in ecumenical dialogue, when catholic theologians join with other Christians in common study of the divine mysteries, while standing fast by the teaching of the church, they should pursue the work with love for the truth, with charity, and with humility. When comparing doctrines with one another, they should remember that in catholic doctrine there exists an order or "hierarchy" of truths, since they vary in their connection *(nexus diversus)* with the foundation of the christian faith. Thus the way will be opened for this kind of friendly emulation to incite all to a deeper awareness and a clearer manifestation of the unfathomable riches of Christ *(UR* 11).

This passage is not referring to the distinction between definitive dogma and nondefinitive doctrine but rather to a hierarchy that exists *among* the dogmas of the Church. The conciliar text insists that Church dogmas must be understood and interpreted in the light of

---

teaching authority and therefore possesses only the status of disciplinary teaching. Cf. Jacob David, *Loi naturelle et autorité de l'église* (Paris: Cerf, 1968).

[24]See Johannes Feiner, "Commentary on the Decree," in *Commentary on the Documents of Vatican II,* ed. Herbert Vorgrimler (New York: Crossroad, 1989) 2:118–21. See also "The Notion of 'Hierarchy of Truths': An Ecumenical Interpretation," (a study commissioned and received by the joint working group between the Roman Catholic Church and the World Council of Churches) Faith and Order Paper 150, (Geneva: WCC, 1990) 16–24.

their relationship to the foundation of Christian faith. But how do we discover this foundation? Since the foundation of the Christian faith *determines* the ordering of the dogmas themselves, this phrase must refer to something more basic than a particular dogma or set of dogmas. The passage from the decree gives us a hint in the use of the phrases "divine mysteries" and "the unfathomable riches of Christ." The foundation of the faith would appear to be not one dogma or another but the entire economy of salvation—what God has done for us in Christ by the power of the Spirit. As we saw in chapter 3, this focus on the economy of salvation is fully in accord with the ancient understanding of Church creeds. The foundation of the Christian faith is the Christian *kerygma*. Vatican II appears to be affirming that Church dogmas have differing relations or links to this foundation. This interpretation is confirmed by the 1973 CDF declaration "In Defense of Catholic Doctrine," article 4, which affirms that some dogmas or "truths" lean on more principal "truths" and are illumined by them.

One way of understanding these different relations to the Christian *kerygma* is to acknowledge that there are certain Church dogmas that are more *confirmatory* in nature. One thinks immediately of the Marian dogmas, the dogmatic content of which is primarily concerned not with any particular biographical facts concerning events in the life of Mary but rather with what the life of Mary says about the nature of Christ's saving work (thus the *immaculate conception of Mary* affirms the comprehensive nature of God's saving grace, which is totally sufficient and available for the salvation of all) and the promise it holds for all humanity (thus *the bodily assumption of Mary* affirms the promise of the integral bodily resurrection of all). Certain needless misunderstandings can be overcome by specifying what precisely is at stake in the formulation of a particular dogma.[25] It is

---

[25]This has important ecumenical implications. If certain dogmatic teachings function in a confirmatory way as would appear to be the case with the Marian dogmas, might it be possible to remove the anathemas attached to these teachings, since the central dogmatic content of these dogmas might be affirmed elsewhere? This distinction between central dogmas and confirmatory dogmas was suggested, albeit, in different terminology, by Heribert Mühlen, "Die Bedeutung der Differenz zwischen Zentraldogmen und Randdogmen für den ökumenischen Dialog," in *Freiheit in der Begegnung*, ed. J. L. Leuba and H. Stirnimann (Frankfurt: Knecht, 1969) 191–227. For more on this proposal to remove certain anathemas as an important ecumenical gesture, see Avery Dulles, "A Proposal to Lift Anathemas," *Origins* 4 (1974) 417–21.

possible that some dogmas may simply reassert or reemphasize in a different form that which is already communicated in other dogmatic teachings.

Definitive Doctrine

We said above that while all Church doctrine was in some way related to divine revelation, the precise relationship may differ. The CDF instruction "The Ecclesial Vocation of the Theologian" recognized as a distinct category of Church doctrine those teachings that were definitive in character (hence irreformable or irreversible) but that communicated nonrevealed truths (see no. 2 in fig. 1):

> By its nature, the task of religiously guarding and loyally expounding the deposit of divine revelation (in all its integrity and purity), implies that the magisterium can make a pronouncement "in a definitive way" on propositions which, even if not contained among the truths of faith, are nonetheless intimately connected with them in such a way that the definitive character of such affirmations derives in the final analysis from revelation itself (16).

This category does not have a formal designation in ecclesiastical documents, but I shall refer to it as *definitive doctrine*. The category itself is somewhat controversial. Definitive doctrines would appear to include teachings that are thought to be necessary for preserving divine revelation but that are not themselves divinely revealed. At the same time, the CDF views these teachings as *definitive* (and therefore *irreformable* or *irreversible*) and holds that in proposing these teachings the Church is protected from the possibility of fundamental error by the infallible assistance of the Holy Spirit. However, unlike dogma, there is no question of these teachings mediating some aspect of God's saving offer. Consequently, whatever their formal status, they cannot attain the central position granted to the Church's core dogmatic teachings.

This category of church teaching was not explicitly developed at Vatican I nor even at Vatican II.[26] In the Latin seminary manuals of

[26]However, there are texts from both councils in which it is implied. At Vatican I in *Pastor aeternus* the council members wrote that the pope had the power to teach infallibly "doctrine concerning faith and morals *to be held* by the whole Church (DS 3074)." The key phrase is "to be held," a translation of the Latin word *tenenda*. This was changed from "to be believed" (*credenda*)

the nineteenth and early twentieth centuries definitive doctrine was often referred to as the secondary object of infallibility. As an *object* of Church teaching it could be taught by an infallible judgment of the magisterium as definitive and irreversible, as *secondary* the manuals were admitting that it did not belong directly to divine revelation. However, when one tries to determine the actual scope of this category of teaching serious difficulties arise. For example, some manualists were inclined to interpret this category very broadly to include the canonization of saints, propositions logically derived from divine revelation, dogmatic facts (e.g., the list of canonical books of the Bible), certain disciplinary decrees, and so on.[27] This broad application raises questions regarding the need for adequate criteria for asserting the definitive and irreversible character of these various teachings.

The recent CDF instruction "The Ecclesial Vocation of the Theologian" (1990) says simply that these teachings are *connected* to divine revelation. Yet Sullivan finds this view at odds with the much more carefully circumscribed view operative at Vatican II and reflected in the earlier CDF declaration "In Defense of Catholic Doctrine" (1973). It is not enough for these doctrines to be simply *connected* to divine revelation as the later CDF instruction implies. The Theological Commission at Vatican II, in an attempt to clear up ambiguity on precisely this matter, wrote that infallible judgments could be made regarding nonrevealed teachings only insofar as they

---

because it was thought that the pope could teach infallibly on matters not strictly revealed but necessary for the preservation of divine revelation. Since these doctrines were not strictly revealed, the proper response of the faithful could not be that of faith or belief. Similarly, at Vatican II, *Lumen gentium* 25 held that the object of infallible teaching "extends as far as extends the deposit of divine revelation, *which must be religiously guarded and faithfully expounded.*" The last clause seems to refer to those nonrevealed truths that can nevertheless be taught with an infallible judgment and are, therefore, definitive and irreversible in nature. See Sullivan, *Magisterium,* 131ff. and his recent note on the subject, "The 'Secondary Object' of Infallibility," *Theological Studies* 54 (1993) 536–50. See also Germain Grisez's refutation of his position and Sullivan's response in Germain Grisez and Francis A. Sullivan, "The Ordinary Magisterium's Infallibility," *Theological Studies* 55 (December 1994) 720–38.

[27]These can all be found in Joseph Salaverri, *Sacrae theologiae summa,* 3rd ed. (Madrid: BAC, 1955) 1:733.

"are required in order that the same deposit (of divine revelation) may be *religiously safeguarded and faithfully expounded.*"[28] This view suggests that in proposing that any teaching is in fact a definitive doctrine, one must demonstrate not only that a teaching is *connected* to divine revelation but that the teaching is *necessary* for safeguarding and faithfully expounding divine revelation. The assumption is that there are doctrines of the Church that, while not divinely revealed, are so bound up with that which is revealed that were they to be proposed falsely, revelation itself would be put in jeopardy. These doctrines are thought to safeguard that which is divinely revealed. Consider, for example, two kinds of formal determinations often mentioned as definitive doctrine. Many hold that while the determination of those books that belong to the canon of the Bible (formally determined by the Council of Trent) is not itself part of divine revelation, were such a determination to be false, divine revelation itself might be compromised. For similar reasons, many insist that the determination of a council's ecumenicity is also a definitive doctrine. These determinations are then considered definitive and irreversible in nature though not divinely revealed.[29]

---

[28]*Acta synodalia,* III/1, 251, as quoted in Sullivan, *Magisterium,* 132. The 1973 declaration "In Defense of Catholic Doctrine," uses a similar phrasing, suggesting that the object of infallible teaching extends "to those matters without which that deposit cannot be rightly preserved and expounded" (110).

[29]I noted above that some theologians in the past have held that every moral norm of the natural law, universal and specific, belongs to divine revelation and may be proposed as definitive and irreversible dogmatic doctrine. While few hold this position today, there are theologians who would suggest that those moral norms that are not divinely revealed may be proposed as definitive doctrine by virtue of *their connection with* divine revelation. This was suggested by Cardinal Umberto Betti in his official commentary on the formula for the Profession of Faith, *L'Osservatore Romano* (February 25, 1989) 6. These concrete norms are held to be so intimately connected with divine revelation that they may be taught as definitive and irreversible. But it is difficult to reconcile this position with the stricter approach of both Vatican II and the 1973 CDF declaration. The council's test of a teaching's necessity for "safeguarding and faithfully expounding" divine revelation must be applied. It is difficult to demonstrate, in the light of what was said above regarding the concern of specific moral norms with questions of objective moral "rightness," how these norms would be considered necessary for "safeguarding and expounding" divine revelation.

I believe that this category of Church teaching contains some serious ambiguities. If these teachings must be necessary to safeguard divine revelation, how do we determine which teachings qualify? Let us consider the example offered above that the determination of a council's ecumenicity belongs in this category of teaching. In this view the determination that a council was ecumenical would not itself be divinely revealed but the truthfulness of that determination would be necessary to protect divine revelation. Yet it is not evident at all that the integrity of divine revelation would be threatened were the ecumenicity of Constantinople IV to be questioned, for example, as it has been by many scholars. In fact, there is significant debate as to the propriety of referring to any but the first seven councils as fully ecumenical.[30] A second frequently cited example is Trent's formal determination of the canon of the Bible. Yet within Christianity there are at least three different lists of canonical books accepted by various traditions. It is not self-evident that these differences have threatened the fundamental integrity of divine revelation either.

Finally, it should be noted that the possibility of infallibly proposing nonrevealed doctrines has never itself been solemnly defined but rather was a position proposed at Vatican I simply as "theologically certain."[31] I believe it is quite possible that many if not all of the doctrinal pronouncements placed in this category could just as easily be placed in the following category, namely, nondefinitive, authoritative doctrine.[32]

Nondefinitive, Authoritative Doctrine

In popular considerations of Catholic doctrine a good deal of attention is given to Church dogma, those teachings that are infallibly taught by the Church as divinely revealed. It is not always recognized that most Church teaching is not taught with the charism of infallibility but belongs to the third category of Church teaching, *nondefinitive, authoritative doctrine* (see no. 3 in fig. 1). As Church doctrines,

---

[30]This does not necessarily imply a denial of the authority of the later councils. I will treat this question further in chapter 7.

[31]Mansi 52, 1226–27.

[32]For a consideration of the difficulties inherent in this category of Church teaching see Spohn, "The Magisterium and Morality," 96–100; Michael J. Buckley and others, *Report of the Catholic Theological Society of America Committee on the Profession of Faith and the Oath of Fidelity* (Washington: CTSA, 1990) 77–84.

these teachings clearly are related *in some fashion* to divine revelation. They may contribute to a fuller understanding of God's word and its implications for the Christian life. They may help to apply God's word to ever-changing human situations and address new questions. Nevertheless, authoritative doctrines are those teachings that for various reasons the Church is not yet ready or able to declare definitively as divinely revealed. It may be that the doctrine's precise relationship to divine revelation is not yet clear. In some instances this may be a doctrine that has not fully "matured" within the consciousness of the Church. Perhaps more scholarly work needs to be accomplished in evaluating its place in Scripture and tradition. It may be a teaching yet to be "received" by the faithful (a concept that we will address more fully in later chapters). Or it may be a doctrine that, by the nature of that with which it is concerned, *cannot* be divinely revealed. Because the Church does not irrevocably bind itself to the revelatory character of such doctrine we must speak of these doctrinal teachings as *nondefinitive* or *reversible.* The possibility of a substantive reversal cannot in principle be excluded.

At the same time, the Church's teaching office is not limited to the charism of infallibility in its recourse to the assistance of the Holy Spirit. The Spirit's assistance is not episodic. As the transcendent subject of Church tradition, the assistance of the Holy Spirit is operative in varying degrees in every exercise of doctrinal teaching. In proposing Church doctrine as nondefinitive, the teaching office of the Church is still guided by the Holy Spirit in its responsibility as guardian of the apostolic faith. Therefore this teaching, though nondefinitive, remains *authoritative.* These teachings continue to provide the norm for Catholic belief and may not be simply dismissed (the proper response of the believer to such teaching will be considered in ch. 9). One example of nondefinitive, authoritative doctrine might help clarify matters.

In Pope Pius XII's 1950 encyclical *Humani generis,* the Pope taught that polygenism, the belief that the origins of humankind lie in more than one set of human parents, could not be reconciled with the Council of Trent's teaching on original sin. Pius XII proposed this conditional condemnation as authoritative doctrine, recognizing that further development both on the scientific and theological fronts may justify a different position. His formulation of this teaching and its authoritative status clearly acknowledged the possibility of a maturation and even shift in the Church's position on the matter.

A reading of contemporary ecclesiastical documents suggests that included within nondefinitive, authoritative doctrine would also be those concrete moral norms that the Church proposes for moral guidance. These norms are composite in character. On the one hand they flow out of universal moral principles as practical guidelines for translating into concrete moral conduct morally "good" dispositions. On the other hand, they are in part dependent upon contingent judgments in concrete and changing moral contexts. This is why, as I proposed above, such norms *cannot,* by their nature, be solemnly defined as divinely revealed teaching. The American bishops provide an example of these teachings from the field of bioethics. They place in this category the prohibition of artificial insemination, in vitro fertilization, and surrogate motherhood.[33] These teachings are concrete applications of that which is divinely revealed regarding the sacredness of human life. At the same time, they are in varying degrees dependent upon changing scientific understandings of human reproduction and reproductive technologies.

Many, perhaps most Church teachings belong in the category of authoritative, nondefinitive doctrine. For that reason it is important to recognize that just as there is a hierarchy or order to the *dogmatic* teachings of the Church, so too, not every teaching in this category should be viewed as equally authoritative. Clearly the Church's teaching on abortion and its teaching on masturbation are not equal in authority or centrality. In fact, some theologians have detected an inconsistency in the authority attached to concrete moral norms. For example, the American bishops have made an important distinction between moral principles and their concrete application in two of their better-known pastoral letters, *The Challenge of Peace* and *Economic Justice for All.*[34] They apparently consider concrete directives in the area of social ethics as examples of prudential judgments in

[33]"The Teaching Ministry of the Diocesan Bishop," 492 n. 25.

[34]In *Economic Justice for All* the bishops write: "In focusing on some of the central economic issues and choices in American life in the light of moral principles, we are aware that the movement from principle to policy is complex and difficult and that although moral values are essential in determining public policies, they do not dictate specific solutions. They must interact with empirical data, with historical, social, and political realities, and with competing demands on limited resources. The soundness of our prudential judgments depends not only on the moral force of our principles, but also on the accuracy of our information" (134).

which responsible disagreement among Catholics is possible. These concrete directives, as they are presented by the bishops, seem to bear more in common with the disciplinary teachings and prudential judgments of the fourth and final category of Church teaching. It is significant that current Church teaching has been reluctant to make this same distinction in either sexual ethics or bioethics.[35]

Prudential Admonitions and Provisional Applications of Church Doctrine

The last category of Church teaching, *prudential admonitions and provisional applications of church doctrine* (see no. 4 in fig. 1), must be distinguished from the first three categories by its explicitly provisional character. These determinations are doctrinal only in an analogous sense. While all Church teaching is in a sense pastoral in character, there are some ecclesiastical pronouncements that are explicitly pastoral, concerned not so much with the proclamation of God's word as with offering prudential judgments regarding the soundness of theological and ecclesiological developments in the Church. Cardinal Ratzinger, in his introduction to the CDF instruction "The Ecclesial Vocation of the Theologian," offers as an example the early twentieth-century censure of the "modernist" theological positions.[36] One might place the recent CDF statements on liberation theology in this category as well.[37] As official teaching of the Church, these pronouncements fall short of explicitly condemning error but simply warn of opinions that are potentially dangerous or misleading.

Legislative determinations regarding the disciplinary life of the Church, as with the requirement of mandatory celibacy for the ministerial priesthood in the Latin Rite, would also fall in this category. The *prudential* character of these pronouncements and disciplinary practices must be emphasized. While the Spirit certainly assists the authoritative teachers of the Church even in its prudential judgments, nevertheless, the guarantee of the Spirit is concerned primarily with

[35]Cf. Charles Curran, "Catholic Social and Sexual Teaching: A Methodological Comparison," *Theology Today* 44 (1988) 425–40.

[36]Joseph Ratzinger, "Theology Is Not Private Idea of Theologian," *L'Osservatore Romano* (July 2, 1990) 5.

[37]Cf. "Instruction on Certain Aspects of the 'Theology of Liberation,'" *Origins* 14 (September 13, 1984) 194–204; "Instruction on Christian Freedom and Liberation," *Origins* 15 (April 17, 1986) 714–27.

preserving the Church in fidelity to the word, not with protecting it from unwise or imprudent disciplinary actions.[38]

Discerning the Authority and Binding Character of Church Teaching

In a speech at the University of Steubenville in February of 1991, Avery Dulles suggested that the teaching authority of the Church was being placed under a severe strain by the proliferation of official teaching statements promulgated by Rome and the various bishops' conferences.[39] With so many official pronouncements, the faithful were being overwhelmed and confused, leading to a disturbing tendency in which many simply ignore the official pronouncements of the ecclesiastical hierarchy. While Dulles has correctly identified one response to this proliferation of Church announcements, there is another response that is equally detrimental to the life of the Church. There is a segment of the Catholic population that tends to flatten out the important distinctions regarding the authoritative character of these ecclesiastical pronouncements. One sometimes hears the opinion that these distinctions between different levels of authoritative teaching are academic and technical in character and can "confuse" the faithful. There is a dangerous paternalism implicit in this view. Every Catholic has a right to know with what doctrinal weight the Church is proposing a particular teaching.

I would like to make two general observations regarding this taxonomy of Church teaching. First, the distinctive character of church dogmas, which alone are proposed by the Church as divinely revealed, must be emphasized much more than it has been. We profess that these teachings faithfully communicate God's offer of salvation and are therefore considered indispensable to the life of the Church. There should be no confusion among the faithful regarding their distinctive status.[40] Honoring the distinctive character of dogmatic teach-

---

[38]Ladislas Örsy, *The Church: Teaching and Learning* (Wilmington: Glazier, 1987) 76–78.

[39]See James Boehm, "Theologian Suggests Fewer Church Teaching Documents," *Catholic News Service* (March 7, 1991) 12–13.

[40]French theologian André Naud contends that the failure to distinguish clearly between definitive dogma and authoritative doctrine constitutes a contemporary Catholic malady (le mal catholique) that compromises the teach-

ing does not mean ignoring other forms of Church teaching, whether it be authoritative doctrine or prudential admonitions, pastoral applications or the regulation of Church discipline. Nevertheless, the pastoral significance of this distinction is evident in the catechetical developments that rightly have abandoned the attempt to communicate the entirety of our Church's doctrinal tradition to catechumens and candidates seeking full communion in the Roman Catholic Church. Mature processes for facilitating admission into the Roman Catholic Church have rightly focused on the lectionary, the creed, and the liturgy as the privileged expressions of the apostolic faith. Other Church teachings are presented as they emerge out of reflection on the Christian *kerygma.* I am not supporting some kind of selective catechesis; rather my desire is to reaffirm the catechetical priority of the Christian *kerygma* transmitted in our Church's central dogmatic teachings.

Second, because so many Church teachings belong in the category of nondefinitive, authoritative doctrine, there is a real danger of the significant gradations of authority *within* this category being overlooked. The taxonomy of Church teaching offered above can be of some help in sorting through these many pronouncements, identifying the binding or authoritative character of each. But this task is still not easy. While few would like to see a return to the seminary manuals of the past, one of the advantages of the manual tradition was its careful delineation of the theological note attached to a particular teaching. Theological notes were formal judgments by theologians or the magisterium on the precise relationship of a doctrinal formulation to divine revelation. When a note took a negative form it was considered a "censure." Their purpose was to safeguard the faith and prevent confusion between binding doctrines and theological opinion. Understood in the broadest sense, the notion of the theological note can be traced back to the very origins of Christianity, in which it became necessary to distinguish between the authentic apostolic message and that which was opposed to it. Designations regarding divine truth and heresy were used quite broadly well into the Middle Ages and did not receive their more specialized meanings until after the Council of Trent. The Counter Reformation saw the first systematic gradations of theological notes and censures in the works of theologians like

---

ing office of the Church and has created "le magistère incertain." André Naud, *Le Magistère incertain* (Montreal: Fides, 1987).

Melchior Cano and Francisco Suarez. One might find the following notes attached to particular teachings in any of a number of seminary manuals in use immediately before Vatican II:[41]

> *fides divina*—that which is immediately revealed by God,
>
> *fides divina et catholica*—that which is immediately revealed by God and is infallibly proposed as such by the magisterium of the Church,
>
> *sententia fidei proxima*—that which is generally taught as belonging to divine revelation but which has not been solemnly defined as such,
>
> *sententia ad fidem pertinens* or *theologice certa*—that which is taught as connected to divine revelation,
>
> *sententia communis*—that which belongs to the field of free opinion but which is generally accepted by theologians as true.

Besides these notes there were numerous others, which proposed the degree of certitude connected with particular theological opinions, for example, opinions that are probable *(sententia probabilis),* more probable *(probabilior),* and well founded *(bene fundata).* This system generally presupposed a propositional view of revelation and was often unwarranted in its confidence regarding a teaching's relationship to divine revelation. Nevertheless, one might wish that official teaching pronouncements of the pope and bishops in our time might be accompanied by a more explicit qualification of their authority. In any event, theologians, catechists, and all who are involved in the teaching ministry of the Church must have an adequate understanding of the different levels of authoritative Church teaching that have been considered in this chapter.

In these past two chapters, constituting the second part of this volume, I have focused on the object of Church teaching. I briefly reviewed the teaching of Vatican II on divine revelation while also

---

[41] A typical example can be found in Ludwig Ott, *Fundamentals of Catholic Dogma,* 4th ed. (St. Louis: Herder, 1960) 9–10. See also Salaverri, *Sacrae theologiae summa,* 1:781–96. For an in-depth treatment of the role of theological notes and censures see Sixtus Cartechini, *De valore notarum theologicarum et de criteriis ad eas dignoscendas* (Rome: Gregorian Univ. Press, 1951).

exploring the role of Church doctrine in mediating divine revelation. In the treatment of Church doctrine I have sought to honor its cognitive, symbolic, and regulative dimensions. By recalling the liturgical and confessional contexts of early creedal statements I have also tried to acknowledge the way in which Church doctrine socializes believers in Christian community by providing an ecclesial identity that shapes attitudes and behaviors. Through the Christian profession of faith the believer is brought into the central mystery of the Christian faith, God's offer of salvation, the shape of which is discovered in the life, death, and resurrection of Jesus Christ.

In part 1 of this volume I concluded that while the ecclesiastical magisterium had an essential role to play in passing on the faith it was by no means an exclusive one. Similarly, I have tried to demonstrate in part 2 that the substance of the apostolic faith is transmitted in many different forms, only one of which is properly doctrinal. As the authoritative and normative teachers of the Church, the college of bishops is charged with the responsibility of faithfully guarding and preserving the apostolic faith in its doctrinal teaching. In part 3 I will turn to consider the concrete *exercise* of the Church's teaching office and the accompanying assistance of the Holy Spirit.

For Further Reading

Boyle, John P. "The Natural Law and the Magisterium." In *Church Teaching Authority: Historical and Theological Studies,* 43–62. Notre Dame: Univ. of Notre Dame Press, 1995.

Congregation for the Doctrine of the Faith. "Declaration in Defense of the Catholic Doctrine on the Church Against Certain Errors of the Present Day." *Origins* 3 (July 19, 1973) 97–112.

_____. "The Ecclesial Vocation of the Theologian." *Origins* 20 (July 5, 1990) 118–26.

Fransen, Piet. "A Short History of the Meaning of the Formula '*Fides et Mores.*'" In *Hermeneutics of Councils and Other Studies.* Ed. H. E. Mertens and F. de Graeve, 287–318. Leuven: Leuven Univ. Press, 1985.

Fuchs, Josef. "Moral Truths—Truths of Salvation?" In *Christian Ethics in a Secular Arena*, 48–67. Washington: Georgetown Univ. Press, 1984.

Hines, Mary. *The Transformation of Dogma: An Introduction to Karl Rahner on Doctrine.* New York: Paulist, 1989.

Joint Working Group Between the Roman Catholic Church and the World Council of Churches. "The Notion of 'Hierarchy of Truths': An Ecumenical Interpretation." Faith and Order Paper no. 150. Geneva: WCC, 1990.

Lonergan, Bernard. "Doctrines." In *Method in Theology,* 295–333. New York: Crossroad, 1979.

National Conference of Catholic Bishops. "The Teaching Ministry of the Diocesan Bishop: A Pastoral Reflection." *Origins* 21 (January 2, 1991) 473–92.

International Theological Commission. "On the Interpretation of Dogmas." *Origins* 20 (May 17, 1990) 1–14.

Rahner, Karl. "What Is a Dogmatic Statement?" In *Theological Investigations.* 5:42–66. Baltimore: Helicon, 1966.

Schillebeeckx, Edward, ed. *Dogma and Pluralism.* Concilium 51. New York: Herder & Herder, 1970.

Sullivan, Francis A. "Some Observations on the New Formula for the Profession of Faith." *Gregorianum* 70 (1989) 552–54.

_____. *Creative Fidelity: Weighing and Interpreting Documents of the Magisterium.* New York: Paulist, 1996.

Part Three

The Exercise of Doctrinal
Teaching Authority

5

How the Church Teaches:
The Assistance of the Holy Spirit

The complex set of questions regarding the structures of ecclesial authority in the early Church has challenged historians and biblical scholars for more than 150 years. The fact is that nowhere do we find a comprehensive and systematic account of ecclesial authority in early Church writings. Scholars have had to be content with piecing together tentative sketches of the nature and exercise of authority in the early Church from fragmentary documentary evidence. If we consider, however, not so much the *structures of ecclesial authority* as ecclesial authority's *inner dynamism*, the testimony of the early Church is more helpful. For example, we find in the early Church's memory of the life and teaching of Jesus several significant themes regarding the nature and exercise of authority. These themes hardly constitute a comprehensive theology of authority, but they do suggest some basic attitudes the early Christians felt ought to characterize all Church authority, regardless of its concrete form. I would like to begin this chapter by considering briefly some of these themes as a way of providing a context for the subsequent treatment of the concrete modalities through which the Church exercises doctrinal teaching authority.

The Exercise of Authority in the Second Testament

There are numerous gospel texts that present Jesus either exercising authority in his ministry or teaching about authority to his disciples.

A careful exegetical study of these texts is not possible here, but a brief consideration of some of these texts may still prove helpful. In particular I want to highlight three central insights about the nature and exercise of authority within the Christian community that emerge from the gospels: (1) authority is characterized as service; (2) the authority of office (*de iure* authority) is most effective when combined with personal or moral authority (*de facto* authority); (3) the exercise of authority demands an openness to the transcendent; there must be a fundamental dependence on God and the assistance of God's Spirit.

Authority as Service

There are several biblical passages in which Jesus speaks of the exercise of authority as service. In Mark 10:42-45 the apostles James and John petition Jesus for places of privilege in Jesus' kingdom.

> Jesus summoned them and said to them, "You know that those who are recognized as rulers over the Gentiles lord it over them, and their great ones make their authority over them felt. But it shall not be so among you. Rather, whoever wishes to be great among you will be your servant; whoever wishes to be first among you will be the slave of all. For the Son of Man did not come to be served but to serve and to give his life as a ransom for many" (cf. also Matt 20:25-28).

The most striking feature in this passage is the contrast between a "worldly" model of authority and that demanded by Jesus. Jesus calls his disciples (and presumably the gospel authors are equally calling the leaders of their communities) to a paradoxical conception of authority—authority as service. The more common model of authority, then as today, separated those in authority from those over whom authority was exercised. However, for the early Christian community, when authority was exercised as service, those in authority were bound to those on behalf of whom this authority was engaged. A servant authority could never exist for its own sake; it existed for the good of the Church.

We can find this view of authority reflected as well in the views of St. Paul. Paul frequently was compelled to justify the authenticity of his own authority (cf. 1 Cor 9), but it was an authority conditioned in two ways. First, Paul's authority was always in service of the gospel that he preached (cf. Gal 1:1-9). Paul never relied on a strictly formal authority; his letters reflect the constant need to cajole and persuade others regarding the authenticity of his message. Second, it was an authority that sought the building up rather than the tearing down of the Church of Jesus Christ (cf. 2 Cor 13:10).[1] This biblical view rejects all forms of authoritarian elitism. Those in authority may be responding to a particular divine calling, but they are not to be identified as a class set apart. This is further developed in a second pericope from the synoptics in which the author of Luke places the discussion of authority in his account of the Last Supper:

> Then an argument broke out among them about which of them should be regarded as the greatest. He said to them, "The kings of the Gentiles lord it over them and those in authority over them are addressed as 'Benefactors'; but among you it shall not be so. Rather, let the greatest among you be as the youngest, and the leader as the servant. For who is greater: the one seated at table or the one who serves? Is it not the one seated at table? I am among you as the one who serves" (Luke 22:24-27).

The setting at the Last Supper suggests an important Eucharistic context for considerations of ecclesial authority. For those who gather at the table of the Lord, there can be no exercise of coercive, dominating authority. Authority in the Eucharistic community is not exercised in relationships of inequality but in relationships grounded in a common discipleship.

Even as the early Church only gradually developed consistent structures and offices for the exercise of ecclesial authority, for centuries it would persevere in its conviction that the Christian exercise of authority was manifested as service within and not above the community of the baptized. St. Augustine gives this conviction classic expression in one of his sermons:

> What I should be for you fills me with anguish; what I can be with you is my consolation. Because for you I am a bishop, but with you a Christian. The first points to my duty, the second to grace. The first shows the danger, the other salvation.[2]

Augustine clearly recognized the dangers of abuse that accompanied the exercise of authority. According to Yves Congar this biblical con-

[1] 2 Cor 13:10 was frequently cited by medieval canonists and theologians intent on warding off abuses in ecclesiastical authority. Cf. Yves Congar, "Reception as an Ecclesiological Reality," in *Election and Consensus in the Church,* Concilium 77, ed. Giuseppe Alberigo and Anton Weiler (New York: Herder, 1972) 61.

[2] Augustine, *Sermons,* 340.

ception of authority as service was not lost until the end of the first millennium:

> We must get back to the true vision of the Gospel: posts of authority in the Church do indeed exist; a real jurisdictional power does exist, which the shepherds of God's people receive from Christ in conformity with the order which Christ willed and instituted (at least in its essential lines). But this power exists only within the structure of the fundamental religious relationship of the Gospel, as an organizational element within the life given to men by Christ, the one Lord and the one Head of his Body, for which each is accountable to all the rest according to the place and measure granted to him. So there is never simply a relationship of subordination or superiority, as in secular society, but always a loving obedience to Christ, shaping the life of each with all and for all, according to the position which the Lord has given him in the Body.[3]

For Congar the witness of the early Church does not challenge the institutional structures of the Church, but it does challenge the way in which authority may actually be exercised in and through these structures.

De Iure *and* De Facto *Authority*

The biblical theme of authority exercised as service is further reinforced by an implicit distinction found in the Gospels between a *de iure* authority, which one possesses by law as a legitimate officeholder, and a *de facto* authority, which one possesses by virtue of moral character. This contrast is highlighted in Matthew's account of Jesus' own exercise of authority. At the end of the Sermon on the Mount we are told, "When Jesus finished these words, the crowds were astonished at his teaching, for he taught them as one having authority, and not as their scribes" (Matt 7:28-9). While the scribes possessed the authority of office, the authority of Jesus was of an entirely different order. It was an authority exercised by force of character.

In Matthew's Gospel Jesus does not reject the need for the authority of office, but he does suggest that it be joined with a moral authority. This is evident in the Matthean passage in which Jesus acknowledges the legitimacy of the authority of the scribes and pharisees while criticizing their hypocrisy:

[3]Yves Congar, *Power and Poverty in the Church* (London: Chapman, 1964) 98.

"The scribes and the Pharisees have taken their seat on the chair of Moses. Therefore, do and observe all things whatsoever they tell you, but do not follow their example. For they preach but they do not practice. They tie up heavy burdens (hard to carry) and lay them on people's shoulders, but they will not lift a finger to move them. All their works are performed to be seen. They widen their phylacteries and lengthen their tassles. They love places of honor at banquets, seats of honor in synagogues, greetings in marketplaces, and the salutation, 'Rabbi'" (Matt 23:1-7).

While the authority of law and office is often necessary, its legitimacy depends on its subordination and reconfiguration before the demands of the gospel.[4]

The Transcendent Ground of Authority

But what is the nature of this moral authority? The authority with which Jesus himself taught (cf. Mark 1:22; Matt 7:28-29; Luke 4:32; John 7:15ff.) was the product of his relationship of perfect intimacy and union with God. His ministry of healing, his freedom to proclaim the forgiveness of sins, his authoritative interpretation of the law—all were derived from his unique relationship with the God whom he addressed as "Abba." The unity of Jesus and the Father was a particularly prominent theme in the Gospel of John. For example, in John 5:17-30 Jesus responds to those who complained of his healing on the Sabbath:

But Jesus answered them, "My Father is at work until now, so I am at work." For this reason the Jews tried all the more to kill him, because he not only broke the sabbath but he also called God his own father, making himself equal to God.

Jesus answered and said to them, "Amen, amen, I say to you, a son cannot do anything on his own, but only what he sees his father doing; for what he does, his son will do also. For the Father loves his Son and shows him everything that he himself does, and he will show him greater works than these, so that you may be amazed. For just as the Father raises the dead and gives life, so also does the Son give life to whomever he wishes. Nor does the Father judge anyone, but he has given all judgment to his Son, so that all may honor the Son just as

---

[4]Raymond E. Brown, *The Churches the Apostles Left Behind* (New York: Paulist, 1984) 134–35.

they honor the Father. Whoever does not honor the Son does not honor the Father who sent him. Amen, amen I say to you, whoever hears my word and believes in the one who sent me has eternal life and will not come to condemnation, but has passed from death to life. . . .

I cannot do anything on my own; I judge as I hear, and my judgment is just, because I do not seek my own will but the will of the one who sent me."

Contemporary biblical scholarship warns us that the primary thrust of this and like passages in John is not an ontological claim about the first two persons of the Trinity but a claim about Christ's radical dependence on the Father and the divine sanctioning of the ministry of Christ. The focal point for the identity of Father and Son in the passage is not the *being* of Father and Son but rather the *work* of Father and Son.[5] What Jesus *does* is in union with what the Father *does*. The authority of Jesus Christ to perform his ministry is grounded in the will and work of God.

Beyond this relationship between Jesus and his "Father in heaven" we must also affirm the significance of Jesus' relationship to the Holy Spirit as reflected in a number of the gospel texts. So dominant had a Logos Christology become by the end of the third century that Western Christianity (with important exceptions) has tended to overlook the early Christian community's intuitions about the relationship between Christ and the Spirit of God. Yet the Gospels attribute a significant role to the Holy Spirit in the life and ministry of Jesus. In the synoptic accounts of Jesus' baptism it is the Spirit of God who anoints Jesus and calls him to mission (cf. Mark 1:9-11; Luke 3:21-22; Matt 3:13-17).[6] While Luke's Gospel attributes the conception of Jesus to the work of the Spirit (Luke 1:35), Luke joins Matthew and Mark in the assumption that Jesus acts in the power of the Spirit only after his baptism.

In the synoptic accounts of Jesus' baptism, the Spirit of God is associated with the word of God.[7] As the Spirit of God comes upon

[5]Raymond E. Brown, *The Gospel According to John* (Garden City: Doubleday, 1966) 1:216–21.

[6]The Johannine version (1:29-34) has a different emphasis. John the Baptist testifies, "I saw the Spirit come down like a dove from the sky and *remain* upon him." The verb "remain" is consistent with a Johannine emphasis on the permanence of Jesus' relationship to the Father as the bearer of the Spirit.

[7]Cf. Yves Congar, *I Believe in the Holy Spirit* (New York: Seabury, 1983) 1:17.

Jesus in the form of a dove we hear the testimony of the Father, "You are my beloved Son: with you I am well pleased," echoing the passage from one of the messianic psalms, "You are my son; today I am your father" (Ps 2:7). It is by the power of the Spirit and the proclamation of a divine word that Jesus is consecrated to his messianic mission.

The biblical tradition that portrays Jesus as fulfilling his mission in the power of the Spirit stands in an unresolved tension with other accounts that portray Jesus as the *giver* of the Spirit (Luke 24:49; Acts 1:4-8; John 16:1-14, 19:30, 20:22). Both at the end of Luke and the beginning of Acts it is Jesus who promises the coming of the Spirit. Similarly, in John's Gospel Jesus gives the Spirit to his disciples during one of the resurrection appearances. This diversity in the biblical tradition helps explain subsequent differences among various theological traditions regarding the role of Christ and the Spirit. While the sacramental theology and ecclesiology of the West will give a priority to the Christological, the East's understanding of Church and sacrament will tend to privilege pneumatology.[8]

The biblical texts that treat both Jesus' relationship to the Father and his relationship to the Spirit remind us above all that his authority was not his own; he truly spoke with the authority of God.[9] Jesus' authority was derived from his unique relationship to God the Father in the power of God's Spirit. This reveals something important about the nature of authority. The word "authority" in the English language comes from the Latin word *auctoritas,* which carries the sense of a source or origination of something.[10] Jesus exercised authority in an authentic and faithful way because he stood in proper relation to his divine source or ground. While Jesus' messianic mission and unique relationship to God means that there are dimensions of his authority proper to him alone, nevertheless, his exercise of authority provides the model for the exercise of all ecclesial authority. As with Jesus, all ecclesial authority comes from God and remains dependent upon the

[8]This is reflected in the West's stress on the institution narrative in its Eucharistic theology while the East focuses more on the *epiklesis.*

[9]For a helpful treatment of the biblical notions of authority and power in the ministry of Jesus see John F. O'Grady, *Disciples and Leaders: The Origins of Christian Ministry in the New Testament* (New York: Paulist, 1991) 39–66.

[10]John E. Thiel, "Responsibility to the Spirit: Authority in the Catholic Tradition," *New Theology Review* 8 (August 1995) 55.

assistance of God. Moreover, as with Jesus, when this authority proceeds from its transcendent ground, this will be evident in its actual exercise. When Jesus acted with authority, those who were witnesses knew from whence that authority came. The same should be true for the Church. When the Church exercises its authority authentically, its transcendent ground should also be evident.

A review of the early Church's recollection of Jesus' teaching on authority highlights the way in which a Christian exercise of authority is distinguished from its worldly counterpart by its orientation (service), its moral character (*de iure* authority must be accompanied by *de facto* authority), and its dependence on the Spirit of God. In the remainder of this chapter I will focus particularly on this third characteristic.

God's Fidelity to the Church

In chapter 1, I spoke of the dangers of an excessively Christomonist ecclesiology that does not pay sufficient attention to the role of the Holy Spirit. This ecclesiology stresses the Church's institution by Christ and gives the impression that in Christ's institution of the Church, the Church received all that it required for its continued existence. In this view there is little need for the Spirit in the life of the Church. Yet a review of the many implicit ecclesiologies of the first millennium suggests that for centuries the role of Christ in the institution of the Church was never separated from the work of the Holy Spirit.[11] In patristic theology the same Spirit who "overshadowed" Mary and came upon Jesus at his baptism also came upon the Church at Pentecost and continues to form the faithful into the body of Christ. The ecclesiologies of the first millennium attended much more fully to the missions of Son *and* Spirit in the life of the Church. Even the ordination of Christ's ministers was thought to be dependent upon the work of the Spirit. The ancient ordination rites gave a prominent role to *epikleses,* invocations of the Holy Spirit.[12]

---

[11]Yves Congar, *L'Ecclésiologie du haut moyen-age* (Paris: Cerf, 1968) 113–16.

[12]Ibid., 115. See also Congar, *I Believe in the Holy Spirit,* 3:268–69; Pierre-Marie Gy, "Ancient Ordination Prayers," *Studia Liturgica* 13 (1979) 70–93; Georg Kretschmar, "Die Ordination im frühen Christentum," *Freiburger Zeitschrift für Philosophie und Theologie* 22 (1975) 35–69.

Properly understood, there is a sense in which one can claim that Christ founded the Church.[13] However, one must avoid any ahistorical misconception that imagines that every aspect of ecclesial life was given explicitly by Christ to the apostles. Similarly, we must avoid the misconception that the entire deposit of faith, conceived as a collection of propositional truths, was dictated to the apostles and then passed on, tag-team fashion, through the apostolic succession of bishops. This view overlooks both the gradual development of ecclesiastical structures and the way in which the Spirit was given to the Church as its animating principle. It is the Spirit who assists the Church in its concrete development.[14] It is through the Spirit that the Church gradually develops and responds to the demands of each time and place. Finally, it is through the Spirit that the Church penetrates ever more deeply the economy of salvation revealed in Christ's paschal mystery. As John Thiel has observed, ecclesial authority involves a "responsibility to the Spirit," an openness to the Spirit's initiative in the life of the Church.[15]

Indefectibility and the Assistance of the Holy Spirit

According to Scripture, Christ promised the continued existence of the Church (cf. Matt 16:18) and implicitly assured that it would remain faithful to the gospel until the end of time. Whether or not one grants this as a statement of the historical Jesus, it certainly reflects the convictions of the early Christian community. As Christians we continue to believe that humanity's ultimate victory over the power of sin and death was assured in Christ's death and resurrection. The ultimate triumph of God's grace has been accomplished and rendered effective in the work of Christ. Insofar as the Church is to be the

[13]Richard McBrien makes a helpful distinction between Christ's "founding" of the Church and his "laying the foundations" for the Church in his gathering of disciples. The latter claim is more faithful to the evidence of historical scholarship. Cf. Richard McBrien, *Catholicism,* rev. ed. (San Francisco: HarperCollins, 1994) 577–79.

[14]One of the most creative Roman Catholic studies on the work of the Spirit in the Church is that of Heribert Mühlen, *Una Persona Mystica* (Munich: Schöningh, 1964). The work of Greek Orthodox bishop and theologian, John Zizioulas, has also had a considerable influence on Orthodox and Roman Catholic theologians alike. See his *Being as Communion* (Crestwood: St. Vladimir's Seminary Press, 1985).

[15]Thiel, "Responsibility to the Spirit," 56–57.

"universal sacrament of salvation" (*LG* 48), the ultimate success of its mission is equally assured. For that reason not only Catholics but many Christians from other traditions share the belief that the Church, relying on the assistance of the Spirit, will never depart fundamentally from the gospel. As we noted earlier, this belief that the Church will be preserved in truth is often referred to as "indefectibility." It is based on Christian convictions regarding the essential nature of the Church.

The Church of Jesus Christ is not merely a social organization or institution; it is also a spiritual reality. As the body of Christ and temple of the Holy Spirit, the Church possesses both human and divine elements. The Church can teach with authority precisely because it is a spiritual as well as a social reality. Our understanding of this exercise of authority, however, will depend on our understanding of the interrelation of the divine and human elements in the Church.

Over the past two centuries, Catholic ecclesiology often patterned the relationship of the human and divine elements within the Church after the model of Christ himself. As Christ was the union of the human and the divine in one person, so too was the Church of Christ a union of the human and divine. This approach can even be found in the documents of Vatican II:

> This society, however, equipped with hierarchial structures, and the mystical body of Christ, a visible assembly and a spiritual community, an earthly church and a church enriched with heavenly gifts, must not be considered as two things, but as forming one complex reality comprising a human and a divine element. *It is therefore by no mean analogy that it is likened to the mystery of the incarnate Word.* For just as the assumed nature serves the divine Word as a living instrument of salvation inseparably joined with him, in a similar way the social structure of the church serves the Spirit of Christ who vivifies the church towards the growth of the body (*LG* 8, my emphasis).

This analogy, although legitimate, has significant limits, which are not always properly recognized. For while in Christ the union of the human and the divine occurs in one person, the Church is not a single moral person but a communion of persons. Second, Christianity holds that Christ's human nature was without sin; the same cannot be said for the humanity of Christ's Church. The Church is composed of sinners, and their sinfulness can never be a merely private matter. Insofar as the mission of the Church is accomplished through its members, the sinfulness of its members compromises the Church's corporate witness.[16] Who can deny that the immorality of many popes and bishops in the Church of the thirteenth through fifteenth centuries compromised the Church's prophetic witness and set the stage for the sixteenth century reformations?

One consequence of uncritically employing the analogy of the incarnation with respect to the Church has been a tendency to consider the Church as a virtual mouthpiece of Christ with little acknowledgment of the way in which the Church's teaching was and is conditioned by its sinful humanity. Herman Schell (1850–1906), an often overlooked German theologian who wrote at the end of the nineteenth and beginning of the twentieth century, already had recognized the shortcomings of this approach to ecclesiology. Schell criticized those ecclesiologists who saw the Church as the continuation of the incarnation. In his mind this view did not pay sufficient attention to the human character of the Church. Schell proposed that the relationship between the human and divine elements in the Church be considered instead according to the model of the *covenantal* union between God and the people of Israel. God remained faithful to the covenant even as Israel continually wandered away. While the infidelity of Israel appeared to place the covenant in jeopardy, the people of Israel were always lured back to the covenant by the God who remained faithful. This model, when applied to the Church, preserves the sense in which the Church is not just another human organization but is a people chosen by God and graced with divine gifts and charisms that enable it to accomplish its mission. At the same time, the model of the covenantal union accommodates the undeniable witness of history that this same Church (and not just individual members) has often departed from God's will in many of its actions (e.g., the Crusades, the Spanish Inquisition, the persecution of Galileo). The indefectibility of the Church is still preserved in this covenantal view of the human and divine elements within the Church. God, through the assistance of the Holy Spirit, promises to remain ever

---

[16]For more on whether we can speak not only of a Church of sinners but of a sinful Church see Karl Rahner, "The Church of Sinners," and "The Sinful Church in the Decrees of Vatican II," in *Theological Investigations* (New York: Crossroad, 1982) 6:253–94; Hans Urs von Balthasar, "Casta Meretrix," in *Sponsa Verbi: Skizzen zur Theologie* (Einsiedeln, 1961) 2:203–305; Yves Congar, "Comment l'église sainte doit se renouveler sans cesse?" in *Sainte Église,* Unam Sanctam 41 (Paris: Cerf, 1963) 131–54.

faithful to the Church. Thus the Church's continued fidelity to the gospel is dependent on the prior fidelity of God to the Church. We must still ask, however, how, concretely, is the Church preserved in fidelity to the gospel? Put differently, how does the Holy Spirit interact with human freedom in such a way as to both preserve that freedom and yet prevent that freedom from leading the Church astray?

The Assistance of the Holy Spirit and Human Freedom

As I noted above, understandings of the assistance of the Holy Spirit have often depended on conceptions of the human-divine relationship in the Church. During the hundred years prior to Vatican II many theologians, influenced by a view of the Church modeled on the incarnation, assumed a somewhat mechanistic understanding of the Church's cooperation with the Holy Spirit. One mid-twentieth-century example of this approach can be found in the work of the influential Swiss theologian Charles Journet (1891–1975). Journet was a pioneer in twentieth-century Catholic ecclesiology who greatly expanded previous neo-Scholastic treatments of the Church by incorporating themes from biblical and patristic sources. He had a tremendous influence on the ecclesiological vision of Pope Paul VI. Nevertheless, Journet's treatment of the Church was configured around Aristotelian conceptions of causality. Consequently, he considered the mediation of the hierarchy in the transmission of divine revelation according to the category of secondary causality.[17] Largely overlooked in his use of Aristotelian-Thomistic understandings of causality was the Thomistic distinction between instrumental causality and a true secondary causality. Instrumental causality involved the relatively passive causality that one might ascribe to an inanimate object like a piece of chalk, or the keyboard with which I am typing these words. True secondary causality, in contrast, engages human freedom. Journet's treatment of the role of the hierarchy in the Church often collapsed secondary causality into instrumental causality. His schema characterized the hierarchy as little more than a pas-

---

[17]Charles Journet, *L'Église du Verbe Incarné*, vol. 1 (Paris: Desclée, 1962–69). Thomas O'Meara has demonstrated the shortcomings of applying Aristotelian categories of causality to the teaching office of the Church in "The Teaching Office of Bishops in the Ecclesiology of Charles Journet," *The Jurist* 49 (1989) 23–47.

sive conduit or instrument of God's grace. There was little or no consideration of human freedom in the cooperation with that grace. Not surprisingly, this approach had little place for the possibility that the Church might err in any of its teaching. The thought of Schell stands in contrast to that of Journet. Writing decades earlier, Schell emphasized that the Spirit operates *through* the exercise of human freedom within the Church. While the pope and bishops are promised the assistance of the Holy Spirit in the exercise of their office as teachers of the faith, this assistance can be inhibited or enhanced by the disposition of the officeholders. Schell wrote:

> The assistance of the Holy Spirit is not, in any case, a replacement for the necessity which is incumbent upon the church teaching office to employ at any given time all the means for the human recognition of truth, but rather the divine assistance operates as it wills to, above all through that which is mediately and immediately called forth in human efforts.[18]

The proclamation of the word of God can be impeded or compromised by failure on the part of the ecclesiastical officeholder to be open to the guidance of the Spirit. The bishops, it is true, teach with the assistance of the Holy Spirit. Yet in certain understandings of this authority divine assistance is thought to be at the automatic disposal of the bishop by virtue of ordination.

At this point it may be helpful to recall the Second Testament portrait of the authority of Jesus. Scripture was consistent in portraying the authority of Jesus as grounded in the authority of God. Divine assistance to those who teach in the name of the Church is no more "automatically" at their disposal than was Jesus' authority "automatically" at his disposal *apart from his relationship with the God whom he addressed as "Abba."* This openness to the Spirit is certainly maintained by the life of prayer, but it is equally dependent upon the engagement of the human processes by which all humans inquire after truth. Through the sacrament of orders, the ordinand is placed in a particular relationship to Christ and the Spirit in virtue of his new ecclesial role, but the celebration of orders does not offer

[18]Herman Schell, "Lehrende und lernende Kirche: Wissenschaft und Autorität," in *Kleinere Schriften,* ed. Karl Hennemann (Paderborn: Schöningh, 1907) 485.

some supernaturally infused knowledge of divine truth. The ordinand's new availability to the influence of the Spirit does not abrogate the necessity of employing human processes in seeking after and expounding divine truth.

Jesuit moral theologian Richard McCormick has remarked on the importance of avoiding two extremes in our consideration of the role of the Holy Spirit in the exercise of the Church's doctrinal teaching office. First, we must avoid any explanations that overlook the important role of ordinary human processes for discovering truth, and second, we must avoid any approach that would reduce this assistance to the exercise of human processes by themselves.[19] If the assistance of the Holy Spirit bypassed human processes, we would have no alternative but to recognize in every hierarchical teaching act the charism of infallibility. If the official teachers of the Church had access to divine truth wholly apart from human processes, it would be difficult to imagine the possibility of error. The second extreme, however, reduces the activity of the Spirit to the exercise of human investigation and can lead to a kind of rationalism.

In between these two extremes it is possible to imagine a real assistance of the Spirit that is an immanent principle active within the exercise of human processes.[20] This full employment of the human processes was alluded to at the Second Vatican Council in *Lumen gentium*: "The Roman pontiff and the bishops, in virtue of their office and the seriousness of the matter, work sedulously through appropriate means duly to investigate this revelation and give it suitable expression" (*LG* 25). The assumption is that the divine assistance promised the Church is only effective when conjoined with the proper cooperation of the Church's ministers.

But what are these "appropriate means"? McCormick divides the relevant human processes into two categories: evidence gathering and evidence assessing. *Evidence gathering* refers to the manifold ways in which the human person inquires after the truth through study, con-

---

[19]I will largely follow McCormick's reflections on this topic, which can be found in his collection "Notes in Moral Theology," which appeared in *Theological Studies* for so many years. Cf. Richard A. McCormick, *Notes on Moral Theology: 1965 through 1980* (Lanham, Md.: Univ. Press of America, 1981) 261ff.

[20]Much of the work of Karl Rahner can be read as an attempt to develop a theology of grace in which grace functions precisely as this kind of immanent principle.

sultation, and investigation. With respect to the exercise of the Church's teaching office, this would involve a study of the Church's tradition (giving primacy of place to the testimony of Scripture), a consultation of scholars and theologians (representing diverse schools of thought and theological/historical perspectives), a consideration of the insights of pertinent related fields (e.g., the contributions of the social sciences, genetics), and an attempt to discern the *sensus fidelium,* the sense of the faithful in and through whom the Spirit speaks. Insufficient attention to this evidence gathering can hamper the activity of the Spirit in bringing forth wisdom and insight.

Evidence assessing involves the proper consideration and assessment of the "evidence" gathered. Here again recourse to a diversity of theological scholarship will be important, but so will patient reflection and authentic conversation in contexts where the free exchange of views is clearly welcomed. The importance of the principle of collegiality is evident in this matter. The value of real conversation and deliberation as a prelude to authoritative teaching was demonstrated at Vatican II. The vast majority of the bishops who traveled to Rome in the fall of 1962 were content to participate in a relatively quick council that would, by and large, continue the status quo. That this status quo was not maintained can be attributed to the conversation and deliberation in which the bishops became engaged. New insight, a new penetration into divine truth, resulted from their interaction.

If the Spirit does work through this kind of human interaction, then one of the most serious handicaps to an authentic exercise of the ecclesiastical magisterium is the limitation of the freedom of bishops to discuss controversial doctrinal matters frankly and openly.[21] While freedom of inquiry is essential for all the baptized, the situation of bishops, who after all *constitute* the ecclesiastical magisterium, is unique. As the authoritative teachers of the faith, the spirit of communion that characterizes the whole life of the Church is particularly concentrated in their episcopal interaction. Their authority to teach the faith depends on their freedom to investigate adequately doctrinal matters under consideration. False notions of obedience to the papacy, perhaps appropriate to the juridical sphere, can seriously inhibit the work of the Spirit in leading the Church to truth.

The emphases on evidence gathering and assessing should not be seen as preludes to the assistance of the Spirit, as if they were mere

[21]For a perceptive treatment of this issue see André Naud, *Le Magistère incertain* (Montreal: Fides, 1987) 123–70.

natural processes necessary before the work of the Spirit could kick in. Rather, the claim here is that the Spirit is operative in and through these human processes. If the teaching ministry of the Church is to be an expression of the Church's essential nature as a communion, then the processes engaged in the teaching ministry must reflect this communion. This is the aforementioned principle of conciliarity. That principle and the whole dynamism of ecclesial communion precludes seeing the authoritative teaching of the Church as isolated ecclesial acts engaged by autonomous authority figures. Consultative activities, dialogue, conversation, and deliberation are constitutive of communion. These are the means by which the Spirit brings the Church to truth. For this reason, when bishops engage in true consultation—with fellow bishops, theologians, and the faithful—they are not merely engaging in prudent gestures, and they are certainly not, as some might suggest, compromising their own prophetic ministry in the Church. If God's word is given to the whole Church, however much the bishops may be the authoritative teachers of that word, they must honor the Church as itself being grounded in the word. In the fulfillment of their teaching ministry they must make themselves available to that word as it emerges within the whole Christian community. Consultation and conversation are integral to the teaching process and must be acknowledged as one of the privileged instruments of the Spirit. This is why many theologians today warn against the dangers of the distinction common since the sixteenth century between the teaching Church *(ecclesia docens)* and the learning Church *(ecclesia discens),* as if they were two distinct entities. In various ways the whole Church teaches and the whole Church learns within the life of communion.[22]

When bishops have been faithful to the processes of evidence gathering and evidence assessing, they can be confident in the activity of the Spirit to work within those human processes to stimulate the emergence of wisdom and insight into God's revelation. When these processes are short-circuited, the work of the Spirit is correspondingly impeded.

Of course the tasks of evidence gathering and assessing will always be somewhat partial and incomplete due to the conditions of human finitude. For that reason the Catholic Church admits that in most exercises of its teaching authority there exists at least the remote

[22]Cf. Ladislas Örsy, *The Church: Learning and Teaching* (Wilmington: Glazier, 1987).

possibility of error. This is not due to a failure of divine assistance but to either human sinfulness or those human limitations inherent in the processes of evidence gathering and assessing. After all, these processes can never be conducted exhaustively. At some point every teacher must put aside, at least temporarily, the tasks of study, conversation, and reflection and actually teach! We can be confident that in the instances when such error does occur, continued fidelity to the human processes for discovering and communicating truth, in communion with the Spirit, will lead to an eventual discovery and correction of this error.

My focus up to this point has been on the discernible human activities inherent in the teaching act. A proper respect for the mysterious activity of God's grace precludes any schematic development of precisely how the Spirit is thought to work through these human processes. The Church looks back over almost two thousand years of history and sees numerous signals of the Spirit's continued guidance of the Church; but in any particular teaching event, we can only trust in the fidelity of the Spirit to operate through the teacher's own faithful inquiry into divine truth.

This brings us to another important question. Is it enough to believe that, *by and large,* when the Church is faithful to the human processes for discovering truth, the Spirit will *generally* be able to insure that this inquiry into divine truth is not frustrated? Can the indefectibility of the Church be preserved while admitting the possibility, however remote, that the Church could still teach error? If the Church is not exempt from error how can this possibility of error be reconciled with the assurance of continued fidelity to the gospel? It is at this point that Roman Catholicism has generally parted company with other Christian traditions and insisted on a doctrine of ecclesial infallibility.

Infallibility: The Church Remains Faithful to the Mediation of the Mystery of Salvation

The official Roman Catholic position, at least since the nineteenth century, is that some notion of infallibility is necessary for the preservation of the Church's indefectibility. In other words, Roman Catholicism contends that the Church cannot remain indefectible as a whole unless there is some sure foundation upon which to base its faith. Edward Schillebeeckx writes that it is hardly possible to accept, from the ecclesiological point of view, that the Church, in its confession of baptism, can "remain in the truth" if there is no promise that its teaching will have a similar lasting value. The Church's "remaining in the truth" implies faithfulness in the teaching Church.[23]

It is true that at times Roman Catholicism has relied excessively on the doctrine of infallibility to support the authority of its teaching office, while Protestantism, reacting to rather maximalist presentations of *papal* infallibility, has by and large rejected the doctrine. Recent ecumenical dialogue, however, gives reason to hope that these differences may someday be overcome. Contemporary Protestant scholars freely grant that the great reformers, Calvin and Luther, both taught that the Church as a whole could not err in matters of faith.[24] Protestant objections have generally focused on the concrete exercise of this ecclesial infallibility. For them, the exercise of infallibility in the Roman Catholic Church, in theory and in practice, lacks the ecclesial and biblical context necessary to protect it from abuse. Orthodoxy continues to question Catholic accounts of infallibility that appear to excise the charism of infallibility given to the pope and college from the Spirit's activity within the whole Church. Beyond these more ecclesial concerns, however, is a whole set of questions that are more linguistic and epistemological in character. These questions generally center on the very possibility of asserting "infallible propositions." Contemporary Roman Catholic theology has sought to attend to these kinds of questions in a more deliberate fashion.

The Epistemic and Linguistic Difficulties in the Doctrine of Infallibility

The epistemic and linguistic challenge to Roman Catholicism's teaching on infallibility was brought to the forefront of debate by

---

[23]Edward Schillebeeckx, "The Problem of the Infallibility of the Church's Office: A Theological Reflection," in *Truth and Certainty, Concilium* 83, ed. Edward Schillebeeckx and Bas van Iersel (New York: Herder, 1973) 80.

[24]George Lindbeck cites Luther in his 1972 Pere Marquette theology lecture, published as *Infallibility* (Milwaukee, Marquette Univ. Press, 1972) 15. For Calvin's attribution of inerrancy to the Church see *Institutes of the Christian Religion*, vol. 2, ed. J. McNeill (Philadelphia, 1969) book 4, 8, 13, p. 1162. For Lindbeck's claim that most Protestant traditions, in fact, accept some notion of infallibility see his essay in *The Infallibility Debate*, ed. John Kirvan (New York: Paulist, 1971) 107–52.

Hans Küng's 1971 book on infallibility. In his controversial work Küng challenged the Roman Catholic belief in the possibility of "infallible propositions." He defines these as "statements which must be considered as guaranteed *a priori* to be free from error: sentences, propositions, definitions, formularies, and formulas, which are not only *de facto* not erroneous but in principle simply cannot be erroneous."[25] Küng rightly criticizes the linguistic impossibility of infallible propositions—human formulations that are immune from error. Since all human speech is governed by human finitude, so are the human articulations of our faith:

> Articles of faith are propositions. Formulas of faith, professions of faith, and definitions of faith, are propositions—simple or complex—and are not *a priori* free from the laws that govern propositions. Nor are propositions of faith ever directly God's word, but at best God's word attested and mediated by man's word: perceptible and transmissable by human propositions. But as such, propositions of faith participate in the problematic of human propositions in general.[26]

The Swiss theologian then goes on to state, presumably as an argument against infallibility, that propositions (1) fall short of reality, (2) are open to misunderstanding, (3) are limited in their capacity for translation, (4) are part of a dynamic linguistic and communicative process, and (5) are ideology prone.[27] Küng's critique of the concept of infallible propositions is very perceptive and rightly rejects this theologically and philosophically problematic concept. However, as numerous critics have observed, while the notion of infallible propositions has often been assumed in Catholic theology, it does not appear in the teaching of either Vatican I or Vatican II.[28] In other words few Catholic theologians would accept Küng's account of the Roman Catholic teaching on infallibility, however much his account is popularly assumed.

[25]Hans Küng, *Infallible? An Inquiry* (Garden City: Doubleday, 1971) 150.
[26]Ibid., 156.

[27]Ibid., 158–62.

[28]Cf. Francis Sullivan, *Magisterium: Teaching Authority in the Catholic Church* (New York: Paulist, 1983) 80–82; John T. Ford, "Infallibility: A Review of Recent Studies," *Theological Studies* 40 (1979) 279–81; "Küng on Infallibility," *Thomist* 35 (1971) 501–12; Walter Kasper, "Zur Diskussion um das Problem der Unfehlbarkeit," *Stimmen der Zeit* 188 (1971) 363–76; Yves Congar, "Infaillibilité et indéfectibilité," *Revue des sciences philosophiques et théologiques* 54 (1970) 614–18.

Properly speaking, infallibility qualifies neither a person nor collective (e.g., the Church itself, the pope, or the college of bishops) nor a doctrine but the act of *judgment,* either in believing or teaching, that a particular doctrine is true.[29] Infallibility does not refer to a proposition. The dogma of the immaculate conception was *taught infallibly*; it is not an *infallible dogma.* Infallibility predicates the act of believing or the act of teaching. The Church's teaching on infallibility requires us to believe only that the judgment regarding the truth or falsity of a particular proposition is not fundamentally erroneous. This is quite different from speaking of an infallible proposition. The propositional statement, as we saw in chapter 4, is subject to all the limitations of human linguistic communication. As such, doctrinal propositions can always be reformulated. Robert Kress writes:

> This [church teaching on infallibility] does not mean that these verbally formulated explications are purely or insurpassably perfect— only that they are adequate and do in fact mediate the truth of God's word mediated by Jesus and the apostles. There could have been other and better expressions. The one *de facto* chosen will be able to be improved upon. Hence, the words of infallibly declared doctrines do not escape the frailty and finitude of human history—no more than the words of Jesus, the apostles and the scripture.[30]

This carefully circumscribed understanding of the topic has been obscured by the terms "infallibility" and "inerrancy" themselves, which often suggest immunity from propositional imperfection. In the *Acta* of Vatican II there was an important *relatio* concerning article 12 of *Lumen gentium* that carefully describes infallibility as the assurance that the Church "cannot fall away from the way of salvation."[31] Echoing what was said in the last chapter on the irreformability of dogma, the Church's teaching on infallibility holds that where the mediation

[29]Cf. Sullivan, *Magisterium,* 80.

[30]Robert Kress, "Infallibility and Sacramentality," in *Papal Infallibility: An Application of Lonergan's Theological Method,* ed. Terry J. Tekippe (Washington: Univ. Press of America, 1983) 299.

[31]Quoted in Harry McSorley, "Some Forgotten Truths About the Petrine Ministry," *Journal of Ecumenical Studies* 11 (1974) 225. McSorley notes the similarity between this position and *Dei verbum* 11's treatment of inerrancy, which does not absolutely preclude Scripture's containing any errors but merely insists that no error will be found that might lead a believer away from salvation.

of God's self-communication is concerned, the Church is assured that *none of its dogmatic formulations will lead the faithful away from the path of salvation.* This view locates the doctrine of infallibility in the notion of fidelity to God's word. No dogmatic formulation of the Church, no matter how imperfect, can be unfaithful to God's offer of salvation as it comes to us through the mediation of the Church. Surely the Church cannot be thought of as remaining in the truth when it professes faith in something pertaining to God's offer of salvation that is illegitimate or contrary to that offer. To resort to the ludicrous, we would be hard pressed to imagine the Church's survival in truth and its continued fidelity to its God-given mission if it could teach that true salvation could be attained only through the acquisition of material wealth!

The question still remains, however, as to how this understanding of infallibility can be reconciled with what was said earlier regarding human freedom. When the Church, in the universal belief of the whole people of God and in its official teaching, infallibly professes and proclaims a teaching, it does so in dependence on the Holy Spirit's assistance. Properly speaking, God alone is infallible; the infallibility of the Church exists purely as gift. However, the notion of infallibility does not imply that in this one instance of divine assistance the human processes for discovering truth may be bypassed. At Vatican I the conciliar text defining papal infallibility itself (*Pastor aeternus,* DS 3074), along with the official commentary or *relatio* of Bishop Gasser, made it clear that infallibility is not exercised either by way of revelation or divine inspiration but by divine assistance. The exercise of the charism of infallibility presumes mental competence and freedom from external coercion along with the good faith engagement of the normal human processes for discovering truth. As Gasser explained:

> Indeed we do not separate the Pope, defining, from the cooperation and consent of the Church . . . because the infallibility of the Roman Pontiff does not come to him in the manner of inspiration or of revelation but through a divine assistance. Therefore the Pope, by reason of his office and the gravity of the matter, *is held to use the means suitable for properly discerning and aptly enunciating the truth.* These means are councils, or the advice of the bishops, cardinals, theologians, etc. Indeed, the means are diverse according to the diversity of situations, and we should piously believe that, in the divine assistance promised to Peter and his successors by Christ, there is simultaneously

contained a promise about the means which are necessary and suitable to make an infallible pontifical judgment (emphasis mine).[32]

After the Second Vatican Council, the examples regarding the "means suitable for properly discerning and aptly enunciating the truth" must be expanded to include recourse to the sense of the faithful.

In the case of the charism of infallibility, when the ordinary human processes for discovering the truth have been properly engaged (and the determination of this fact will not always be an easy matter), the assistance of the Spirit is actualized in a way that overcomes those human limitations inherent in the quest for truth. Put negatively, the Spirit guarantees that a teaching or belief of the Church is not inimical to the way of salvation.

The Ecclesial Context of the Doctrine of Infallibility: Infallibility in Believing and Teaching

Infallibility is best understood when it is coordinated with the more fundamental belief in the Church's indefectibility.[33] One of the common concerns of those who speak outside of the Roman Catholic tradition regards Catholic understandings of infallibility conceived as a power exercised external to the Church in a separate and absolute way. As we shall see in chapter 7, this was also the concern of many of the minority bishops at Vatican I, who initially opposed the definition on papal infallibility. One of the most important developments in Catholic teaching on infallibility came with Vatican II's explicit acknowledgment that since it is the Church as a whole that is to be preserved in truth, it is to the Church as a whole that the charism of infallibility is given.

---

[32]Mansi 52, 1213D. Gasser seems to view infallibility as a primarily negative assistance of the Holy Spirit. Many of the later manualists concurred in this view. Cf. Hermann Dieckmann, *De ecclesia* (Freiburg: Herder, 1925) 2:36–7; Joseph Salaverri, *Sacrae theologiae summa* (Madrid: BAC, 1952) 1:563. However, Charles Journet would insist on a more positive understanding of divine assistance. Cf. Charles Journet, *L'Église du Verbe Incarné,* 1:433–34. John Boyle sees in Journet the beginning of a trajectory toward a more expansive understanding of divine assistance that has come to its term in the 1990 CDF instruction "The Ecclesial Vocation of the Theologian." Cf. John P. Boyle, *Church Teaching Authority: Historical and Theological Studies* (Notre Dame: Univ. of Notre Dame Press, 1995) 195 n. 26.

[33]Sullivan considers the relationship between indefectibility and infallibility in his *Magisterium,* 4–23.

The holy people of God has a share, too, in the prophetic role of Christ, when it renders him a living witness, especially through a life of faith and charity, and when it offers to God a sacrifice of praise, the tribute of lips that honour his name. *The universal body of the faithful who have received the anointing of the holy one, cannot be mistaken in belief* (*LG* 12, my emphasis).

From the sixteenth to the nineteenth century this infallibility of the whole people of God was often referred to as an infallibility in believing *(in credendo)* in order to distinguish it from the infallibility exercised by the authoritative teaching office of the Church (an infallibility *in docendo*). This distinction is legitimate, but one must be wary of attributing to the former a kind of passivity or docility. Some of the nineteenth-century Latin manuals conceived of the infallibility in believing as nothing more than a passive acceptance and submission to the teaching of the hierarchy. Vatican II avoided this more passive view of the infallibility of the whole people of God. Rather, the infallible belief of the people of God involves a dynamic process by which the whole Church participates in the discovery, penetration, and profession of the gospel of Jesus Christ.

The distinction between the infallibility of the whole people of God and the infallibility of the Church's teaching office is located in part in the different expressions or manifestations of that belief. The infallibility in belief of the whole people of God will have many different concrete objectifications (e.g., narratives, exemplary life witness, pious practices, characteristic actions and gestures, creative expressions in art and literature). The discernment of this belief, given its pluriform character, will always be a very difficult matter. It is the task of the authoritative teaching office of the Church to give these diverse objectifications of infallible believing expression in propositional statements (dogmas). For that reason, while we may rightly speak of infallibility as given to the whole Church, Roman Catholicism recognizes the need for a particular exercise of infallibility in the fulfillment of its teaching office.

Insisting on the need for an infallible teaching office need not denigrate the importance of the infallibility of the whole people of God. The infallibility of the whole people of God is largely descriptive in character. When the whole people of God are united in belief regarding a matter of faith (cf. *LG* 12), their belief cannot lead them from the path to salvation. However, it is difficult to determine when this infallibility is actually operative. As many have pointed out today, the sense of the faithful cannot be determined by merely polling Christians. Such methods do not take into account the differences between baptized believers who actively and prayerfully practice their faith and those who are only nominally identified with the Church. Neither do they acknowledge the way in which the concrete implications of the gospel require time in order to emerge within the consciousness of the Church. For these reasons, it is almost impossible to develop an adequate criteriology that enables us to recognize clearly when the infallibility of the whole people of God is actually operative.

In contrast to the infallibility of the whole people of God, the infallibility of the teaching office of the Church has an explicit criteriological dimension. That is, there must be clear conditions for its exercise, the fulfillment of which are readily recognizable by the faithful.[34] This criteriological function was affirmed in the 1983 Code of Canon Law: "No doctrine is understood to be infallibly defined unless it is clearly established as such" (can. 749.3). Since it is the principal task of the Church's teaching office to preserve the apostolic faith from error, it is necessary that the faithful be able to identify without ambiguity when in fact it is that the Church's teaching office intends to bind itself irrevocably to the revelatory character of a particular teaching.

These two exercises of infallibility should not be opposed to one another, for they exist in a fundamental unity. While the infallibility of the Church's teaching office has a distinct criteriological function, its exercise is grounded in the infallibility of the whole people of God.[35] That is, the infallibility of the Church's teaching office is ordered toward bringing to normative and propositional expression what is infallibly believed by the whole people of God. This relationship is quite different from the common nineteenth-century conception in which the people of God are thought to be infallible in their passive adherence to that which is taught by the magisterium.

---

[34] I will suggest in chapter 6 that the ordinary universal magisterium of bishops represents an important exception.

[35] That the proper movement is from the infallibility of the whole people of God to the infallibility of the pope and college and not in the other direction is confirmed by the rejection of the proposed emendation to the *De ecclesia* text at Vatican II that infallibility in believing has its source in the "active" infallibility of the magisterium. This emendation was rejected as foreign to tradition. *Acta synodalia* III/1, 198–99.

A renewed emphasis on the infallibility of the whole people of God entails a discernible shift (though not an opposition) from *orthodoxy* as a stress on the infallible judgment of propositional claims, to *orthodoxy* in its second meaning as "right worship," and finally, to *orthopraxy* and the infallibility of lived Christian faith.[36] It is this shift that has led many theologians to speak of infallibility more in terms of ongoing fidelity to the gospel and less in terms of the inerrancy of discrete statements. The intention is not to reject an infallibility operative in doctrinal judgment but to recognize that this doctrinal exercise serves the lived Christian witness.

Is there a priority then given to either the infallibility of the teaching office of the Church or the infallibility of the whole people of God? Wolfgang Beinert contends that each can claim a kind of priority, depending on what is being considered.[37] As a norm for preserving the unity of the Christian faith, the conceptual clarity offered in the doctrinal teaching of the magisterium gives to the teaching office a certain priority. By giving this faith conceptual form the ecclesiastical magisterium can provide a function regulatively or criteriologically in a manner not available to the often prethematic, preconceptual faith of believers. Because the faith of believers, precisely as a lived faith, admits of a great diversity of expression, it is not well suited for "norming" the faith. However, because the living faith of the whole people of God is more richly variegated in its concrete realization than any doctrinal expression of it, from the perspective of comprehensiveness the infallibility of the whole people of God possesses a priority. In an ecclesiology of communion these different manifestations of the charism of infallibility will always mutually condition one another.

While affirming the unity of these two manifestations of ecclesial infallibility, we must also acknowledge the possibility of conflict. Church history offers numerous instances of a palpable tension or conflict between the teaching of the ecclesiastical magisterium and

---

[36]Cf. Herbert Vorgrimler, "From *Sensus Fidei* to *Consensus Fidelium,*" in *The Teaching Authority of Believers,* Concilium 180, ed. Johann Baptist Metz and Edward Schillebeeckx (Edinburgh: T. & T. Clark, 1985) 3–11; Stephen Duffy, "Interpretation: Second Vatican Council," in *Papal Infallibility: An Application of Lonergan's Theological Method,* 83.

[37]Wolfgang Beinert, "Bedeutung und Begründung des Glaubensinnes (Sensus fidei) als eines dogmatischen Erkenntniskriteriums," *Catholica* 25 (1971) 271–303.

the belief of the people. Edward Schillebeeckx has remarked on the ecclesiological difficulties that such a situation presents. He warns of the dangers of a too-idyllic conception of the unity between the infallibility of the Church's teaching office and that of the people of God:

> For as a result of it [this idyllic view] any actual conflict between believers and hierarchy, and any conflict between a local church community and the top of the church, is assigned to the order of sinfulness: disobedience on the part of the underlings. The conflict is thought soluble by the hierarchy, which, sometimes to the point of arrogance, appeals to the believers for obedience. . . . In this view, the actual history of conflicts is then seen *a priori* as the fruit of sin, in such a way that any conflict within this logic is resolved in favour of the stronger, i.e. hierarchical, position, and declared by this powerful side to be sin on the part of the grass roots. . . . The "laity," too, sense that there can be conflicts which have nothing to do with sinfulness but derive from differences of insight and assessment of salvation history, for example the pastoral interest of the people and the specific interests of the hierarchical organs.[38]

When one insists, in a naive and simplistic way, that the teaching office and the true sense of the faithful can never differ, the result of any actual conflict is likely to be the magisterium's judgment in its own favor and a dismissal of the sense of the faithful as defective by virtue of sin or as distorted in its presentation (e.g., by the media or public pollsters). A certain tension will always be present within this unity. A healthy acceptance of this tension is only possible from within an ecclesiology of communion in which reciprocity and the give and take of respectful conversation are the norm.

The gospel testimony is clear: the exercise of authority within the Church is not to follow the example of secular models of authority. In particular, the ecclesial exercise of authority depends on the assistance of the Holy Spirit given to the Church. In this chapter I have tried to develop a theology of the assistance of the Holy Spirit that both honors the real cooperation of human processes in the discovery and proclamation of God's word and yet affirms that the Church is truly not left to its own resources but trusts in the assistance of the Holy Spirit to preserve it in truth. Contemporary Catholic theology

---

[38]Edward Schillebeeckx, *Church: The Human Story of God* (New York: Crossroad, 1990) 208.

must work to overcome a monochromatic theology of the assistance of the Holy Spirit that employs an all-or-nothing approach: either the Church infallibly proclaims God's word or it is left utterly to its own devices. The concluding chapters of this volume will consider in more detail this interplay between teaching office and the whole people of God. Chapters 6 and 7 consider the various ways in which the Church's teaching office is exercised, while chapters 8 and 9, in Part 4, develop the role of the *sensus fidelium* in the reception of Church teaching.

For Further Reading

Authority in the Early Church

Congar, Yves. "The Historical Development of Authority in the Church: Points for Christian Reflection." In *Problems of Authority.* Ed. John M. Todd, 119–56. Baltimore: Helicon, 1962.

_____. *Power and Poverty in the Church.* London: Geoffrey Chapman, 1964.

O'Grady, John F. *Disciples and Leaders: The Origins of Christian Ministry in the New Testament.* New York: Paulist, 1991.

The Work of the Spirit in the Church

Congar, Yves. *I Believe in the Holy Spirit.* 3 Vols. New York: Seabury, 1983.

Zizioulas, John D. "The Pneumatological Dimension of the Church." *Communio* 1 (1974) 142–58.

Infallibility

Butler, Christopher B. *The Church and Infallibility.* Rev. ed. London: Sheed & Ward, 1969.

Chirico, Peter. *Infallibility: The Crossroads of Doctrine.* Wilmington: Glazier, 1983.

Journal of Ecumenical Studies 8 (1971) 751–871. Whole issue is dedicated to the question of infallibility.

Kirvan, John J., ed. *The Infallibility Debate.* New York: Paulist, 1971.

Tekippe, Terry J., ed. *Papal Infallibility: An Application of Lonergan's Theological Method.* Washington: Univ. Press of America, 1983.

Ford, John T. "Infallibility: A Review of Recent Studies." *Theological Studies* 40 (1979) 273–305.

——————. "Küng on Infallibility." *Thomist* 35 (1971) 501–12.

Küng, Hans. *Infallible? An Inquiry.* Garden City: Doubleday, 1971.

Lindbeck, George. *Infallibility.* Milwaukee: Marquette Univ. Press, 1972.

Schillebeeckx, Edward. "The Problem of the Infallibility of the Church's Office: A Theological Reflection." In *Truth and Certainty, Concilium* 83. Ed. Edward Schillebeeckx and Bas van Iersel, 77–94. New York: Herder & Herder, 1973.

6

How the Church Teaches: The Ordinary Magisterium

The first chapter of this work treated the historical subject of the Church's teaching ministry, namely the whole Christian community. The second chapter addressed the particular ministry of the college of bishops as the authoritative teachers of that word that is given to the whole Church. Now it may be helpful to say more about this distinction.

The word *magisterium* means literally, the authority of the master or teacher.[1] It has a long and complicated history. In classical Latin the term simply referred to the dignity, authority, or office of the teacher or *magister.* In the usage of the early Church it did not have the specialized meaning it carries today; more often when one wished to refer to the teaching office of the bishops one would use the Greek, *didaskalos,* or the Latin, *praedicatio ecclesiae.* When the term *magisterium* was used it often referred to an authority pertaining not only to teaching but to many other forms of pastoral ministry. This usage gradually narrowed so that by the late Middle Ages "magisterium" primarily referred to the office and authority of teachers, both bishops and scholars. Then in the nineteenth-century "magisterium" as a

---

[1] The classic essays on this topic are both by Yves Congar, "A Semantic History of the Term 'Magisterium'" and "A Brief History of the Forms of the Magisterium and Its Relations with Scholars," in *The Magisterium and Morality,* Readings in Moral Theology No. 3, ed. Charles E. Curran and Richard A. McCormick (New York: Paulist, 1982) 297–313 and 314–31.

term began to be employed in reference to the officeholders themselves (namely, the bishops and pope). This more narrow usage is the
most common one today.

Even though the college of bishops has become the primary referent of the term "magisterium," this should not blind us to other legitimate conceptions of teaching authority. Since God's word is given to
the whole Christian community, the whole Christian community is
responsible for giving witness to that word.[2] The authority that every
believer possesses to pass on the faith follows from the Christian conviction that through baptism every believer is given a sense or instinct
of the faith *(sensus fidei)*. In this sense, every baptized believer participates in the magisterium, or teaching authority of the Church. As
Bishop Christopher Butler has observed: "[E]veryone in the Church
who has reached maturity has, at some time or another, to play the
role of the teacher, the *magister,* the *ecclesia docens.*"[3]

Vatican II's Decree on the Pastoral Office of Bishops in the Church,
Christus Dominus, says that the goal of catechetical ministry is to
make Christian faith "become living, conscious and active" (*CD* 14)
in the hearts and minds of believers. This catechetical ministry is the
responsibility of every Christian by virtue of baptism.[4] Some of the
baptized will fulfill this responsibility in a formal way as catechists,
pastoral ministers, and preachers, but for most the role of teacher will
be less formal. For example, when we pause to reflect on how, concretely, our Christian faith is passed on within the Christian community, we must acknowledge the central role of the family. Vatican II
affirms this in its retrieval of the ancient notion of the family as a "domestic church": "[The Christian family] is, as it were, the domestic
church in which the parents must be for their children, by word and
by example, the first preachers of the faith; encouraging each in her
or his vocation and paying special attention to a sacred vocation" (*LG*
11). An important feature of this passage is its emphasis on the evan-
gelical aspect of the family as Church, noting that the parents are the
first to proclaim the gospel to their children.

---

[2]Ladislas Örsy, *The Church Learning and Teaching* (Wilmington:
Glazier, 1987) 65.

[3]Christopher Butler, "Authority and the Christian Conscience," in *The
Magisterium and Morality,* 182.

[4]See also *Sharing the Light of Faith: National Catechetical Directory for
Catholics of the United States* (Washington: USCC, 1979) no. 32, 204.

Beyond the authority to teach that pertains to the baptized, we can also speak of the authority of theologians. They too are teachers of the faith. Avery Dulles once proposed that in our tradition one could find evidence of two magisteria, one for theologians and the other for the hierarchy.[5] The teaching responsibilities of bishops and theologians are obviously distinct, and their authority derives from different sources (one from ordination and the other from scholarly competence), but theologians too possess a proper magisterium, or authority to teach. That having been said, in practice this broader usage is likely to blur the distinctive teaching roles of theologians and the college of bishops. Therefore, I will continue to use the term "magisterium" in its more contemporary and restricted sense to refer to the teaching authority of the college of bishops. We should not forget, however, that the bishops are not the sole possessors of an authority to teach. Theologians and all believers share a responsibility to teach the faith. In an ecclesiology of communion these different teaching ministries and the kinds of ecclesial authority associated with them will not be placed in competition but will be seen as each in their proper fashion contributing to the living tradition of the Church. If this book focuses on the doctrinal teaching ministry of the college of bishops, it does so with the recognition that to the extent that these other authorities are not honored, the unique teaching authority of the college of bishops will likewise suffer.

Even when the focus of attention is limited to the teaching authority of the college of bishops, this authority cannot be understood univocally. Over almost two thousand years, the Roman Catholic tradition has come to differentiate many ways in which this authority may be exercised. Some of the differences have to do with personal style, while other distinctions are more formal in character. The careful distinctions that have developed regarding the various exercises of ecclesial authority can appear rather technical to the nonspecialist, and indeed, some of them have probably become superfluous. But the more central distinctions, properly understood, serve the purpose of

---

[5]Avery Dulles, "The Two Magisteria: An Interim Reflection," *CTSA Proceedings* 35 (1980) 155–69. This was an attempt to retrieve St. Thomas's distinction between the *magisterium cathedrae pastoralis* and the *magisterium cathedrae magistralis*. Cf. IV *Sent.* D. 19, q. 2, a. 2, qᵃ 2 ad 4 and *Quodlibet* III, 9 *ad* 3. Dulles has since distanced himself from this proposal. Cf. Avery Dulles, "Criteria of Catholic Theology," *Communio* 22 (Summer 1995) 303–15.

balancing the authoritative proclamation of the gospel by the bishops with the honest admission that this exercise of authority has real limits or boundaries. These distinctions can only be defended to the extent that they are not merely formal but actually arise from our understanding of the nature of the Church's teaching office. Consequently, I will devote the rest of this chapter and all of the next to a consideration of several distinct modalities of the bishops' doctrinal teaching authority.

The Ecclesiastical Magisterium

It has become common for theologians to differentiate between an *extraordinary* and an *ordinary* magisterium. Briefly, the exercise of the *extraordinary* magisterium involves a solemn and infallible act of defining a matter of faith on the part of either the whole college of bishops, usually in ecumenical council, or the pope as head of that college when he teaches *ex cathedra,* that is, from the chair of St. Peter. Since the exercise of the extraordinary magisterium involves a number of special questions, I will defer discussion of it to chapter 7. The *ordinary* magisterium designates all other exercises of the bishops' teaching authority.[6] It too can be divided into two categories (see

[6]The terminology employed here is by no means universally accepted among theologians. Indeed, contemporary discussions of issues related to the magisterium have been hampered considerably by a lack of terminological consistency. On the meaning of the terms "ordinary" and "extraordinary" as applied to the ecclesiastical magisterium, I am essentially following Yves Congar and Francis Sullivan, both of whom appear to identify the exercise of the extraordinary magisterium with solemn judgments of pope and council. Cf. Yves Congar, *The Meaning of Tradition* (New York: Hawthorn, 1964) 65; Francis A. Sullivan, *Magisterium: Teaching Authority in the Catholic Church* (New York: Paulist, 1983) 120–21. John Boyle has challenged this restriction of the extraordinary magisterium to solemn definitions. Boyle contends that *all* conciliar teaching is the fruit of an extraordinary exercise of teaching authority even if this teaching does not take the form of a solemn judgment. Cf. John P. Boyle, *Church Teaching Authority: Historical and Theological Studies* (Notre Dame: Univ. of Notre Dame Press, 1995) 189–90 n. 30. It seems to me that in terms of ecclesiology, Boyle's identification of the extraordinary magisterium with all conciliar teaching puts the focus on the ecumenical council itself as a distinct ecclesiastical event. However, I believe that ecumenical councils are better understood as concentrated, visible expressions of both that conciliarity that belongs to the Church itself and that collegiality

fig. 2): that ordinary teaching of bishops which does not explicitly engage the whole college (the ordinary *nonuniversal* magisterium) and that which does (ordinary *universal* magisterium). [7] This chapter will consider these two broad categories of the ordinary magisterium.

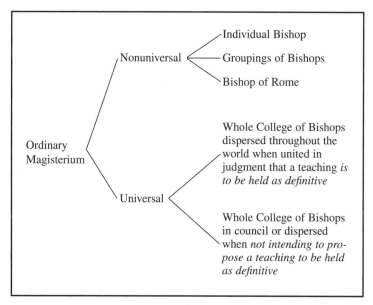

Figure 2

that belongs to the college of bishops, whether in council or dispersed throughout the world. The distinguishing factor between the extraordinary and ordinary magisteria is not a particular ecclesiastical event but whether the bishops are exercising the *suprema potestas* given to them in solemnly defining the teaching of the Church.

[7] The term "ordinary magisterium" first appeared in an ecclesiastical document in Pius IX's 1863 papal brief, *Tuas libenter,* in which it referred to the infallible exercise of the college of bishops when dispersed throughout the world. At Vatican I, the word "universal" was added to the term "ordinary magisterium" in order to more accurately designate this infallible exercise of the college of bishops. In common usage today, the ordinary magisterium (as distinguished from the ordinary and universal magisterium) now refers to that teaching of the bishops that is proposed authoritatively but that does not exclude the possibility of error.

The Ordinary (Nonuniversal) Magisterium

The many exercises of the ordinary nonuniversal magisterium, those that do not involve the teaching of the whole college, can be further divided into three categories: (1) the teaching of individual bishops, (2) the teaching of groups of bishops, and (3) the teaching of the bishop of Rome. I will consider each in turn.

Ordinary Teaching of Individual Bishops

The Second Vatican Council considered the pastoral teaching office of the bishop in several texts.[8] *Lumen gentium* states of this teaching office:

> Among the principal tasks of bishops the preaching of the gospel is pre-eminent. For the bishops are the heralds of the faith who bring new disciples to Christ. They are the authentic teachers, that is, teachers endowed with the authority of Christ, who preach to the people entrusted to them the faith to be believed and put into practice; they illustrate this faith in the light of the holy Spirit, drawing out of the treasury of revelation things new and old, they make it bear fruit and they vigilantly ward off errors that are threatening their flock (*LG* 25).

In The Decree on the Pastoral Office of Bishops, *Christus Dominus*, the council notes, "[I]n discharging their obligation to teach, they [the bishops] should proclaim to humanity the gospel of Christ. This stands out among the most important duties of bishops" (*CD* 12). These passages reflect Vatican II's consistent focus on the bishop's pastoral obligations to his flock. He is first a pastor and only secondarily an administrator or bureaucrat. This teaching ministry can be comprehended under several distinct but closely related aspects.

The primary aspect of the bishop's teaching ministry is *kerygmatic/catechetical*. Episcopal teaching is oriented toward the proclamation of God's saving word. As an authoritative witness to the faith, the bishop is the chief evangelist and chief catechist in the local Church. He must oversee the preaching and catechetical ministry of the Church and insure that through that ministry all within the local Church hear of God's saving offer. The bishop himself will perform this *kerygmatic/catechetical* ministry in his own preaching and catechesis and in the publication of pastoral letters and other ecclesiastical directives. Beyond his direct ministry of preaching and teaching,

[8]See *Christus Dominus,* 11–14 and *Lumen gentium,* ch. 3.

the bishop is further charged with safeguarding the authentic exposition of Church teaching as that ministry is carried out by others within the local Church. The bishop's ministry therefore, is truly episcopal, a word derived from the Greek word *episkope,* meaning "oversight"; the bishop is responsible for pastoral oversight of the local Church.[9]

For the most part, the success of the bishop's *kerygmatic/catechetical* ministry will depend not so much on his formal authority as a bishop of the Church but on his moral authority as one who has truly internalized Church teaching, made it his own, and therefore teaches it with personal conviction. This aspect of episcopal teaching is often overlooked. That bishop who is truly an effective teacher will always do more than reiterate "official Church teaching." As Vatican II taught, the bishop is more than a spokesperson for the pope. The goal of his teaching is to bring to light the profundity of the Catholic tradition both in his ministry within the local Church and in his conveying the faith of his Church to the Church universal through his participation in the college of bishops. The bishop must aspire to advance the cause of the faith through a prayerful and informed articulation of the Catholic tradition that does not simply repeat past formulations but seeks to bring new insight to Church teaching. This means that while the bishop need not be a professional theologian, theological competency will be important to the effective fulfillment of his teaching ministry. It also means that the bishop must be attuned to the particularity of his community's own testimony to the gospel of Jesus Christ. For each local Church, living the gospel in a particular cultural setting, has the potential of offering to the Church universal its own incarnation of the one gospel. When the bishop heeds this testimony and gives voice to it in his own teaching, the unique testimony of the local Church can potentially enrich the faith consciousness of the whole Church.

This *kerygmatic/catechetical* aspect of his teaching is, of course, part of the fulfillment of his apostolic office and the content of that teaching is therefore authoritative, but it generally will not involve any formal judgment on disputes related to matters of doctrine. Consequently, while the substance of the Christian faith that the bishop proclaims is normative for the believer, the bishop may employ

[9]Cf. Raymond E. Brown, *Priest and Bishop* (New York: Paulist, 1970) 34ff.

anecdotes, images, theological approaches, personal reflections, and the like, which he would not wish to make binding on those who would echo the faith of the Church.

A second aspect of the bishop's teaching office is *pastoral,* in the more narrow sense of the term. This pastoral dimension is directly concerned with the reflective application of Church doctrine to the changing conditions and circumstances in the lives of believers. It is precisely in the fulfillment of this aspect of episcopal teaching that the role of the bishop as *local* pastor becomes most prominent. Frequently bishops will feel compelled to address not so much a disputed doctrinal matter as a question of how an accepted teaching of the Church applies in a particular pastoral situation. This is particularly true with respect to the Church's moral teaching, where the broad contours of Christian morality will require concrete moral judgments with respect to particular questions and issues arising within a local Church. One can easily imagine an individual bishop addressing a wide range of issues concerning immigration or welfare policy, the distribution of contraceptive devices in public schools, and so on.

Finally, along with the kerygmatic/catechetical, and pastoral aspects of the bishop's teaching ministry, we must acknowledge a third aspect, namely that of *doctrinal judgment.* This dimension of a bishop's teaching ministry involves a formal judgment (not to be confused with a solemn judgment, which belongs to the extraordinary magisterium) that a particular theological position does or does not accord with the Catholic doctrinal tradition. Regarding this third component of episcopal teaching, Edmund Hill writes: "Formal judgment, . . . *iudicium,* is by its nature something much more occasional. It is a precise act of a distinct personage, delivered only after hearing argument and discussion and evidence by several other personages."[10] These formal judgments themselves possess varying degrees of authority. However, when a bishop makes a formal doctrinal judgment, he does so specifically with the intent of proclaiming Church doctrine in an authoritative and normative manner. This may be exercised by an individual bishop, a group of bishops, or even the whole college of bishops. These pronouncements are intended to articulate and/or clarify the official teaching of the Catholic Church on a disputed matter. This is true even though these judgments are not

[10]Edmund Hill, "Who Does the Teaching in the Church?" *New Blackfriars* 70 (February 1989) 72–73.

proposed infallibly. For example, when an individual bishop publicly denounces a local theologian's position on abortion, though he does not teach with the charism of infallibility, he does offer a formal doctrinal judgment regarding the teaching of the Catholic Church, and this judgment must be seen as normative in a more directly binding manner than in the exercise of either the kerygmatic/catechetical or the pastoral dimensions of his teaching ministry.

These three aspects of ordinary episcopal teaching overlap considerably, yet it is fair to say that most teaching of the individual bishops would involve the first two components much more than the third. As dimensions of episcopal ministry they apply not only to the teaching ministry of the individual bishop but also to the teaching of groups of bishops and the teaching of the bishop of Rome.

The Ordinary Teaching of Groups of Bishops

Chapter 3 of *Lumen gentium* attended to the teaching authority of bishops, considered both individually and as a whole college. Not resolved, however, was the authoritative status of the teaching of various groupings of bishops that represented something less than the whole college. The two principal instances of this would be the teaching of episcopal conferences and the teaching of the world synod of bishops.[11]

Episcopal Conferences

The last thirty years have seen a greatly expanded teaching role for episcopal conferences. With that expanded role have come numerous questions regarding the authority of conferences when they teach. Episcopal conferences as we know them today first emerged in the early nineteenth century, though one can find similar episcopal structures dating back to the particular synods of the early Church.[12] These structures have long been accepted in the Church for their practical pastoral value. It is only in the past two decades, however, that the ecclesiological significance of these conferences has become a serious theological question. This issue was raised, at least indirectly, at the

[11]The following material is drawn substantially from an essay of mine, "An Ecclesiology of Communion and Ecclesiastical Structures: Towards a Renewed Ministry of the Bishop," *Église et Théologie* 24 (1993) 194–99.

[12]For a history of episcopal conferences see Giorgio Feliciani, *Le conferenze episcopali* (Bologna: Il Mulino, 1974).

Second Vatican Council when in The Constitution on the Sacred Liturgy, *Sacrosanctum concilium,* the council members granted to episcopal conferences significant authority over a variety of liturgical matters (*SC* 22.2). This new development was coupled with the recommendation in *Christus Dominus* 36–38 for the further development of episcopal conferences and the broad ecclesiological trend to reaffirm the principles of collegiality and subsidiarity. Together these new developments greatly enhanced the status of episcopal conferences in the eyes of many.[13] However, since the council the differing responses of several episcopal conferences to *Humanae vitae* and the increased teaching role of conferences like that of the American bishops have revived questions about the authority of these conferences.

At the 1985 Extraordinary Synod the bishops requested a study of the status and authority of episcopal conferences. The result was a working paper introduced in 1988 by the Congregation of Bishops on the juridical and theological status of episcopal conferences. This draft document was criticized by many theologians as fundamentally flawed in its historical and theological argumentation.[14] The draft was withdrawn, and as of early 1996 Rome has yet to produce an official document on the matter. Since the debate regarding the authority of episcopal conferences brings to the surface some fundamental ecclesiological issues, it will be useful to briefly rehearse the central questions being raised.

At Vatican II, then theologian Joseph Ratzinger gave a very important lecture on episcopal collegiality and used the theological sta-

[13]See Remigiusz Sobanski, "The Theology and Juridic Status of Episcopal Conferences at the Second Vatican Council," in *The Nature and Future of Episcopal Conferences,* ed. Hervé Legrand, Julio Manzanares, and Antonio García y García (Washington: The Catholic Univ. of America Press, 1988) 68–106; R. Kutner, *The Development, Structure, and Competence of the Episcopal Conference* (Washington: Catholic Univ. of America Press, 1972).

[14]"Draft Statement on Episcopal Conferences," *Origins* 17 (1987–88) 731–37. A good overview of the debate concerning the ecclesiological status of episcopal conferences is provided by Joseph Komonchak in his introduction to *Episcopal Conferences: Historical, Canonical, and Theological Studies,* ed. Thomas Reese (Washington: Georgetown Univ. Press, 1989) 1–22. This collection contains several other important essays on the topic. See also Hervé-M. Legrand, Julio Manzanares, and Antonio García y García, eds., *The Nature and Future of Episcopal Conferences,* and Hubert Müller and Hermann J. Pottmeyer, eds., *Die Bischofskonferenz: theologischer und juridischer Status,* (Düsseldorf: Patmos, 1989).

tus of episcopal conferences as a test case.[15] The debates on chapter 3 of the Dogmatic Constitution on the Church were going on, and he was committed to a retrieval of the patristic ecclesiology of communion. Ratzinger criticized a narrow and primarily juridical view of collegiality that saw its sole expression limited to the formal acts of the whole college of bishops in communion with its head, the bishop of Rome. Instead, he hearkened back to the more fluid notion of collegiality manifested in the regional synods of the early Church. This view called for a more elastic understanding of collegiality correlated to the ecclesiological principle of communion. Every relationship between one bishop and another was considered an expression of the *communio ecclesiarum*, the spiritual communion among the Churches. This is why the participation of three bishops was deemed sufficient at episcopal consecration. To those who contended that collegiality could be applied only to the entire episcopate, Ratzinger, echoing the views of another theologian, Dominican Jerôme Hamer,[16] responded that every exercise of collegiality need not be an exercise of the *suprema potestas,* the supreme power and authority properly attributed only to the whole episcopate. On this point Ratzinger writes:

> We should rather say that the concept of collegiality, besides the office of unity which pertains to the pope, signifies an element of variety and adaptability that basically belongs to the structure of the Church, but may be actuated in many ways. The collegiality of bishops signifies that there should be in the Church (under and in the unity guaranteed by the primacy) an ordered plurality. The bishops' conferences are, then, one of the possible forms of collegiality that is here partially realized but with a view to the totality.[17]

If Ratzinger and Hamer were two proponents of the collegiality of episcopal conferences in the 1960s, by the mid-1970s their views had changed. After having become prefects for the Congregation for the

[15]The substance of Ratzinger's view at that time may be found in two essays, "Konkrete Formen bischöfliche Kollegialität," in *Ende der Gegenreformation?* ed. Johann Christophe Hampe (Stuttgart: Kreuz-Verlag, 1964) 155–63, and "The Pastoral Implications of Episcopal Collegiality," in *The Church and Mankind,* Concilium 1 (Glen Rock: Paulist, 1964) 39–67.

[16]Cf. Jerôme Hamer, "Les conférences épiscopales exercice de la collégialité," *Nouvelle revue théologique* 85 (1963) 966–69.

[17]Ratzinger, "Pastoral Implications," 64.

Doctrine of the Faith and the Congregation for Religious respectively, they revised their positions. This rethinking was instigated by a number of new considerations, not the least of which was the postconciliar writing of Henri de Lubac.[18]

De Lubac considered the theological status of episcopal conferences from the perspective of a Eucharistic ecclesiology. In every celebration of the Eucharist two ecclesial modalities can be identified: first, there is the communion of all believers gathered at the local celebration of the Eucharist, and second, there is the communion that exists among all local Eucharistic communities. This communion of Eucharistic communities is none other than the universal Church of Christ. The Church is at the same time one and many, universal and local, but it is never something in between, at least not in the theological sense. Since episcopal collegiality flows out of the more fundamental principle of ecclesial communion, what holds for the communion of Churches holds for the college of bishops. The individual bishop expresses collegiality precisely as bishop of a local Church, and the whole episcopate expresses collegiality as a college. De Lubac concluded that a bishop can realize the collegial character of his ministry in only two ways: through the exercise of his ministry within the local Church and through his participation in the activity of the whole college. He admitted that episcopal conferences and world synods were collective acts of bishops that might be useful, but he resisted attributing to them a properly theological significance, since they were not manifestations of the whole college.[19] Furthermore, de Lubac noted that episcopal conferences, as ecclesial structures, did not belong to divine law but rather were the product of ecclesiastical law.

While following de Lubac's line of argument, in their more recent writings Ratzinger and Hamer have also complained that the enhanced role of episcopal conferences may bring about a return to the kind of Church nationalism that appeared in times past under the

[18]See Henri de Lubac, *The Motherhood of the Church Followed by Particular Churches in the Universal Church* (San Francisco: Ignatius, 1982, originally published in French, 1971). For a recent reformulation of de Lubac's perspective as it applies to the status of episcopal conferences see Susan Wood, "The Theological Foundations of Episcopal Conferences and Collegiality," *Studia Canonica* 22 (1988) 327–38.

[19]One should note, of course, that most if not all ecumenical councils would have failed a strict criterion of universality.

guise of Gallicanism and Febronianism.[20] They further noted the real danger of the bureaucratization of the ministry of the bishop in which individual bishops can become little more than functionaries who hide behind episcopal committees and vague declarations that inevitably lose their prophetic bite in the process of achieving episcopal consensus.[21] Hans Urs von Balthasar gives voice to precisely this concern:

> Let us read the Gospel again: Jesus always designated persons for service, not institutions. The persons of bishops belong to the fundamental structure of the church, not bureaucratic offices. There's nothing more grotesque than to think of a Christ who would want to establish committees! We have to rediscover a Catholic truth: in the church everything is personal, nothing should be anonymous. Instead, today so many bishops are hiding behind anonymous structures.[22]

The fundamental issue has revolved around the ecclesial significance of gatherings of individual bishops that fall short of a full convocation of the college of bishops. With regard to the magisterium, the question is, do these episcopal conferences, partial realizations of the college of bishops, have a *mandatum docendi* (a mandate to teach)? Do they have authority to teach Christian doctrine that would be binding for the faithful or do they merely serve the practical order?

Unfortunately, the Second Vatican Council was not particularly helpful on this question. A review of the council *Acta* regarding the debates on the ministry of bishops suggests that many council members desired a more specific reference to the teaching authority of episcopal conferences. However, additional material that would have offered helpful clarification on this topic did not survive the final draft of the Decree on the Pastoral Office of Bishops in the Church. The official explanation given for its exclusion mentioned only considerations regarding the length of the text.[23] In the final version *Christus*

---

[20]Joseph Ratzinger with Vittorio Messori, *The Ratzinger Report,* 58–61; Jerôme Hamer, "La responsabilité collégiale de chaque évêque," *Nouvelle revue théologique* 105 (1983) 641–54.

[21]Ratzinger, *The Ratzinger Report,* 67.

[22]Hans Urs von Balthasar with Vittorio Messori, *Un Papa nutrito di preghiera per questa Chiesa offesa e ferita* (Milano: Avenire, 1985) 11, as quoted in Komonchak, "Introduction," *Episcopal Conferences,* 9.

[23]*Acta synodalia* III/6, 204. See Julio Manzanares in *The Nature and Future of Episcopal Conferences* for a more detailed treatment of these debates.

Dominus 38.1 simply defined episcopal conferences as assemblies of bishops of a given nation or territory that collaboratively exercise their "pastoral office" *(munus pastorale)*. It goes on to note that certain "decisions" *(decisiones)* of these conferences may have binding force of law. This is the closest the council came to addressing the specific teaching role of these conferences. Unfortunately, as Avery Dulles has pointed out, the meaning of the two key terms here, "pastoral office" and "decisions," is notoriously ambiguous. It is difficult to know whether they were intended to include doctrinal teaching or concerned only Church legislation.[24] Because of this ambiguity, much attention has been given to the 1983 Code of Canon Law's treatment of the subject. Of particular importance is canon 753:

> Although they do not enjoy infallible teaching authority, the bishops in communion with the head and members of the college, whether as individuals or gathered in conferences of bishops or in particular councils, are authentic teachers and instructors of the faith for the faithful entrusted to their care; the faithful must adhere to the authentic teaching of their own bishops with a sense of religious respect *(religioso animi obsequio)*.[25]

For many scholars this canon clearly grants a doctrinal teaching authority to episcopal conferences.[26] Others say that it only affirms two different modes by which an individual bishop may teach: on his own or in conjunction with other bishops.[27] In either case the authority can be only that of the individual bishop.

[24] Avery Dulles, "Doctrinal Authority of Episcopal Conferences," in *Episcopal Conferences: Historical, Canonical, and Theological Studies*, 207–13.

[25] The English translation is taken from the *Code of Canon Law: Latin-English Edition* (Washington: CLSA, 1983).

[26] For scholars favoring this view see Manzanares, "The Teaching Authority of Episcopal Conferences," in *The Nature and Future of Episcopal Conferences*, 234–63; Francisco J. Urrutia, "De exercitio muneris docendi a Conferentiis Episcoporum," *Periodica* 87 (1987) 605–36. The Urrutia essay is part of a debate over a position taken against the doctrinal teaching authority of episcopal conferences offered by James P. Green, "Conferences of Bishops and the Exercise of the "munus docendi" of the Church" (J.C.D. diss., Gregorian University, 1987). Green was largely following a similar position taken by his dissertation director, Gianfranco Ghirlanda, whose views on the subject may be found in "De Episcoporum Conferentia deque exercitio potestatis magisterii," *Periodica* 87 (1987) 573–604.

[27] See Ghirlanda, "De Episcoporum."

So what is the state of the question? The arguments against granting a doctrinal teaching authority to episcopal conferences might be summarized as follows. First, episcopal conferences, which are almost always created along national lines, can encourage a kind of nationalism that can undermine the universality of the Church. Second, episcopal conferences have become dominated by bureaucracies that can eclipse the proper pastoral teaching office of the individual diocesan bishop. Third, the institution of episcopal conferences, unlike that of the college of bishops, does not belong to divine law but rather is a product of ecclesiastical law. And fourth, episcopal conferences, since they fall short of a full realization of the episcopal college, can lay no claim to the supreme teaching authority promised the college of bishops as a college.[28]

These concerns must not be easily dismissed, but important arguments have been marshaled against this position and in favor of granting a true doctrinal teaching authority to episcopal conferences. Aside from the most obvious argument that the new Code of Canon Law appears to grant such an authority, the most important argument in favor of granting a doctrinal teaching authority looks to the parallel situation of particular synods or councils in the early Church. These regional gatherings of bishops, while clearly not representing the whole college, were considered authoritative and often addressed properly doctrinal concerns.[29] Those who support this view follow the position taken by the early Ratzinger and Hamer in arguing for a more fluid understanding of collegiality, one grounded in the principle of ecclesial communion. This approach would recognize a gradation in the various exercises of collegiality, some of which may fall short of a full and formal collegiality (that possessed by the whole college) but which nevertheless possess a true theological character.[30]

---

[28]This last argument seems to rely on the *nota explicativa praevia* attached to *Lumen gentium* that refers to a "strict collegial act" engaged by the whole college in communion with the pope.

[29]Hermann J. Sieben, "Episcopal Conferences in Light of Particular Councils During the First Millennium," and Antonio García y García, "Episcopal Conferences in Light of Particular Councils During the Second Millennium," in *The Nature and Future of Episcopal Conferences,* 30–67.

[30]It must be admitted, however, that there are important differences between episcopal conferences as they are presently constructed and the particular synods of the early Church. While those particular synods met only occasionally to address common pastoral/doctrinal concerns, the modern

Since the Vatican has yet to follow up on the 1988 working paper, the matter must still be viewed as an open theological question. I would propose the following points as the starting point for a possible consensus position:

(1) There is no question but that the full exercise of the supreme teaching authority given to the college of bishops requires the participation of the whole college and therefore is not applicable to episcopal conferences. The teaching of episcopal conferences does not have recourse, then, to the charism of infallibility. (2) One must distinguish between the collegial activity of the whole college and other expressions of collegiality, whether by referring to one as "direct and formal" and the other as "indirect," as Willy Onclin does,[31] or by distinguishing between "effective" and "affective" collegiality, as a number of other theologians have done.[32] Nevertheless, a study of early Church practice would seem to justify a properly theological and dynamic understanding of collegiality that falls short of the exercise of the whole college. (3) Because groupings of bishops are truly if not formally collegial in character, we can acknowledge that in certain instances episcopal conferences do have a *mandatum docendi* and their teaching must be seen as an exercise of the ordinary magisterium. (4) Because of the proliferation of documents issued by episcopal conferences, it is particularly important that the bishops clearly specify when they are articulating doctrinal principles in conference documents. It might also be helpful to articulate certain safeguards that would limit the possibility of divergence from the teaching of the universal Church.[33]

---

episcopal conference has become a huge bureaucracy. The relatively short meetings of the bishops' conferences make extended deliberation over important issues difficult. Cf. James H. Provost, "Episcopal Conferences as an Expression of the Communion of Churches," in *Episcopal Conferences: Historical, Canonical, and Theological Studies*, 282f.; Hervé Legrand, "Synodes et conseils de l'après-concile," *Nouvelle revue théologique* 98 (1976) 193–216.

[31]Willy Onclin, "Collegiality and the Individual Bishop," in *Pastoral Reform in the Church,* Concilium 8 (New York: Paulist, 1965) 81–91.

[32]Walter Kasper, "Der theologische Status der Bischofskonferenzen," *Theologische Quartalschrift* 167 (1987) 3; Angel Antón, "The Theological Status of Episcopal Conferences," in *The Nature and Future of Episcopal Conferences,* 205.

[33]For example, regarding the issuance of general decrees, canon 455 requires a two-thirds majority vote and approval by the Holy See. Dulles argues

The World Synod of Bishops

The world synod of bishops is the fruit of the positive experience many bishops had of finding a forum at Vatican II in which it was possible to freely and openly consider issues of considerable import for the life of the Church.[34] Immediately preceding the council, Cardinal Bernard Alfrink of Utrecht had already called for a permanent body of bishops to assist in the government of the universal Church loosely based on the model of the permanent synods of the Eastern Churches. Various versions of this idea were proposed during council debates, and many bishops considered a formal request for the creation of a permanent body of bishops to participate with the pope in his pastoral ministry over the whole Church. This would constitute a concrete institutional structure reflecting the important ecclesiological conviction voiced at the council that the college of bishops, under the headship of the bishop of Rome, possessed supreme authority over the whole Church. This proposal found an advocate in Patriarch Maximos IV, Melkite patriarch of Antioch. What is of particular interest is the patriarch's contention that it would be only proper that the Roman congregations be subordinate to such a body.[35] However, before this controversial proposal could be considered, Pope Paul VI himself established the world synod of bishops in the *motu proprio, Apostolica solicitudo* (September 15, 1965).[36]

The nature of this synod differs from an episcopal conference or a particular council inasmuch as it is explicitly concerned with the universal Church. Furthermore, according to Paul VI's *motu proprio,* the synod was not to be a decision-making body but a consultative body, though the possibility that the Holy See might confer upon it a deliberative power was left open.

---

that in the case of doctrinal teaching the approval of the Holy See would be particularly important, while Hermann Pottmeyer views such approval as unnecessary. See Dulles, "Doctrinal Authority," 220; Hermann Pottmeyer, "Das Lehramt der Bischofskonferenz," in *Die Bischofskonferenz,* 132.

[34]Peter Hebblethwaite, "The Synod of Bishops," in *Modern Catholicism: Vatican II and After,* ed. Adrian Hastings (New York: Oxford Univ. Press, 1991) 200–209. For a comprehensive study see D. Foley, *The Synod of Bishops: Its Canonical Structure and Procedures* (Washington: Catholic Univ. of America Press, 1973).

[35]René Laurentin, *Bilan de la deuxième session* (Paris: Seuil, 1964) 118.

[36]*AAS* 57 (1965) 775–80.

The debate over the theological status and authority of the synod of bishops involves issues similar to the debate regarding the authority of episcopal conferences. Those who would grant collegiality only to an exercise of the whole college generally would not attribute collegial authority to the world synod.[37] Some have emphasized the synod's strictly consultative capacity and the prominence of the Holy See in determining the timing of the synod's convocation, its agenda, and the confirmation of its membership as indications that it should more appropriately be considered as a participation in papal primacy.[38] Other theologians have offered a more positive assessment, emphasizing the passage in Paul VI's *motu proprio* in which the synod is said to function as "representative of the entire Catholic episcopacy." These theologians suggest that the acts of an episcopal synod may be considered truly collegial as long as the pope accepts the counsel of the synod.[39]

Too often, however, arguments on both sides suffer from the problem addressed above regarding episcopal conferences, namely, the evaluation of collegiality strictly in terms of the juridical criteria for an exercise of the college's *suprema potestas*. When collegiality is evaluated in relationship to the communion of Churches, it becomes possible to more accurately assess collegial acts in terms of their service to the *communio ecclesiarum* and to admit degrees of collegial exercise. From this perspective it is difficult to refute the collegial character of the world synod of bishops and difficult to challenge the authoritative status of its documents.[40]

[37] Joseph Ratzinger, "The Structure and Task of the Synod of Bishops," in *Church, Ecumenism, and Politics: New Essays in Ecclesiology*, (New York: Crossroad, 1988) 46–62.

[38] Cf. V. Ferrara, "Il Sinodo dei Vescovi tra ipotesi e realtà: Natura teologico-giuridico del Sinodo," *Apollinaris* 42 (1969) 491–556; W. Bertrams, "De synodi episcoporum potestate cooperandi in exercitio potestatis primatialis," *Periodica de re morali, canonica, liturgica* 57 (1968) 528–49.

[39] Edward Schillebeeckx, "The Synod of Bishops: One Form of Strict but Non-Conciliar Collegiality," *IDO-C Dossier* nos. 7–9 (March 12, 1967); Angel Antón, "Episcoporum synodus: 'Partes agens totius catholici episcopatus,'" *Periodica de re morali, canonica, liturgica* 57 (1968) 495–527.

[40] In my conclusion to this volume I will consider some of the practical shortcomings of the current structure and conduct of these synodal gatherings, not the least of which is the practice of synods deferring to the pope in the composition of postsynodal documents.

Ordinary Teaching of the Bishop of Rome

Up to this point I have not differentiated between the ordinary teaching of the bishops and ordinary papal teaching.[41] However, *Lumen gentium* makes it clear that ordinary papal teaching does have a special status:

> The religious assent of will and intellect *(Hoc vero religiosum voluntatis et intellectus obsequium)* is to be given *in a special way* to the authentic teaching authority of the Roman pontiff even when he is not speaking *ex cathedra;* in such a way, that is, that his supreme teaching authority is respectfully acknowledged, and sincere adherence given to decisions he has delivered, in accordance with his manifest mind and will which is communicated chiefly by the nature of the documents, by the frequent repetition of the same doctrine or by the style of verbal expression *(LG* 25, emphasis mine).

The constitution states clearly that the response the faithful must give to ordinary episcopal teaching is owed, "in a special way," to the ordinary exercise of the "supreme teaching authority" of the pope, that is, to the supreme teaching authority exercised apart from a solemn *(ex cathedra)* judgment. This ordinary exercise of the pope's supreme teaching authority does not involve the charism of infallibility; the remote possibility of error is not excluded in these instances. But what distinguishes ordinary papal teaching from the ordinary teaching of other bishops? In other words, what justifies the "special" response owed to noninfallible *papal* teaching?

To begin with, *Lumen gentium* is referring to properly papal teaching, that is, teaching of the pope when he acts as universal pastor of the Church. The pope actually wears many ecclesiastical hats. Vatican I specified as a condition for the exercise of a papal infallibility that the pope teach "as pastor and teacher of all Christians" (DS 3074). This presumes that there might be instances in which he would not teach in this capacity. While nowhere is this explicitly developed in Church documents, one can imagine several instances in which the teaching of the pope might not be teaching offered in his capacity as universal pastor.

---

[41]John Boyle contends that the explicit mention of an ordinary papal magisterium appears for the first time in a papal document in Pius XII's 1950 encyclical *Humani generis.* Cf. Boyle, *Church Teaching Authority,* 190 n. 30.

The Pope as Private Doctor

The first instance was actually considered by Bishop Gasser in his official *relatio* at Vatican I. There he observed that the conciliar definition on papal infallibility excluded any instances in which the pope would teach as a doctor or theologian, stating that

> it [infallibility] does not belong to the Roman Pontiff inasmuch as he is a private person, nor even inasmuch as he is a private teacher, since, as such, he is equal with all other private teachers and, as Cajetan wisely noted, equal does not have power over equal, not such power as the Roman Pontiff exercises over the Church Universal.[42]

Gasser presumed that a pope might speak or write as a private doctor or teacher and not as universal pastor. As an example of the pope writing as a private doctor, one might consider the ample writings of Pope Gregory the Great. Clearly his exegetical writings like his *Commentary on the First Book of Kings* or his *Dialogues* describing the lives of Italian saints would be examples of a pope writing not as universal pastor but as private doctor. Any scholarly publication of papal writing would obviously fall in this category. Pope John Paul II's recent *Crossing the Threshold of Hope*[43] is particularly difficult to categorize. This volume is a collection of written responses to interview questions given to him by Catholic journalist Vittorio Messori. On the one hand, the pope is not writing on a scholarly topic as a private doctor. He is being interviewed precisely in his capacity as pope, as "pastor and teacher of all Christians." On the other hand, these interviews are a blend of personal reminiscence and authoritative reaffirmation of Church teaching, drawing heavily on the teaching of Vatican II. Consequently it is difficult to see this collection of often inspiring meditations as a formal exercise of papal teaching.

Pope, Patriarch, Primate, and Bishop: The Significance of the Various Ecclesiastical Titles Held by the Bishop of Rome

A second teaching role of the pope is as bishop of the local Church of Rome. Admittedly the pope's responsibilities to the Roman Church are largely delegated to the cardinal vicar of Rome. Nevertheless, in

---

[42]Mansi, 52, 1213.
[43]John Paul II, *Crossing the Threshold of Hope* (New York: Knopf, 1994).

theory it would be possible for the pope to address a pastoral situation in Rome that would be a true exercise of episcopal teaching but not necessarily "papal."

In addition to his formal responsibilities as bishop of the local Church of Rome, the pope also possesses titles as primate of Italy and patriarch of the Western Church.[44] One can make the case that the apostolic constitution *Sacrae disciplinae leges,* by which Pope John Paul II formally promulgated the 1983 Code of Canon Law,[45] was not an exercise of papal authority but rather an exercise of John Paul II's authority as patriarch of the West, since the Eastern Rite Churches in communion with Rome are not bound by that code. Might not certain recent statements of the Pope concerning the Mafia and organized crime in Italy be considered the pastoral teaching exercise of the primate of Italy rather than of the universal pastor and teacher of all Christians? Admittedly most of these distinctions reflected in papal titles are not observed in practice. At present popes rarely distinguish between the different offices to which they might appeal in their teaching. Yet the recovery of these distinctions in the various titles held by the bishop of Rome might do much to overcome the often monolithic conception of papal authority held by many within and without Roman Catholicism.

My more immediate point, however, is to demonstrate that the distinct character of *papal* teaching lies in its exercise of that "supreme teaching authority" of the pope, which is his *when he is teaching as pastor of all Christians.* The pope exercises this supreme authority not just in a solemn definition, when he relies on the infallible assistance of the Holy Spirit, but in that ordinary exercise of his teaching office for which the possibility of error is not excluded. The pope's exercise of supreme teaching authority occurs whenever he explicitly teaches as universal pastor, as with the issuance of a papal encyclical. In these instances ordinary papal teaching serves as a concrete manifestation of the pope's universal solicitude, his unique ministry to stand watch over the faith of the universal Church. As such, papal teaching is rightly owed a special respect, for it represents an exercise of that supreme teaching authority and universal pastoral solicitude that cannot be claimed by any other individual bishop.

---

[44]Cf. Yves Congar, "Le Pape comme patriarche d'Occident: Approche d'une réalité trop négligée," *Istina* 28 (October-December, 1983) 374–90.

[45]*AAS* 75/2 (1983) vii–xiv.

Even when the bishop of Rome does exercise his teaching authority as pope, according to *Lumen gentium* 25 not every instance of this ordinary papal teaching will be equally authoritative. The precise character of the believer's assent is to correspond to "the manifest mind and will" of the pope as communicated by "the nature of the documents, by the frequent repetition of the same doctrine or by the style of verbal expression." This passage assumes a gradation of teaching authority *within* the exercise of the pope's ordinary teaching. This gradation is determined formally by the documents themselves. Constitutions are the most authoritative of papal documents, followed by encyclicals. Then there are a number of other media for papal teaching, which include apostolic exhortations, pastoral letters, occasional addresses, and so on. One would generally expect, for example, that a new doctrinal formulation appearing in an encyclical would carry more weight than that offered in a weekly papal address.

The Exercise of Universal Papal Ministry and the Ministry of the Local Bishop

There is still the question of when and how the pope ought to exercise his "pastoral solicitude" for the universal Church. In the second chapter I sketched out a theology of the papacy within the context of Vatican II's teaching on episcopal collegiality. Vatican II insisted that bishops were not delegates of the pope but were themselves "vicars of Christ." As such, they are called to exercise a teaching authority that is properly theirs as pastors of a local flock and members of a college that itself possesses supreme teaching authority within the Church. It is only within the context of that conciliar teaching that a proper understanding of papal ministry can emerge.

The ecclesiology of Vatican II began a shift away from a monolithic, pyramidical conception of the Church in which pastoral initiative began at the top (the papacy) and descended down to the local Church. What emerged at the council was a view of the universal Church as manifested *in and through* the local Churches (cf. *LG* 26). Consequently, the council gave unprecedented authority to local bishops to take pastoral initiative in their Churches. This shift in ecclesiology reflects the beginning of what Karl Rahner called a true "world Church."[46] It acknowledges that in a Church no longer sharing a

---

[46]See Rahner's essays "A Basic Theological Interpretation of the Second Vatican Council" and "The Abiding Significance of the Second Vatican

common Western European cultural thought-world, the locus for Church teaching will lie increasingly in the local Church, where the local bishop will have a better opportunity of bringing the gospel of Jesus Christ to bear on the particular issues and concerns of a local Christian community. As sensitivity to cultural context increases, one would expect a greater implementation of the principle of subsidiarity, in which the pastoral authority with direct responsibility for a local community would have the primary responsibility for pastoral ministry within that community and would be expected to address, without external intervention, the pastoral issues that emerge. It is only when these issues appear insoluble at the local level and/or threaten the faith and unity of the Church universal that one should expect the intervention of "higher authority." It follows that the exercise of papal authority ought to be limited to those instances when the "faith and communion" of the Church universal is in jeopardy. As this principle of subsidiarity becomes the norm, intermediate ecclesiastical structures that in recent times have fallen into neglect, like the ancient patriarchate and the convening of regional synods, may need to be restored in new forms.[47]

The Papal Exercise of Doctrinal Judgment

The three components of the teaching of individual bishops considered earlier also apply to papal teaching. Much confusion has arisen because of an unfortunate blurring of the distinction between the more broadly conceived kerygmatic/catechetical and pastoral ministries of the bishop of Rome, which certainly include the presentation of Christian doctrine, and the exercise of doctrinal judgment itself. Since the emergence of the papal encyclical tradition in the nineteenth century, there has been a growing trend to accompany doctrinal judgments with protracted theological exposition. Two recent examples can be offered. No one doubts that in Pope Paul VI's 1968 encyclical on birth regulation, *Humanae vitae,* the Pope offered a properly doctrinal judgment regarding the permissibility of recourse

---

Council," in *Theological Investigations* (New York: Crossroad, 1981) 20:77–102.

[47]Joseph Ratzinger at one time proposed the creation of new patriarchates in order to facilitate better this principle of subsidiarity. See Joseph Ratzinger, *Das neue folk Gottes: Entwürfe zur Ekklesiologie* (Düsseldorf: Patmos, 1969) 141–45.

to artificial contraception. In that encyclical he also offered an extended theological consideration of human love and sexuality that blended Thomistic and personalist considerations of the topic. This extended theological exposition, certainly a legitimate manifestation of papal teaching, nevertheless must be distinguished from the doctrinal judgment itself. In this instance the Pope was employing the contributions of several theological schools in the service of his properly kerygmatic/catechetical ministry. Similarly, in Pope John Paul II's 1993 encyclical, *Veritatis splendor,* there are clear doctrinal judgments (e.g., a condemnation of schools of thought that would propose an unfettered freedom of conscience, severing the conscience's necessary servitude to the truth). However, in that very dense 178-page encyclical, the Pope also offers a developed theological perspective that certainly does not qualify as a strict doctrinal judgment. That is, few would hold that henceforward every theologian must give an account of the "good" only in the context of the kind of personalist phenomenology employed by the Holy Father. A failure to distinguish between doctrinal judgment and the kerygmatic/catechetical dimension of papal ministry has led to an excessively broad and unwarranted view of the way in which papal teaching "norms" Catholic theological discourse.

The exercise of formal doctrinal judgment is fundamentally conservative in character. I do not use the word "conservative" here in its ideological sense (conservative as opposed to liberal) but in its most fundamental meaning. As Francis Sullivan has observed, "its [the ecclesiastical magisterium's] primary function is not to penetrate into the depths of the mysteries of faith (the task of theology) but rather to safeguard the priceless treasure of the word of God and to defend the purity of the faith of the Christian community."[48] The essentially cautious and conservative character of the teaching responsibilities of the magisterium also suggests that one of the most significant exercises of the ecclesiastical magisterium in general and the papal magisterium in particular may be the *refusal* to offer a doctrinal judgment on a controverted issue. Historically, one thinks of the sixteenth-and seventeenth-century *de auxiliis* controversy between the Jesuits and the Dominicans regarding the relationship between divine providence and human freedom. After considerable theological debate and a se-

---

[48]Francis A. Sullivan, "Magisterium," *Dictionary of Fundamental Theology,* 616.

ries of ecclesiastical investigations, Pope Paul V simply prohibited either side from condemning the views of the other. This papal act implicitly acknowledged the difficult and speculative theological issues being considered.

In today's Church the genie of theological pluralism cannot be put back in the bottle. A more modest papal exercise of doctrinal judgment in keeping with this new pluralism may be necessary. This need not mean an abdication of papal responsibility. Circumstances may dictate the need for a clear and formal doctrinal judgment on a matter of faith and morals. Nevertheless, the papacy may best fulfill its responsibility as servant of faith and communion by facilitating open and respectful conversation among bishops and theologians representing different schools of thought. This ministry would be inspired by the conviction that this kind of free and respectful dialogue could yield a greater consensus on essentials and a more mature respect for legitimate theological differences. The creation and support of the International Theological Commission by Pope Paul VI was apparently conceived with this view of papal ministry in mind. One could easily see, in this light, the tremendous potential for the various pontifical councils relating to Christian unity, religion and science, faith and culture, and so on, as papally supported forums for free and respectful theological conversation.

In conclusion, I agree with David Cunningham when he suggests that the authority of the pope ought to be exercised in a way that creates a "free and ordered space" within which theologians can advance theological argumentation from different perspectives.[49] If, as *Dei verbum* insisted, the magisterium is "servant of the Word of God" and must hear the word in order to proclaim it, then papal ministry must go beyond insuring the authoritative proclamation of the word. Papal ministry, precisely as a ministry of universal pastoral solicitude, must also encourage and facilitate processes that enable the Church and its teachers to "hear the Word of God with reverence." Respectful disagreement must not merely be tolerated but welcomed as a natural by-product of the kind of honest conversation through which God's word can often be heard. Formal condemnations,

---

[49]David Cunningham, "Coercion or Persuasion? In Search of the Authority of Dogma," *Pro ecclesia* 3 (1994) 318. Cunningham borrows the phrase "free and ordered space" from A. Bartlett Giamatti, *A Free and Ordered Space: The Real World of the University* (New York: Norton, 1988).

though occasionally necessary, ought to be the instrument of last resort in the fulfillment of the magisterium's unique responsibility for safeguarding the faith.

The Ordinary Universal Magisterium

Up to this point discussion has been limited to the teaching of individual bishops, groupings of bishops, and the teaching of the bishop of Rome in his various capacities. All are exercises of the *ordinary* magisterium, as I have been employing the term, because all fall short of the fullest engagement of supreme teaching authority in the Church, the solemn and infallible definition of Church dogma. Furthermore, all of these have been exercises of the ordinary *nonuniversal* magisterium because they have not explicitly engaged the whole college of bishops.[50] However, there are two conceivable exercises of the ordinary magisterium in which the whole college might be engaged without issuing a solemn definition. In the first instance the bishops, while dispersed throughout the world, could, in their daily teaching activities, propose a teaching *to be held as definitive* and in doing so would have recourse to the charism of infallibility. In the second instance the whole college of bishops, either in council or while dispersed throughout the world, might teach authoritatively *without* either solemnly defining a teaching or proposing a teaching as something to be held as definitive. This exercise of the ordinary universal magisterium would not have recourse to the charism of infallibility.

Ordinary Universal Teaching of the College of Bishops When Teaching Definitively

As with the pope, it is possible for the whole college of bishops to exercise its *potestas suprema* apart from a solemn judgment. Since this teaching exercise would not yield a solemn definition it must be

[50]Admittedly one does not commonly find these exercises of ecclesiastical teaching authority referred to as exercises of the ordinary *nonuniversal* magisterium. I am making explicit use of the term here because I believe that implicit in Vatican I's qualification of the infallible ordinary magisterium of bishops as *universal* was the fact that the whole college was being engaged in this teaching. Logically, it seems to me that all other exercises of the ordinary magisterium must be considered *nonuniversal*.

qualified as *ordinary*. Since it would explicitly engage the whole college it must be qualified as *universal*. Now, *Lumen gentium* states that the whole college can teach with the charism of infallibility apart from a solemn judgment when, while dispersed throughout the world, the bishops are of one judgment that a teaching is *definitively to be held*:[51]

> Although the bishops, taken individually, do not enjoy the privilege of infallibility, they do however proclaim infallibly the doctrine of Christ

[51]The first appearance of the expression *magisterium ordinarium* in an ecclesiastical document occurs in a letter of Pius IX, *Tuas libenter*, to Gregor von Scherr, archbishop of Munich, in 1863. The letter was a response to a theological congress held in Munich with the approval of the local archbishop. This congress had as one of its principal goals a critique of neo-Scholastic thought. The letter to von Scherr reflected the concern of the Pope, under the influence of various curial officials and the papal nuncio in Munich, that the German bishops had been too lax in their oversight of theologians. The letter praised the work of the congress participants but admonished the theologians not to limit their obligations of fidelity to solemnly defined Church teaching alone. The Pope maintained that a response of divine faith was owed as well to those teachings that had been handed on by the *ordinary magisterium* of the Church scattered throughout the world. Vatican I confirmed the teaching of Pius IX in *Dei Filius,* Vatican I's Dogmatic Constitution on the Catholic Faith: "Wherefore, by divine and catholic faith all those things are to be believed which are contained in the word of God as found in scripture and tradition, and which are proposed by the church as matters to be believed as divinely revealed, whether by her solemn judgment or in her ordinary and universal magisterium." See Norman Tanner, ed., *Decrees of the Ecumenical Councils* (Washington: Georgetown Univ. Press, 1990) 2:807. Vatican I added the qualifier "universal" to clearly distinguish this teaching from papal teaching. If the term "ordinary and universal magisterium" was new, the concept was quite ancient. That is, the early Church had a firm conviction that the normative expression of the Christian faith could be found in the universal teaching of the bishops. It should be remembered, however, that in the early centuries of the Church there was no clear distinction between ordinary and extraordinary means of teaching the faith. The teaching of Vatican I was reaffirmed in the 1917 Code of Canon Law (can. 1323.1) and was alluded to in the writings of later popes. Cf. Pius XI, *Mortalium animos,* DS 3683; Pius XII, *Munificentissimus Deus,* AAS 42 (1950) 757. For historical background regarding the origins of this term, see Boyle, *Church Teaching Authority,* 10–42; Richard R. Gaillardetz, *Witnesses to the Faith: Community, Infallibility, and the Ordinary Magisterium of Bishops* (New York: Paulist, 1992) 18–35.

on the following conditions: namely, when, even though dispersed throughout the world but preserving for all that amongst themselves and with Peter's successor the bond of communion, in their authoritative teaching concerning matters of faith and morals, they are in agreement that a particular teaching is to be held definitively and absolutely (*LG* 25).[52]

After Vatican II this third mode of infallible teaching would receive new attention from theologians, largely due to issues raised in the area of moral theology.

Interest in the infallible exercise of the ordinary universal magisterium greatly increased after Pope Paul VI's teaching on artificial contraception in *Humanae vitae*. In the face of widespread dissent, some theologians claimed that the Church's teaching on birth regulation had *already* been taught infallibly by the ordinary universal magisterium. John C. Ford and Germain Grisez offered the most developed exposition of this position in an important article published in *Theological Studies* in 1978.[53] Ford and Grisez found in *Lumen gentium* 25 four conditions for the exercise of the ordinary universal magisterium, which, they maintained, served as a kind of criteriology: "first, that the bishops remain in communion with one another and with the pope; second, that they teach authoritatively on a matter of faith or morals; third, that they agree in one judgment; and fourth, that they propose this judgment as one to be held definitively."[54] They then concluded that in the Church's teaching on artificial contraception even prior to *Humanae vitae*, these conditions had been fulfilled. Other theologians, however, have raised questions about Ford and Grisez's application of these conditions to controversial teaching.[55] It is difficult to see in the teaching of Vatican II the kind of clear criteriology suggested by Ford and Grisez. The fact that the bishops are teaching while dispersed throughout the world and the fact that their common teaching does not issue in a solemn definition raises numerous difficulties regarding

[52]The translation is taken from Austin Flannery, *Vatican Council II: The Conciliar and Post-Conciliar Documents* (rev. ed., Grand Rapids: Eerdmans, 1992).

[53]John C. Ford and Germain Grisez, "Contraception and the Infallibility of the Ordinary Magisterium," *Theological Studies* 39 (1978) 258–312.

[54]Ibid., 272.

[55]For a more in-depth analysis of the position of Ford and Grisez see Sullivan, *Magisterium*, 142–52; Gaillardetz, *Witnesses to the Faith*, 127–38.

verification. How are we to discern the unity of the bishops on a particular matter when their teaching is not manifested in a formal teaching act as is the case with a solemn definition? Do we resort to polling the bishops on a given matter or do we simply assume that lack of public dissent among the bishops in and of itself constitutes agreement? And even if we were able to ascertain that the bishops were in agreement on a doctrinal matter, *Lumen gentium* 25 also holds that the bishops must be in agreement that what is taught be "held definitively." This would appear to exclude any common teachings of the bishops in which the particular teaching is considered by some bishops to be only "probable" or "safe."

These difficulties in verification suggest that appeal to this exercise of episcopal teaching is in fact illsuited for resolving controversial points of doctrine. I agree with Peter Chirico, who describes the ordinary universal magisterium as a kind of "concentrated *sensus fidelium*."[56] Put simply, the bishops exercise their ordinary universal magisterium infallibly when they propose in their daily teaching those truths of the faith that have never been solemnly defined by pope or council only because they have never been seriously challenged. Francis Sullivan has suggested that examples of such teaching would include many of the articles of the ancient baptismal creeds like the bodily resurrection of Jesus or the Catholic Christian belief in the communion of saints.[57] Such teachings, though never seriously challenged, are nevertheless central to our faith and, most would agree, have dogmatic status. It is with respect to these central and noncontroversial teachings that it can be said that all the bishops, though dispersed throughout the world, are in agreement that they should be held as definitive by the faithful.

[56] Peter Chirico, *Infallibility: The Crossroads of Doctrine* (Wilmington: Glazier, 1983) 245ff.. Cf. Gaillardetz, *Witnesses to the Faith,* 169–72.

[57] Sullivan, "Magisterium," 618. More recently, Sullivan has considered the possibility that John Paul II gave expression to three moral teachings of the ordinary universal magisterium in his encyclical *Evangelium vitae.* Those three teachings involved condemnations of the "direct and voluntary killing of an innocent human being," the claim that "direct abortion . . . always constitutes a grave moral disorder," and that "euthanasia is a grave violation of the law of God." These condemnations can be found in "Evangelium vitae," *Origins* 24 (April 6, 1995) 689–727 at 709, 711, and 712. Sullivan's analysis of these condemnations can be found in his article "The Doctrinal Weight of *Evangelium Vitae," Theological Studies* 56 (1995) 560–65.

Ordinary Universal Teaching of the College of Bishops When Not Teaching Definitively

Apart from the *infallible* exercise of the ordinary universal magisterium discussed above, there is a second way in which the bishops might exercise their ordinary and universal magisterium.

At Vatican II the bishops, following the injunction of Pope John XXIII that the council be pastoral in character, determined not to offer any solemn dogmatic judgments. Since this was the first council in the history of the Church expressly to avoid dogmatic judgments in favor of a consistent pastoral orientation, there were some who contended that the council documents had the status of mere pastoral directives.[58] Because of this, the theological commission, under the authority of the secretary general of the council, made the following statement on March 6, 1964:

> Taking into account conciliar custom and the pastoral aim of the present council, this holy synod defines as binding on the church only those matters concerning faith and morals which it openly declares to be such. The other matters which the synod puts forward as the teaching of the supreme magisterium of the church, each and every member of the faithful should accept and embrace according to the mind of the synod itself, which is clear either from the subject matter or from the way it is said, in accordance with the rules of theological interpretation.[59]

From this text we may conclude that the college of bishops may exercise its supreme teaching authority in an ecumenical council even when the council members are not promulgating a solemn definition (extraordinary magisterium) and are not proposing a teaching as something to be held as definitive (*infallible* exercise of the ordinary universal magisterium). Nondefinitive conciliar teaching, even though it is not protected by the charism of infallibility, is truly authoritative and can lay claim to the assent of the faithful. While to my knowledge it has never been described in this fashion, it follows that the teaching of ecumenical councils *when not issuing a solemn judg-*

---

[58]Gérard Philips, "History of the Constitution," in *Commentary on the Documents of Vatican II,* ed. Herbert Vorgrimler (New York: Crossroad, 1989) 1:135.

[59]*Acta synodalia* III/8, 10. The English translation is taken from *Decrees of the Ecumenical Councils,* 898.

ment must also be an exercise of the ordinary and universal (because it engages the whole college) magisterium.

In a similar way, it is possible to imagine the bishops, while dispersed throughout the world, agreeing on a particular matter but *not proposing it as a matter to be held definitively.* As this common episcopal teaching would not involve a solemn definition it would be an exercise of the *ordinary* magisterium. As a common teaching of the whole college of bishops it would be an exercise of the ordinary and *universal* magisterium. However, if the bishops did not propose this teaching as a matter *to be held as definitive,* it would have to be yet another example of a *noninfallible* exercise of the ordinary and universal magisterium.

The focus of this chapter has been on the different modes by which the ordinary magisterium of bishops may be exercised. Precisely because these are the more common ways in which the Church authoritatively presents its doctrinal belief, a proper understanding of these various modes of exercise is essential for anyone involved in the Church's pastoral ministry. Unfortunately, until recently the various expressions of the ordinary magisterium have been obscured by the more controversial questions surrounding the extraordinary magisterium (e.g., papal infallibility), particularly in ecumenical dialogue. Many non-Catholics and Catholics alike have had the impression that the charism of infallibility is operative in virtually any exercise of authoritative Church teaching. In this chapter I have tried to correct this misunderstanding by giving extended consideration to the importance of the many noninfallible exercises of the Church's doctrinal teaching office while acknowledging when the charism of infallibility may be operative. In the next chapter I will consider the two modes of promulgating solemn judgments generally viewed as exercises of the *extraordinary* magisterium.

For Further Reading

The Ordinary Magisterium

Boyle, John P. "The Ordinary Magisterium" and "The Influence of Joseph Kleutgen, S.J." In *Church Teaching Authority: Historical and Theological Studies,* 10–42. Notre Dame: University of Notre Dame Press, 1995.

Congar, Yves. "A Semantic History of the Term 'Magisterium'" and "A Brief History of the Forms of the Magisterium and Its Relations with Scholars." In *The Magisterium and Morality*. Readings in Moral Theology No. 3, ed. Charles E. Curran and Richard A. Mc-Cormick, 297–31. New York: Paulist, 1982.

Ford, John C., and Germain Grisez. "Contraception and the Infallibility of the Ordinary Magisterium." *Theological Studies* 39 (1978) 258–312.

Gaillardetz, Richard R. *Witnesses to the Faith: Community, Infallibility, and the Ordinary Magisterium of Bishops*. New York: Paulist, 1992.

Sullivan, Francis A. "The Infallibility of the Ordinary Universal Magisterium," and "The Non-definitive Exercise of Papal and Conciliar Teaching Authority." In *Magisterium: Teaching Authority in the Catholic Church*, 119–73. New York: Paulist, 1983.

The Ordinary Papal Magisterium

Dionne, J. Robert. *The Papacy and the Church: A Study of Praxis and Reception in Ecumenical Perspective*. New York: Philosophical Library, 1987.

Granfield, Patrick. *The Limits of the Papacy*. New York: Crossroad, 1987.

Komonchak, Joseph A. "Ordinary Papal Magisterium and Religious Assent." In *The Magisterium and Morality*. Readings in Moral Theology No. 3, ed. Charles E. Curran and Richard A. Mc-Cormick, 67–90. New York: Paulist, 1982.

Küng, Hans, ed. *Papal Ministry in the Church*. Concilium 64. New York: Herder & Herder, 1971.

Episcopal Conferences and the Synod of Bishops

Foley, D. *The Synod of Bishops: Its Canonical Structure and Procedures*. Washington: Catholic University of America Press, 1973.

Green, James P. *Conferences of Bishops and the Exercise of the "munus docendi" of the Church*. Rome: Gregorian University, 1987.

Kutner, R. *The Development, Structure, and Competence of the Episcopal Conference*. Washington: The Catholic Univ. of America Press, 1972.

Legrand, Hervé-Marie, Julio Manzanares, and Antonio García y García, eds. *The Nature and Future of Episcopal Conferences*. Washington: The Catholic University of America Press, 1988.

Reese, Thomas, ed. *Episcopal Conferences: Historical, Canonical, and Theological Studies.* Washington: Georgetown Univ. Press, 1989.

Schotte, Jan P. "The Synod of Bishops: A Permanent yet Adaptable Church Institution." *Studia canonica* 26 (1992) 289–306.

7

How the Church Teaches:
The Extraordinary Magisterium

In the previous chapter I examined the many ways in which the bishops realize their responsibility to teach Christian doctrine in their ordinary teaching ministry. The very use of the term "ordinary," however, suggests that the Church may have to resort to more extraordinary means for teaching the faith. In Catholic teaching one of the distinctive characteristics of the extraordinary magisterium is the belief that in its exercise the Holy Spirit will protect the magisterium from leading the faithful away from the path of salvation.

Any consideration of the infallibility of the extraordinary magisterium must begin with the honest admission that we are dealing with the development of a doctrine that cannot be found explicitly in Scripture. Traditional Catholic apologetics, which appealed to biblical texts like Matthew 16:18-20, Luke 22:32, or Acts 15, will no longer suffice.[1] It would be historically irresponsible to claim that the early Church explicitly professed the doctrine of infallibility for either pope or council. Nevertheless, one can make a claim to a real continuity between some of the central faith convictions of the early

[1] For a balanced treatment of the biblical texts regarding the Petrine ministry from an ecumenical perspective, see Raymond E. Brown, Karl Donfried, and John Reumann, eds., *Peter in the New Testament* (New York: Paulist, 1973). The most useful study since the Brown volume is that of Rudolph Pesch, *Simon-Petrus: Geschichte und geschichtliche Bedeutung des ersten Jüngers Jesu Christi.* Papste und Papsttum 15 (Stuttgart: Hiersemann, 1980).

Church and the subsequent development of the doctrine of infallibility. Most basic among these convictions was the belief in the Church's continued fidelity to the apostolic faith. The Holy Spirit was Christ's gift to the Church and provided assurance that the Church would never depart fundamentally from the proclamation of God's offer of salvation. From this conviction came the gradual recognition that there must be specific instances in which the Church's formal teaching is protected by the Spirit. Over the span of nineteen hundred years the consciousness of the Church grew to recognize two ways of pronouncing on disputed doctrinal matters (by pope or council) with the assurance of continued fidelity to the apostolic faith through the assistance of the Spirit. This chapter will consider these two exercises of the extraordinary magisterium (see fig. 3).

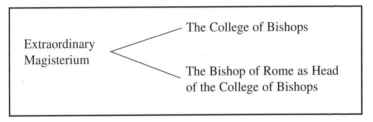

Figure 3

The Extraordinary Magisterium of the College of Bishops

The gathering of bishops in regional synods began in the late second century as bishops sought to address important pastoral and doctrinal matters. As we saw in chapter 2, these gatherings had their theological foundation in the ancient notion of communion. The bishops saw themselves following in the tradition of Acts 15 and the so-called Council of Jerusalem. While the meeting at Jerusalem would not qualify as a council by modern standards (since it involves not bishops of local Churches but the apostolic leadership), by the late second century we do have evidence of an episcopal synod called to respond to the Montanist threat, and we know that in 190 Bishop Victor of Rome called for a series of regional synods to address the discrepancies in the dating of Easter. Yet as important as many of these early synods were, they have never been considered "ecumenical" councils.

The Historical Development of Ecumenical Councils and the Determination of Ecumenicity

The adjective "ecumenical" is derived from the Greek word *oik-oumene,* which meant "universal," or "pertaining to the whole world." When applied to a gathering of bishops, the term initially lacked the technical meaning it currently has and simply denoted a gathering of significance for the whole Church. Most Christian traditions recognize the fourth-century Council of Nicaea as the first ecumenical council. However, this designation can give the impression that participants at that council understood themselves to be inaugurating some new ecclesiastical institution. In fact, there was no distinct canonical or structural difference between the Council of Nicaea and the earlier regional synods. All of the first seven "ecumenical" councils were, objectively, little more than regional gatherings of bishops not unlike the previous synods.[2]

The ecumenicity that was ultimately conferred on these councils was derived not from some juridical feature of the councils themselves but from both the weighty doctrinal problems addressed by the councils and the fact that the solutions these councils provided were ultimately accepted and *received* by the whole Church. "Reception" here refers to the process by which the local Churches take a teaching of pope or council and make it their own.[3]

At the Second Council of Nicaea (753) the participants sought to refute the legitimacy of a prior gathering of iconoclast bishops at Constantinople. Toward this end the council proposed three criteria for determining whether a council was truly "ecumenical": (1) there must be participation, either personal or through ecclesiastical representative, of the five patriarchal sees, and in particular, the See of Rome; (2) the decisions of the council must be "received" by the whole Church; (3) the council teachings must be in agreement with those of the previous councils whose ecumenicity was accepted.[4] The

---

[2] See Georg Denzler, "The Authority and Reception of Conciliar Decisions in Christendom," in *The Ecumenical Council,* Concilium 167, ed. Peter Huizing and Knut Walf (New York: Seabury, 1983) 13–18.

[3] This notion of "reception" has received a good deal of attention over the last thirty years. It will be considered in more detail in the next chapter.

[4] These criteria are developed in Luis Bermejo, *Infallibility on Trial: Church, Conciliarity, and Communion* (Westminster: Christian Classics, 1992) 71. The conciliar text from which he develops these criteria can be found in Mansi, 13, 208–9.

first criterion was concerned with the question of participation or representation at a council. In the Western Church the question of participation/representation focused on the role of the See of Rome, whereas the Eastern Church would continue to insist on the importance of the whole pentarchy, the five ancient patriarchal sees (Rome, Alexandria, Antioch, Constantinople, and Jerusalem). The second and third criteria involve a twofold consensus, first a horizontal consensus among all the Churches, and second a vertical consensus with the apostolic tradition, particularly as enshrined in the teaching of previous councils.

These three criteria were not equally important. For example, ecumenicity was granted to several of the first seven councils when the first criterion, participation by the pope and the other four patriarchal sees, could not clearly be demonstrated. The twofold universal *reception* was ecclesiologically more significant than universal representation/participation. Hermann Josef Sieben, one of the foremost scholars on the history of ecumenical councils, has explored in some detail the character of this twofold reception. Sieben too contends that the authority or ecumenicity of a council was determined not primarily by who was present at the council but by a *consensio antiquitatis et universitatis* (a consensus with antiquity and with the universal Church). The authority of the council itself depended on whether the determinations of the council were accepted as expressions of this twofold consensus.[5] *Universitas* involved the horizontal consensus of the whole Church. When a council sought to teach a matter of doctrine authoritatively, it did so out of the conviction that it was teaching the faith of the Churches. Council participants never believed themselves to be imposing something foreign to the faith of their respective communities. While a council presumed itself to be expressing this *universitas,* or horizontal consensus, in its teaching, the verification of that authority demanded that the local Churches receive the teaching of the council and come to profess it as their own. This could take considerable time. Often a key moment in the reception of a council's teaching would be its acceptance at a subsequent council. Yves Congar offers the example of the creed of the Council of Nicaea, which was only truly "received" fifty-six years later when it was accepted at the Council of Constantinople (381). The reception

---

[5]Hermann Josef Sieben, *Die Konzilsidee der Alten Kirche* (Paderborn: Schöningh, 1979) 511–16.

of the teaching of Constantinople, in turn, only occurred at the Council of Chalcedon (451).[6]

If the *consensio universitatis* was authenticated by the council's reception by the Churches, the *consensio antiquitatis,* or agreement with the apostolic tradition, had to be demonstrated by the council itself. The burden was on the council to demonstrate how its teaching was faithful to that tradition.[7] In defending the Council of Nicaea, St. Athanasius felt compelled to write: "The Fathers, in matters of faith, never said: Thus it has been decreed, but: This is what the Catholic Church believes; and they confessed what they believed directly, so as to show unmistakably that their thought was not new, but apostolic."[8] It fell again to the local Churches to determine whether a council had preserved this agreement with antiquity. It is a consistent theme in the theological reflection on teaching authority of the first millennium that authoritative proclamation of the apostolic faith could not be divorced from the authentic reception of that teaching by the Christian communities. This is not due to some liberal democratic conviction but rather to the nature of divine revelation itself, which always resides in the consciousness of the whole Church. This conviction permeates the many writings of Yves Congar on ecumenical councils.

> In a council it is either a question of clarifying the tradition of the Church or the *sensus ecclesiae,* or of producing a solution to a contemporary question. Both the *sensus ecclesiae* and the desired solution lie hidden in the memory or consciousness of the Church—or rather, in the memories or consciousness of the persons who compose the Church. These memories and consciousnesses must communicate in order to produce a common expression and sum total, so to speak, of

[6]Yves Congar, "Reception as an Ecclesiological Reality," in *Election and Consensus in the Church,* Concilium 77, ed. Giuseppe Alberigo and Anton Weiler (New York: Herder, 1972) 46–48. In this last case, Congar notes the significance of the fact that Constantinople was eventually accepted as ecumenical in spite of the complaints of Ambrose and others of serious deficiencies in representation.

[7]Edward Kilmartin, "Reception in History: An Ecclesiological Phenomenon and Its Significance," *Journal of Ecumenical Studies* 21 (1984) 48–50.

[8]*De Synodus 5,* as quoted in Yves Congar, "A Brief History of the Forms of the Magisterium and Its Relations with Scholars," in *The Magisterium and Morality,* Readings in Moral Theology No. 3, ed. Charles E. Curran and Richard A. McCormick (New York: Paulist, 1982) 316.

the memory and consciousness of the Church. This is not a collection of personal convictions, for although it only exists personified in actual men—and, at the highest level in the consciousness of Christ and in his Spirit, but I shall speak of this later—it nonetheless transcends these men and through them belongs to the Church. The council aims at achieving a totalization of the memory of the Church, by a communication of the consciences which house this memory.[9]

Here again we see collegiality, the interaction among the bishops, as but the external expression of the communion of the Churches.

The place of universal reception in determining the authority of councils has remained important for the Eastern Churches, leading them to accept the ecumenicity of only the first seven councils. They argue that all subsequent councils lacked the reception of the Eastern Churches and therefore could not be considered ecumenical. In fairness, many Orthodox theologians have similarly refused to grant ecumenicity to the gathering of bishops at Constantinople convened in 867 by Photius, the patriarch of Constantinople, on the grounds that this council has not been received in the West.

Over the past few decades there have been attempts in Roman Catholicism to honor Orthodoxy's emphasis on universal reception as a condition for the ecumenicity of a council. One way of doing this has been to distinguish between *ecumenical* councils, properly speaking, and *general* councils. Those councils conducted without the participation and/or reception of non-Catholic Christian traditions would be considered *general* rather than *ecumenical* councils. This distinction is no novelty but in fact represents what was the common practice before the Reformation. It was only in the late sixteenth century that it became common to include in a listing of ecumenical councils those councils conducted by the Roman Catholic Church alone.[10] A precedent for this distinction between general and ecumenical councils may have been set by the letter of Pope Paul VI to Cardinal Willebrands on the occasion of the seventh centenary of the Second Council at Lyon. In that letter the Pope conspicuously referred to that council as "numbered six among the general synods celebrated in the

[9]Yves Congar, "The Council as an Assembly and the Church as Essentially Conciliar," in *Theologians Today: Yves Congar* (London and New York: Sheed & Ward, 1972) 110–11.

[10]Cf. Yves Congar, "1274–1974: Structures ecclésiales et conciles dans les relations entre orient et occident," *Revue des sciences philosophiques et théologiques* 58 (1974) 378ff.

West."[11] This terminological distinction, however, has yet to be commonly employed in theological discourse.

In the second millennium, faced first with the schism between East and West followed by the sixteenth-century Protestant Reformation, Roman Catholicism gradually relied on a more formal criterion of ecumenicity, namely papal participation and approval.[12] Most of the councils conducted by the medieval Church were so papal in character as to barely qualify as councils. The notion of a council's teaching needing to be received by the local Churches became irrelevant as the ecumenical council had been reduced to an instrument for the furtherance of papal policy. This papal domination would be less pronounced, however, in the cases of both the Council of Trent and Vatican I.

As a modern example of conciliar reception we can look to the circumstances surrounding the definitions of papal infallibility and papal primacy at Vatican I.[13] It is well known that a sizable number of bishops chose to depart early from that council before the final vote on the definition on papal infallibility in *Pastor aeternus*. Presumably these bishops were opposed to the definition but did not wish to register a negative vote. This was a cause for concern for theologians like John Henry Newman, who felt that a significant lack of unanimity among the council members could call the definition into question.[14]

[11]*AAS* 66 (1974) 620.

[12]While the Eastern Churches have objected to the West's reliance on papal participation and approval, many Eastern theologians have also reacted against the more radical approach of the nineteenth-century Slavophile movement. This movement, represented by the writing of Alexei Khomiakov, held that the authority of an ecumenical council depended solely on the universal assent of the whole Church manifested in a corporate consciousness. To many Orthodox thinkers this too is a novelty that does not honor the traditional role of the bishops and the pentarchy in particular. See W. Hryniewicz, "Die ekklesiale Rezeption in der Sicht der orthodoxen Theologie," *Theologie und Glaube* 65 (1975) 250–65; B. Schultze, "Orthodoxe Kritik an der Ekklesiologie Chomjakovs," *Orientalia Christiana periodica* 36 (1970) 407–31; P. Duprey, "La structure synodale de l'Église dans la théologie orientale," *Proche Orient Chrétien* 20 (1970) 123–45.

[13]See John P. Boyle, *Church Teaching Authority: Historical and Theological Studies* (Notre Dame: Univ. of Notre Dame Press, 1995) 124–41.

[14]Newman wrote: "If, on the other hand, I find that there was a concerted and organized protest against it [the definition] on the part of a considerable number of bishops of various countries, then I should find it difficult to determine

Clearly it was a matter of great import for officials in the Vatican as well. Those bishops who departed early were pressured to publicly state their submission to the council's definition. The willingness of those bishops to do so (though some were clearly more willing than others!) can be seen as a limited exercise of reception, since they were technically assenting to a conciliar determination in which they had no direct part. Nevertheless, even as an exercise of ecclesial reception, the circumstances surrounding this act of reception reflect the juridical state of ecclesiology at the time; reception meant submission or juridical obedience and applied to the bishops without reference to the local Churches themselves.[15]

However one may evaluate the role of reception at Vatican I, in the 1917 Code of Canon Law the determination of the ecumenicity of a council still depended exclusively on the participation and approval of the papacy. There was no mention of universal representation by the ancient pentarchy or the episcopal college in general. Neither was there any mention of the need for the reception of a council's teaching by the local Churches. This juridical and papocentric approach to ecumenical councils was accepted into the 1983 Code of Canon Law, which still insists on papal participation and approval as the determining factors in a council's ecumenicity: "It is for the Roman Pontiff alone to convoke an ecumenical council, to preside over it personally or through others, to transfer, suspend or dissolve it, and to approve its decrees" (can. 338). In spite of this formal dependence on the papacy Catholicism has remained surprisingly vague in its teaching on ecumenical councils. Apart from the determinations of canon law there is no formal doctrinal definition of the criteria for ecumenicity, nor is there a definitive list of ecumenical councils.[16]

---

the ground on which it was binding on my faith." John Henry Newman, *The Letters and Diaries of John Henry Newman,* ed. Charles Dessain and Thomas Gornall, (Oxford: Clarendon, 1973) 25:179.

[15]Bermejo, *Infallibility on Trial,* 186ff.

[16]See Remigius Bäumer, "Die Zahl der allgemeinen Konzilien in der Sicht der Theologen des 15. und 16. Jahrhunderts," *Annuarium historiae conciliorum* 1 (1969) 288–313. The accepted list of twenty-one councils is based on a list of Robert Bellarmine that eventually won a practical acceptance. This list has been questioned by many today. As just one example, a growing number of scholars have questioned the ecumenicity of Constantinople IV.

The strictly juridical and formal approach to ecumenical councils reflected in the 1983 code raises important questions in light of one of the most far-

Vatican II and the Formal Authority of Ecumenical Councils

Vatican II reaffirmed what had become a common conviction of the Church since around the tenth century, namely that in an ecumenical council the college of bishops may teach with the charism of infallibility. In *Lumen gentium* 25, after considering the infallible exercise of the ordinary universal magisterium, the council explains that the exercise of an infallible teaching judgment by the college of bishops "takes place even more clearly when they are gathered together in an ecumenical council and are the teachers and judges of faith and morals for the whole Church. Their definitions must be adhered to with the obedience of faith *(obsequio fidei)*." The council's treatment of the authority of ecumenical councils *after* consideration of the authority of the bishops when dispersed throughout the world is noteworthy. It suggests that it is the college of bishops itself that is central rather than a given ecclesiastical institution (an ecumenical council) in and through which the college exercises its authority. This is consistent with Vatican II's shift away from a juridical view of authority preoccupied with ecclesiastical institutions.

While in canon law the determination of a council's ecumenicity continues to lie with the pope, this must be coupled with the teaching of Vatican II, which consistently situates the pope *within* the college

---

reaching new developments in the ecclesiology of Vatican II, the council's treatment of the relationship of the Church of Jesus Christ to the Roman Catholic Church and other Christian traditions. Pius XII, in his encyclical *Mystici corporis* (1943), had claimed an absolute identity between the Church of Christ and the Roman Catholic Church. In *Lumen gentium* 8 the council significantly modified this position by teaching instead only that the Church of Christ *subsists in* the Roman Catholic Church. The council acknowledged that there were many ecclesial elements like the belief in Scripture and the celebration of sacraments that were present within other Christian traditions. These elements were sufficiently ecclesial in character to warrant referring to these other Christian traditions as "Churches or ecclesiastical communities" *(LG* 15). If other Christian traditions may truly be called Churches, then what is the significance of their exclusion from a council for the determination of a council's ecumenicity? For a treatment of this problem see Bermejo, *Infallibility on Trial,* 185–236; Harry McSorley, "Some Forgotten Truths About the Petrine Ministry," *Journal of Ecumenical Studies* 11 (1974) 234–36; Francis A. Sullivan, *Magisterium: Teaching Authority in the Catholic Church* (New York: Paulist, 1983) 109–11; Boyle, *Church Teaching Authority,* 138–39.

of bishops as member and head. According to *Lumen gentium* 22, the authority of the ecumenical council is derived not from the authority of the pope but from the authority of the whole college of bishops under the headship of the pope. The ecclesiology of Vatican II clearly resists separating pope and college.

One final observation on current teaching regarding ecumenical councils must be made. There are no clearly developed criteria for determining *when* a valid ecumenical council is in fact teaching with the charism of infallibility. This ambiguity has often resulted in an unjustified attribution of infallibility to all conciliar teaching. For example, some of the manualists assumed that any conciliar canon with an anathema attached was a solemn infallible judgment. Scholars now acknowledge that only after a careful study of the conciliar *acta* and the historical and theological context of a council can one determine when councils intended to make a solemn infallible judgment on a matter of faith and morals.[17] *Lumen gentium* specifies that this charism of infallibility is involved only when the bishops in council act as "teachers and judges of faith and morals for the whole Church" (*LG* 25). The 1964 declaration of the council's theological commission emphasized this distinction: "Taking into account conciliar custom and the pastoral aim of the present council, this holy synod defines as binding on the Church only those matters concerning faith and morals which it openly declares to be such."[18] In the future one might hope that any council wishing to exercise its extraordinary magisterium by means of a solemn judgment would use a formula that would make that intention manifestly evident. This would seem to be demanded by canon 749.3 of the new Code of Canon Law: "No doctrine is understood to be infallibly defined unless it is clearly established as such."

In conclusion, the development of the authority of ecumenical councils mirrors the significant shifts that have occurred in Roman Catholic ecclesiology itself. In the early Church councils were viewed as concentrated expressions of the faith of the whole Church. This was in keeping with the patristic ecclesiology of communion. During the Middle Ages when an ecclesiology of communion was gradually supplanted by a more juridical and hierarchical ecclesiol-

[17]Cf. Piet Fransen, "The Authority of the Councils," in *Problems of Authority*, ed. J. M. Todd (Baltimore: Helicon, 1962) 43–78.

[18]Norman Tanner, ed., *Decrees of the Ecumenical Councils* (Washington: Georgetown Univ. Press, 1990) 2:898.

ogy, the ecumenical council was reduced to a tool of the papacy. Though both Trent and Vatican I functioned as much more than instruments of papal policy, by the mid-twentieth century, reflecting the Ultramontane tendencies of the time, it was common for theologians to suggest that a strong papacy rendered ecumenical councils unnecessary. The important contributions of Vatican II have certainly challenged that view.

The Extraordinary Magisterium of the Bishop of Rome as Head of the College of Bishops

The history of the emerging doctrine of papal infallibility is extremely complex and would take us well beyond the scope of this book.[19] However, given the controversial character of Roman Catholicism's

---

[19]Major works on the topic include Gustave Thils, *Primauté et infaillibilité du pontife Romain à Vatican I* (Leuven: Leuven Univ. Press, 1989); Margaret O'Gara, *Triumph in Defeat: Infallibility, Vatican I, and the French Minority Bishops* (Washington: Catholic Univ. of America Press, 1988); Terry J. Tekippe, ed., *Papal Infallibility: An Application of Lonergan's Theological Method* (Washington: Univ. Press of America, 1983); Ulrich Horst, *Papst-Konzil-Unfehlbarkeit* (Mainz: Grünewald, 1978); idem, *Unfehlbarkeit und Geschichte: Studien zur Unfehlbarkeitsdiskussion von Melchior Cano bis zum I. Vatikanischen Konzil* (Mainz: Grunewäld, 1982); August B. Hasler, *Pius IX (1846–1878), päpstliche Unfehlbarkeit, und I. Vatikanisches Konzil: Dogmatisierung und Durchsetzung einer Ideologie* (Stuttgart: Hiersemann, 1977); Franz Xaver Bantle, *Unfehlbarkeit der Kirche in Aufklärung und Romantik: Eine dogmengeschichtliche Untersuchung für die Zeit der Wende vom 18. zum 19. Jahrhundert* (Freiburg: Herder, 1976); Klaus Schatz, *Kirchenbild und päpstliche Unfehlbarkeit bei den Deutschsprachigen Minoritätsbischöfen auf dem I. Vatikanum* (Rome: Gregorian Univ., 1975); Hermann Josef Pottmeyer, *Unfehlbarkeit und Souveränität: Die päpstliche Unfehlbarkeit im System der ultramontanen Ekklesiologie des 19. Jahrhunderts* (Mainz: Grünewald, 1975); Brian Tierney, *Origins of Papal Infallibility, 1150–1350* (Leiden: Brill, 1972); Frederick J. Cwiekowski, *The English Bishops and the First Vatican Council* (Louvain: Publications Universitaires de Louvain, 1971); E. Castelli, ed., *L'Infaillibilité: Son aspect philosophique et théologique* (Paris: Aubier, 1970); Gustave Thils, *L'Infaillibilité pontificale: Source-conditions-limites* (Gembloux: Duculot, 1969); Roger Aubert, *Vatican I* (Paris: Editions de l'Orante, 1964); James Hennesey, *The First Council of the Vatican: The American Experience* (New York: Herder & Herder, 1963); Jean-Pierre Torrell, *La théologie de l'épiscopat au premier*

teaching on papal infallibility, it will be helpful to consider briefly the main features of this doctrine's development, culminating in its solemn definition at Vatican I and recontextualization at Vatican II.

The Historical Origins of the Doctrine of Papal Infallibility

As was noted in chapter 2, the influence of the Church of Rome and its bishop on other Churches is evident already by the end of the second century. Much has been made of St. Ignatius of Antioch's opening greeting to the Church of Rome, which he describes as "pre-eminent in love." It is a greeting that, at the least, suggests the high esteem with which the Church of Rome was held. The *Ecclesiastical History* of Eusebius confirms the outstanding reputation of Rome in the second century.[20] Rome's reputation for doctrinal integrity in particular is affirmed in the late second-century writings of St. Irenaeus of Lyon.[21] The late second century also saw a significant exercise of the authority of the bishop of Rome regarding an important regional conflict, known as the Quartodeciman controversy, over the proper dating of liturgical feasts. In the dispute, Bishop Victor of Rome sought to sever communion with the bishops of Asia minor who refused to adopt the Roman practice. While this action did not go unchallenged, it is one of the first instances we have of the bishop of Rome exercising ecclesiastical authority beyond the boundaries of his local Church. The exercise of some kind of "papal" authority over regional disputes would continue in the third and early fourth centuries. By the mid-fourth century Roman bishops were themselves articulating a ministry of universal primacy, justified in part by reference to Petrine biblical texts. These assertions of papal authority, however, were not always accepted, particularly in the East.

The development of papal authority cannot be separated from the developing authority of the so-called patriarchal sees, the ancient Churches that each held a special claim to apostolicity. Of the five patriarchal sees that emerged (Rome, Constantinople, Alexandria, Antioch, and Jerusalem), only Rome lay in the West.[22] As the Churches of

---

concile du Vatican (Paris: Cerf, 1961); Georges Dejaifve, *Pape et évéques au premier concile du Vatican* (Brussels: Desclée, 1961).

[20]For a summary assessment of these texts see Robert B. Eno, *The Rise of the Papacy* (Wilmington: Glazier, 1990) 34ff.

[21]Irenaeus, *Adversus haereses* III, 3, 1–2.

[22]O. Kéramé, "Les chaires apostoliques et le role des Patriarcats dans

the East and West became separated both politically and culturally, a natural tension evolved between the apostolic see of Rome and the apostolic sees in the East. In the fourth through sixth centuries the succeeding bishops of Rome came to play significant roles in the great Christological and Trinitarian debates of the period. Indeed, it may well have been the papacy's steadfast support of what became the orthodox position that did more than anything to enhance the papacy's prestige. While the East would stress the role of the councils in resolving these doctrinal disputes, the bishops of Rome, at least, were equally insistent that it was the authority of the papacy that played the determinative role. Increasingly strong claims to a universal primacy were made by popes of this period like Damasus (366–84) and Leo the Great (440–61).

Beyond these claims to primacy we also find an important assertion of the doctrinal trustworthiness of the Roman See in the formulary of Pope Hormisdas (514–23). The formulary states that the apostolic faith has been preserved "without spot" in the Church of Rome.[23] A century and a half later a similar claim would be made by Pope Agatho (678–81), who insisted that just as Jesus prayed that Peter's faith would not fail, so too Rome's own faith had been preserved without blemish (Luke 22:32).[24] By the end of the first millennium claims to the inerrancy of the Roman apostolic tradition would become quite common, often relying on this text from Luke.

In spite of these increasingly common claims to the trustworthiness of the Roman profession of faith, it would be historically inaccurate to speak of an explicit doctrine of papal infallibility during the first millennium. The witness of the See of Rome was quite important because of its *principalitas,* or origin as the Church of Sts. Peter and Paul (though by the fourth century the significance of the Pauline connection had diminished). Rome was considered the outstanding example of fidelity to the apostolic *kerygma.* Consequently, the West generally acknowledged the right of the pope to settle matters of faith authoritatively. But it would be a mistake to imagine a formal doctrine of papal infallibility at work here. The emphasis still lay not on

---

l'Église," in *L'Épiscopat et l'Église universelle,* ed. Yves Congar and B.-D. Dupuy, *Unam Sanctam* 39 (Paris: Cerf, 1962) 261–78.

[23]This formulary is treated in Trevor Jalland, *Church and Papacy* (London: SPCK, 1944) 338.

[24]*Patrologia Latina* 87:1169, 1205.

the formal authority of the pope alone but on the faith of the whole Church of Rome and on that apostolic tradition to which the Roman Church and its bishop gave witness.[25] Perhaps the dominant view at the end of the first millennium can be summarized as follows. While there was a widespread belief that Rome *had not erred* and therefore was trustworthy in its apostolic witness, it would be some time before there was a serious consideration of the possibility that Rome *could not err.*

Moving ahead to the thirteenth century, we must consider the viewpoint of the century's most luminous theological figure, St. Thomas Aquinas. While Thomas did not offer a developed doctrine of papal infallibility, one can find all of the major premises for such a doctrine in his writing.[26] Thomas defends the right of the pope to make definitive pronouncements on the faith of the Church, but in a period prior to the antagonistic opposition of pope and council, he simply assumes that this papal exercise would normally occur in conjunction with an ecumenical council.[27] Furthermore, Thomas believes that this authority to make a definitive judgment on matters of faith derives from the inerrancy of the faith of the universal Church.[28] According to Congar, Thomas insists that inerrancy is applied to the pope only "insofar as he is a personification or a figure of the universal Church."[29] This use of symbolic representation, common to the patristic Church, grounded the authority of the bishop/pope firmly in the Church itself.

The ecclesiology of St. Thomas, however, was not the dominant school of thought in the thirteenth century. Already that ecclesiology of communion that characterized the Church of the first thousand years was giving way to a more hierocratic or pyramidical ecclesiology that stressed the authority of the papacy. It is not surprising that an explicit doctrine of papal infallibility would emerge in this climate. What is surprising is that a doctrine of papal infallibility would develop as a means of *limiting* papal sovereignty rather than enhanc-

[25]Yves Congar, *L'Ecclésiologie du haut moyen-âge* (Paris: Cerf, 1968) 160.

[26]Terry Tekippe, "History: The Medieval Period," in *Papal Infallibility,* 145–47.

[27]Yves Congar, "St. Thomas Aquinas and the Infallibility of the Papal Magisterium," *Thomist* 38 (1974) 92.

[28]*Quodlibet* IX, 16.

[29]Congar, "St. Thomas Aquinas and the Infallibility of the Papal Magisterium," 92.

ing it. This was the conclusion of Brian Tierney in his influential study of the origins of papal infallibility.[30]

Tierney contends that in the thirteenth century an explicit theological argument for the infallibility of the pope was first proposed by the spiritual Franciscans. These mendicants wished to embrace St. Francis' commitment to radical poverty. Their position had been given official approbation by Pope Nicholas III in his papal bull, *Exiit qui seminat* (1279). Since their status was quite controversial, they wanted to ensure that future popes could not renounce Pope Nicholas' decision. If the pope's approval of the radical poverty of the spiritual Franciscans was proposed infallibly, then future popes would not be free to condemn the position. It is no coincidence that the Franciscan theologian Peter Olivi pens an explicit exposition of this doctrine of papal infallibility in 1280, immediately after the papal decree.[31] Olivi argued that the infallibility of papal teaching followed from the inerrancy or indefectibility of the faith of the whole Church. How could the Church be sure that its faith was without error unless there was an authority who could teach that faith without error? Olivi anticipates Vatican I's teaching on infallibility by limiting the scope of papal infallibility to "faith and morals" and distinguishing between "private error" and "magisterial error." Papal infallibility excluded only the latter. However, Olivi offers a somewhat distinctive approach to the possibility of error in papal teaching. While on the one hand he insists that a pope cannot err on matters of faith and morals, he does admit the possibility of a heretical, pseudo-pope who could teach error. "Olivi's doctrine of infallibility also implied—and this was new—that any pontiff who departed from the doctrinal decisions of a predecessor would, by doing so, automatically fall into heresy and so cease to be the true head of the Church."[32] Olivi was understandably preoccupied with the possibility of a future pope withdrawing support from the Franciscans. He suggested that the norm for determining whether a pope was heretical and therefore not truly pope was the faith of the universal Church. This view would later be developed by the Franciscan William of Ockham.

In the early fourteenth-century writing of the Carmelite Guido Terreni, this doctrine of papal infallibility would be purged of the peculiarities associated with its Franciscan formulation. Terreni built a whole

---

[30]Tierney, *Origins of Papal Infallibility.*
[31]Ibid., 122.
[32]Ibid., 126.

ecclesiology around the doctrine of papal infallibility.[33] Against Olivi and
the Franciscans, Terreni contended that while there might be a heretical
pope, there could not be heretical papal teaching. The Holy Spirit would
never allow even a heretical pope to err in his doctrinal determinations.[34]
Also significant was his insistence that all papal determinations protected
by infallibility must be in some way derived from Scripture.[35] He explicitly distinguished between the pope as head of the Church and the pope
as private doctor and attributed infallibility only to the former.

Significantly lacking in all medieval treatments of the subject is the
modern distinction between an infallible and fallible exercise of papal
teaching in matters of doctrine. There is a common assumption
shared by the Franciscans as well as Terreni that "every official doctrinal definition of a true pope was necessarily unerring."[36] Any papal
teaching not taught infallibly was usually considered an exercise of
papal disciplinary authority.[37]

After Terreni, while the doctrine would reappear from time to time,
particularly in response to conciliarism, it would find little explicit
development until the sixteenth and seventeenth centuries. The topic
then reemerges as it is defended by the Catholic apologists against the
attacks of the Protestant reformers. While Melchior Cano treats papal
infallibility in some length in his *De locis theologicis,* the most significant exposition of the doctrine during this period is found in
Robert Bellarmine's late sixteenth-century *De controversiis.* There
Bellarmine submits papal infallibility to his own rigorously systematic analysis. Bellarmine follows the medieval tradition in limiting
the charism of papal infallibility to teaching on faith and morals. He
also distinguishes between the pope as a private doctor and as universal pastor.[38] He follows Terreni, against Olivi, in claiming that

[33]Ibid., 238ff.

[34]See Terreni, *Quaestio de magisterio infallibili,* ed. B. M. Xiberta (Mün-
ster, 1926) 25.

[35]This is the interpretation of Tierney, who rejects Xiberta's claim that Terreni assumes a nascent two-source theory. Cf. Tierney, *Origins of Papal Infallibility,* 257.

[36]Tierney, 269.

[37]For medieval understandings of papal teaching authority see James Heft,
John XXII and Papal Teaching Authority (Toronto: Mellon, 1986).

[38]Later Bellarmine does allow for the pious belief that even as a private
doctor the pope cannot err. Cf. *De controversiis* (Naples: Pedone Lauriel,
1872) bk. 4, ch. 6, 484.

whether or not a pope can himself be heretical, he cannot teach heretical doctrine.[39] Bellarmine also appears to distinguish between the popes teaching on "particular facts" and papal teaching on matters of faith. Finally, he will insist that inerrancy applies not only to the teaching of the pope but to the inerrancy of the faith of the local Church of Rome.[40] His nuanced treatment of this topic will anticipate Vatican I on many points.

In the seventeenth and eighteenth centuries there emerged an alternative theological tradition associated with Gallicanism and Febronianism with roots in the conciliarism of the fourteenth and fifteenth centuries. This ecclesiology sought to ground papal infallibility in the infallibility of the Church. The best-known exposition of this view is found in the writings of Jacques Bossuet and the famous Gallican Articles of 1682, which he helped compose. There the exercise of papal infallibility was bound to the consent of the universal Church.[41]

By the end of the eighteenth century one could recognize a broad consensus in favor of the infallibility of the Church and of ecumenical councils, but belief in papal infallibility was more uneven. Much depended on the way in which the doctrine was formulated. While a belief in a separate papal infallibility was strong in Italy and Spain, there was serious disagreement in other regions.[42]

[39]Ibid., 477–78.

[40]Ibid., 482.

[41]Richard F. Costigan, "Bossuet and the Consensus of the Church," *Theological Studies* 56 (December 1995) 652–72. Costigan argues against the view common to both early propapalist writers and many modern scholars that Bossuet and Gallicanism was committed to a *consensus subsequens,* that is, the need for a formal and juridical consent of the whole Church (meaning the bishops) subsequent to a papal definition. Costigan points out that this question was given a far more complex consideration by Bossuet and others than is generally granted. "Gallican authors do indeed at times describe the consensus of the Church in these terms [*consensus subsequens*], and Bossuet is one of these. . . . But this is not the only, or principal, way in which Gallicans describe the *consensus ecclesiae.* It is actually more complex and nuanced, and the focus is really placed most often on *consensus antecedens,* which is the underlying or pervasive agreement of the Church as a whole on the basic truths of faith" (666). See also Richard Costigan, "The Consensus of the Church: Differing Classical Views," *Theological Studies* 51 (March 1990) 25–48.

[42]Michael Place has written an informative dissertation on the eighteenth-century views of papal authority, surveying the writings of Pietro Ballerini,

The Definition of Papal Infallibility at Vatican I

In the nineteenth century the theoretical underpinnings for a doctrine of papal infallibility underwent a profound transformation at the hands of the French Ultramontane philosopher Joseph de Maistre. De Maistre was a proponent of the restoration of the French monarchy. He saw in the French Revolution and in the Enlightenment itself an individualism corrosive to the fabric of society. As a figure of the nineteenth century, de Maistre subscribed to that period's romantic preoccupation with notions of organic unity. According to de Maistre, every society must possess a unifying principle that vivifies the organism. This is as true of the Church as it is of civil society. As outlined in his *Du pape* (1817), the pope exists as the unifying principle within the Church just as the monarch functions as the unifying principle in civil society. The effective interaction of these two societies requires a strong alliance between pope and king. De Maistre employed his monarchalist view of sovereignty to justify the doctrine of papal infallibility.[43] Recall that according to Tierney, the doctrine of papal infallibility emerged in the thirteenth century as a way of *limiting* papal sovereignty. In the thought of de Maistre, however, infallibility is conceived as a necessary condition for papal sovereignty. For him, sovereignty requires absolute authority, and absolute authority yields infallibility.

What de Maistre succeeded in doing was to recast the infallibility issue as a debate over papal sovereignty. And in a contentious century in which the papacy was being threatened by the incursion of liberalism and nationalism, there was a real sympathy in the Church for the plight of Pius IX and a desire to rally around the Pope. Many were convinced that only a strong papacy could withstand the attacks of liberalism and modernity. An adequate interpretion of the development of the definition on papal infallibility at Vatican I must take into

Alphonsus Liguori, Francesco Zaccaria, and Mauro Cappellari (later Pope Gregory XVI). He finds a consistent belief in papal infallibility but significant differences in the understanding of the scope and exercise of that infallibility. Michael D. Place, "The Response Due Noninfallible Papal Solicitude in Matters of Faith and Morals: A Study of Selected Eighteenth-Century Theologians" (Ph.D. diss., Catholic University of America, 1978) Ann Arbor: University Microfilms.

[43]For an excellent study of de Maistre's influence on Catholic Ultramontanism and the teaching of Vatican I, see Pottmeyer, *Unfehlbarkeit und Souveränität*.

account the influence of Ultramontanism, the name given to this program to strengthen papal authority.

The first council to be held in three hundred years, Vatican I, like Trent, was clearly a council of "reaction." Pope Pius IX's determination to snuff out the liberalizing tendencies of the age, reflected in his 1864 *Syllabus of Errors,* was the driving impulse behind his public announcement in 1867[44] of an impending council. It was relatively clear to all even before the council began that, apart from addressing the most pressing theological problem of the day, the relationship between faith and reason, Pius IX was bent on further centralizing Church authority in the papacy. Nevertheless, at the outset of the council it was not certain whether the question of papal infallibility would come up. There was already considerable politicking on both sides of the issue. Ultramontane journalists like Louis Veuillot, theologians like William George Ward, and prelates like Archbishop Manning of Westminster and Bishop Senestrey of Ratisbon were promoting rather sweeping views of papal authority that appeared to grant to the pope an absolute, personal, and separate infallibility. Dom Cuthbert Butler writes:

> Of course no trained theologian would accept such aberrations. Still the excesses of the New Ultramontanism, whether Veuillot's entirely untheological extravagances, or Ward's undue straining of infallibility beyond the traditional teaching of Catholic Ultramontane schools, or the extreme interpretations of the political and social import of the *Syllabus* . . . did exercise a profound influence on the atmosphere in which the Council was held.[45]

In response to these Ultramontane positions, theologians like Ignaz von Döllinger and bishops like Charles-Henri Maret and Felix Dupanloup of France protested vigorously against, at the minimum, the opportuneness of a council definition on the matter.[46]

During the council itself a long schema on the Church consisting of fifteen chapters was proposed for consideration. The draft was

[44]Already as far back as December 1864 Pius IX had informed the cardinals in Rome of his intention to convene a council.

[45]Dom Cuthbert Butler, *The Vatican Council* (London: Longmans, Green, 1930) 1:77.

[46]For a fuller consideration of this fear of the French bishops regarding extravagant claims to a doctrine of papal infallibility before the council see O'Gara, *Triumph in Defeat,* 68–85.

composed by the Roman theologian Clemens Schrader but met with early difficulties and was sent back to committee. Early in the council a petition was circulated requesting that the bishops define papal infallibility.[47] In fact, a separate text on papal infallibility had been drafted by members of the Ultramontane camp prior to the council. Against the protest of many bishops who were opposed to a definition, a decision was made to have all the material on the papacy, including the independent text on papal infallibility, considered before the rest of the schema on the Church. This material was eventually divided into four chapters, with the last dedicated to papal infallibility. The bishops were not able to consider the rest of the schema on the Church, as the council was suspended when the Italian troops entered Rome.

Among those in favor of a definition on papal infallibility there was a small group of extreme Ultramontanists who saw the enhancement of papal authority as the Church's best defense against nationalism and the liberal spirit of the age. Beyond these few, however, a greater majority of the bishops who supported a definition did so as much out of personal loyalty to the papacy as out of their own personal convictions regarding papal infallibility. The arguments of the minority opposed to the definition were quite varied. There were those who personally accepted at least some understanding of papal infallibility but thought that a solemn definition would likely be misunderstood both by governmental officials and by non-Catholic Christians. Others thought the doctrine was a novelty unsubstantiated by Scripture and tradition. Still others, especially among the French minority, were convinced that such a doctrine violated the fundamentally ecclesial character of the charism of infallibility. Stephen Duffy attributes this view to the minority bishops in general:

> The real concern of the minority was that somehow pope and Church not be severed. They wanted it clearly understood that when defining *ex cathedra* the pope is articulating the *sensus ecclesiae;* that he is acting not only as head, but as mouth of the body of Christ; that he teaches in union with the Church and under magisterium and infallibility. In other words, it was their concern to avoid the establishment of a papal infallibility that would be personal, absolute, and separate.[48]

The concerns of the minority led to the proposal of numerous emendations to the schema. While many of the minority left the council

---

[47] Ibid., 1–6.

[48] Stephen Duffy, "Interpretation: Vatican I," in *Papal Infallibility,* 64.

rather than vote against the final constitution, the fact that all these bishops eventually came to accept the council's teaching suggests that they were able to recognize in its final form a tolerable formulation of papal infallibility.[49]

What did Vatican I finally teach? In the beginning of the fourth chapter of *Pastor aeternus* the council moved from a consideration of papal primacy in general to the supreme teaching authority of the pope as part of that primacy. The purpose of this supreme teaching authority was to make "the saving teaching of Christ" available, un-contaminated, to the whole world.[50] The council wrote that in times past popes have

> defined as doctrines to be held those things which, by God's help, they knew to be in keeping with sacred scripture and the apostolic traditions. For the holy Spirit was promised to the successors of Peter not so that they might, by his revelation, make known some new doctrine, but that, by his assistance, they might religiously guard and faithfully expound the revelation or deposit of faith transmitted by the apostles.[51]

This represented a very important qualification. That which is defined must belong to Scripture and tradition (or be necessary for its faithful exposition); it cannot be a doctrinal novelty. The formal definition itself then reads as follows:

> Therefore . . . we . . . teach and define as a divinely revealed dogma that when the Roman Pontiff speaks *ex cathedra*, that is, when, in the exercise of his office as shepherd and teacher of all Christians, in virtue of his supreme apostolic authority, he defines a doctrine concerning faith or morals to be held by the whole church, he possesses,

---

[49]This is the central thesis of Margaret O'Gara's important work, namely that the French minority were operating out of a nascent ecclesiology of communion that saw the doctrine of papal infallibility, at least in its earliest formulations, as placing the papacy outside of the Church. She disputes August Hasler's view that the French bishops effectively "sold out" in subsequently accepting the papal definition. O'Gara persuasively demonstrates that the French bishops, at any rate, were able to accept the papal definition because its final form was open to an interpretation sympathetic to their more ecclesial view of infallibility, even if this view was not as explicitly developed as they would like. For a summary of her thesis see *Triumph in Defeat*, 221–55.

[50]The English translation I am using here comes from Tanner, *Decrees of the Ecumenical Councils*, 2:815–16.

[51]Ibid., 816.

by the divine assistance promised to him in blessed Peter, that infallibility which the divine Redeemer willed his church to enjoy in defining doctrine concerning faith or morals. Therefore, such definitions of the Roman pontiff are of themselves, and not by the consent of the church, irreformable.[52]

The definition follows the medieval tradition, which relates infallibility to the pope only insofar as he is "shepherd and teacher of all Christians." This infallibility can only be considered "personal" inasmuch as it pertains to the pope as officeholder. As Bishop Gasser noted, infallibility does not apply to the pope as private doctor.[53] More importantly, the council connected papal infallibility with that infallibility "which the divine Redeemer willed his church to enjoy." This clause was crucial to those minority bishops seeking to find an acceptable interpretation of the conciliar definition. It meant that papal infallibility could not be absolutely separated from the infallibility given to the whole Church. Many of the minority bishops wanted this connection between Church (and by Church most meant the bishops) and pope made more explicit.[54] Though their request for greater development of this connection was rejected, they were somewhat reassured by Bishop Gasser's insistence that the final text did not preclude the pope's general consultation of the bishops.

The most difficult pill for the minority bishops to swallow was the eleventh-hour addition of the final clause in the definition stating that these solemn definitions are irreformable "of themselves, and not by the consent of the Church *(ex sese autem non ex consensu ecclesiae)*." Following in the wake of attempts by the minority to introduce clauses that would strengthen the relationship between papal infallibility and the *consensus ecclesiae,* many viewed this late addition as a blatant act of insensitivity to their concerns.

There is a growing agreement among commentators that this final condition must be read in the light of a certain obsession at the council with the possible recurrence of Gallicanism. This late addition was

[52]Ibid.

[53]Mansi, 52, 1213.

[54]This was true not only of the French minority but of some German bishops as well, particularly Bishop Karl Joseph von Hefele of Rottenburg. For a study of the German minority at the council see Klaus Schatz, *Kirchenbild und päpstliche Unfehlbarkeit.*

a repudiation of the Gallican Articles and its presumed demand for a juridical determination of ecclesial consensus subsequent to a papal definition. It is only this kind of extrinsic juridical requirement that was being rejected. Gasser's authoritative interpretation confirms this reading. He states that what the council actually rejected in this clause was only the "strict and absolute necessity of seeking that consent."[55] The assumption embedded in this restrictive clause was that the pope possessed sufficient means for discerning the *sensus ecclesiae;* juridical validation, either before or after the definition, was both unnecessary and unduly restrictive. Georges Dejaifve contends that Vatican I accepted the *moral* necessity of the consent of the Church, rejecting only a *juridical* necessity.[56] Gustave Thils concurs and writes of this final condition:

> Moreover, that which is rejected by the Catholic conciliar declarations is the *absolute* necessity of a formal approbation of the church as a *sine qua non* condition of the value and validity of an infallible definition. . . . A theologian can perfectly defend the idea of the relative necessity (but not absolute) of the assent of the church, as a habitual condition (but not a *sine qua non*) of the value of infallibility.[57]

In the light of Gasser's *relatio* the conclusions of theologians like Dejaifve and Thils seem justified. Nevertheless, this reading is by no means explicit in the text, a fact that would have important consequences for subsequent interpretations of the teaching of Vatican I. It is ironic that the most controversial clause in the conciliar definition was included in reaction to what now appears to have been a simplistic reading of Gallicanism. Richard Costigan has made the case that the consent of the Church that Bossuet had in mind was, for the most part, *not* a subsequent juridical consent but the kind of natural consent that occurs whenever the faithful immediately recognize in a

---

[55]Mansi, 52, 1216.

[56]Georges Dejaifve, *Pape et éveques,* 130. Cf. Georges Dejaifve, "ex sese, non autem ex consensu ecclesiae," *Eastern Churches Quarterly* 14 (1962) 360–78; Heinrich Fries, "Ex sese, non ex consensu ecclesiae," in *Volke Gottes: Zum Kirchenverständnis der katholischen, evangelischen und anglikanischen Theologie,* ed. R. Bäumer and H. Dolch (Freiburg: Herder, 1967) 480–500; Avery Dulles, "A Moderate Infallibilism: An Ecumenical Approach," in *A Church to Believe In* (New York: Crossroad, 1982) 144–45.

[57]Thils, *Primauté et infaillibilité,* 190–91. See also Thils, *L'Infaillibilité pontificale,* 172–75.

formal teaching the substance of what they already in fact believe. He supports this with a compelling quotation from Bossuet's massive defense of the Gallican Articles: "When the successor of Peter pronounces from the common tradition in such a way that all recognize the sense of their own faith in his statement, then there is that consensus which provides pontifical judgments with their firm and unbendable strength."[58] This passage is remarkable for its similarity to Vatican II's claim that in any exercise of papal infallibility the consent of the faithful can never be lacking. Had the participants at Vatican I had a fuller appreciation of the ecclesiological subtlety of many of the Gallican writers, the controversial *ex sese* clause might have been avoided.

As it was, after Vatican I there developed two distinct lines of interpretation regarding papal infallibility. The first line of interpretation was decidedly "maximalist" in its assessment of papal authority. This view stressed the significance of the *ex sese* clause and was based on some of the more ecclesiologically questionable features of the council's treatment of the topic. First, the definition on papal infallibility was set in the context of a doctrine of papal primacy that lacked any extended consideration of the papacy's relationship to the whole college of bishops. Consequently the papacy was viewed as an altogether distinct locus of power and authority. Second, papal primacy was conceived in juridical categories without any substantial theological grounding. Third, the definition itself did not include explicitly the conditions and limits on the exercise of papal infallibility that were widely assumed by the council bishops in approving the definition (e.g., that episcopal consultation would be the norm prior to a solemn definition). These defects and lacunae left the door open for an Ultramontane, maximalist reading of the definition that was far more sweeping than the text itself warranted.

In the aftermath of the council one can also discover a second, alternative interpretation of the council definition. This interpretation, it now appears, was much more faithful to the intentions of the council fathers themselves. The German bishops published a pastoral letter on the council's teachings in 1870 that represented a more moderate reading of the definition on papal primacy and infallibility. Quite significantly, the letter received the official endorsement of

<hr/>

[58]Jacques-Bénigne Bossuet, *Defensio declarationis cleri Gallicani de ecclesiastica potestate* (Paris: Louis Vives, 1862–66) 9:162, as quoted in Costigan, "Bossuet and the Consensus of the Church," 667.

Pope Pius IX.[59] A similar interpretation was adopted by many members of the French minority. In fact, Margaret O'Gara attributes to the French minority a nascent ecclesiology of communion in which their understanding of the definition presupposed the collegiality of pope and bishops.[60] In England John Henry Newman also proposed a much more cautious and moderate interpretation of the conciliar definition.[61] It is this more moderate interpretation that would be accepted and reinforced at Vatican II.

Vatican II and the Recontextualization of Papal Infallibility

One of the oft noted ironies of the last two ecumenical councils is that the ecclesiological framework of the *minority* bishops at Vatican I, those bishops operating out of a more collegial understanding of Church authority and a strong sense of the Church's fidelity to Scripture and tradition, became the framework of the *majority* bishops at Vatican II. From this point of view Newman was indeed prescient in predicting that a future council would "trim the boat," redressing the papocentric imbalance created by Vatican I.[62] When Vatican II began its consideration of the Church, it became evident early on that the teaching of Vatican I on the papacy needed to be complemented by a much more developed understanding of two other components in the teaching ministry of the Church, namely the college of bishops[63] and the *sensus fidelium*.

The new *minority* at Vatican II, however, saw this attempt to recontextualize Vatican I as a thinly veiled conspiracy to undermine

---

[59]The bishops' letter and the pope's endorsement can be found in Mansi, 53, 917–23. These texts are discussed in Boyle, *Church Teaching Authority,* 134–35.

[60]O'Gara, *Triumph in Defeat,* 245–46.

[61]See especially his "Letter to the Duke of Norfolk," in *Newman and Gladstone: The Vatican Decrees,* (Notre Dame: Univ. of Notre Dame Press, 1962) 72–203. For more on Newman's understanding of papal infallibility see Wolfgang Klausnitzer, *Päpstliche Unfehlbarkeit bei Newman und Döllinger: Ein historisch-systematischer Vergleich* (Innsbruck: Tyrolia, 1980); John R. Page, *What Will Dr. Newman Do? John Henry Newman and Papal Infallibility, 1865–1875* (Collegeville: The Liturgical Press, 1994).

[62]Newman, *Letters and Diaries,* 27:310.

[63]This need to attend to the role of the episcopacy in particular was stressed by Paul VI in his opening address at the third session of the council. *Acta synodalia* III/1, 140–51.

papal primacy and infallibility. In light of the concerns of the minority, the politics of compromise required what Hermann Pottmeyer has called a method of "juxtaposition." According to this method, theological formulations reflecting two distinct schools of thought were not so much reconciled as juxtaposed to one another.[64] The bishops at Vatican II were careful to reiterate the teaching of Vatican I on papal primacy and papal infallibility. Thus *Lumen gentium* affirms the following: "For the Roman pontiff has, by virtue of his office as vicar of Christ and shepherd of the whole church, full, supreme and universal power over the church, a power he is always able to exercise freely" (*LG* 22).[65] However, juxtaposed to this reaffirmation of Vatican I's view of papal primacy is the following:

> [T]he order of bishops, which succeeds the college of apostles in teaching authority and pastoral government, and indeed in which the apostolic body continues to exist without interruption, *is also the subject of supreme and full power over the universal church*, provided it remains united with its head, the Roman pontiff, and never without its head; and this power can be exercised only with the consent of the Roman pontiff (*LG* 22, my emphasis).

This juxtaposition continues later, when, *after* considering the infallibility of the whole college of bishops, the council repeats Vatican I on papal infallibility but with some significant additions:

[64]"Special attention must be paid here to the method the Council used in linking two concerns: renewal of the Church and preservation of continuity. The method is essentially that of juxtaposition: alongside a doctrine or thesis couched in pre-conciliar language is set a doctrine or thesis that formulates some complementary aspect." Hermann J. Pottmeyer, "A New Phase in the Reception of Vatican II: Twenty Years of Interpretation of the Council," in *The Reception of Vatican II*, ed. Giuseppe Alberigo, Jean-Pierre Jossua, and Joseph A. Komonchak (Washington: Catholic Univ. of America Press, 1987) 37.

[65]In order to reassure the minority that this doctrine was not being compromised on the order of "higher authority," a *nota* was attached to the constitution that insisted that ecclesial communion, while spiritual, is nonetheless hierarchical and requires a "juridical form." It also reasserted the independence of the papacy: "The supreme pontiff, as supreme pastor of the Church, can exercise his power at all times as he thinks best, as is required by his very function" (no. 4). This *nota* reflects a regrettable instance of the more juridical view of papal authority.

The Roman pontiff, head of the college of bishops, by virtue of his office, enjoys this infallibility when, as supreme shepherd and teacher of all Christ's faithful, who confirms his brethren in the faith, he proclaims in a definitive act a doctrine on faith or morals. Therefore, his definitions are rightly said to be irreformable of themselves, and not from the consent of the church, for they are delivered with the assistance of the Holy Spirit which was promised to him in blessed Peter; and therefore they have no need of approval from others nor do they admit any appeal to any other judgment. For then the Roman pontiff is not delivering a judgment as a private person, but as the supreme teacher of the universal church, in whom the church's own charism of infallibility individually exists, he expounds or defends a doctrine of the catholic faith. The infallibility promised to the church exists also in the body of bishops when, along with the successor of Peter, it exercises the supreme teaching office. The assent of the church, however, can never fail to be given to these definitions on account of the activity of the same holy Spirit, by which the whole flock of Christ is preserved in the unity of faith and makes progress.

But when the Roman pontiff or the body of bishops together with him define a decision, they do so in accordance with revelation itself, by which all are obliged to abide and to which all must conform. This revelation, as written or as handed down in tradition, is transmitted in its entirety through the lawful succession of bishops and in the first place through the care of the Roman pontiff himself; and in the light of the Spirit of truth, this revelation is sacredly preserved in the church and faithfully expounded. The Roman pontiff and the bishops, in virtue of their office and the seriousness of the matter, work sedulously through the appropriate means duly to investigate this revelation and give it suitable expression. However, they do not accept any new public revelation as belonging to the divine deposit of faith (*LG* 25).

The council incorporated into its formulation of the doctrine of papal infallibility several clarifications that at Vatican I were left to Bishop Gasser to introduce in his explanatory *relatio:* (1) the council explicitly distinguished between the pope as universal pastor and as private person; (2) it mentioned the need for the pope to employ the appropriate means for investigation, and more importantly, (3) it claimed that in the proper exercise of the extraordinary magisterium the consent of the whole Church can never be lacking.

Vatican II's teaching on collegiality makes explicit what one could only infer from Vatican I. The bishops at Vatican II affirmed that the pope and college can be distinguished but not separated, that even a papal exercise of the extraordinary magisterium in some way involves the whole college, and consequently that consultation and ongoing conversation between pope and college is a moral if not a juridical necessity for a solemn papal definition. From the perspective of Vatican II's understanding of collegiality, it is evident that the famous *ex sese* condition, that papal definitions are irreformable in themselves and not by the consent of the Church, qualifies only the definitions themselves, which need no further juridical validation. It does not refer to the teaching activity of the pope, who must continue to manifest a real communion with the college.[66]

This consent of the Church must always accompany a valid solemn definition because of the unity of the Holy Spirit, who assists the whole Church in coming to truth. This leads us to perhaps the most significant "new context" for considering papal infallibility, the infallibility of the whole people of God. I have already considered this infallibility in chapters 3 and 5, and I will return to it in the next chapter, so it must be sufficient here to stress this teaching's implications for papal infallibility. Even Vatican I explicitly related papal infallibility to that infallibility given to the whole Church. Vatican II simply amplified that claim in terms of the doctrine of the *sensus fidelium*. The shift in Vatican II's consideration of papal infallibility can be formulated in this way: since the pope always acts as head of the college, papal infallibility is only intelligible in the light of the infallibility of the whole college of bishops. Since the college of bishops is inextricably linked to the communion of Churches, the infallibility of the college of bishops, in turn, depends on the infallibility of the people of God. Only from within an ecclesiology of communion can the teaching of the pope and bishops, who function as judges of the faith *(judices fidei),* be properly correlated to the testimony of all the baptized, who serve as witnesses to the one apostolic faith *(testes fidei).*

The Problem of Verification

Finally, it is necessary to return to a problem alluded to in the last chapter with respect to the ordinary universal magisterium, namely, the problem of verification. There is an important difference between the actual fulfillment of certain conditions for the exercise of the

[66]Karl Rahner, "Dogmatic Constitution on the Church: Chapter Three," in *Commentary on the Documents of Vatican II,* ed. Herbert Vorgrimler (New York: Crossroad, 1989) 1:213.

charism of infallibility (e.g., those outlined by Vatican I for an *ex cathedra* definition) and the verification of that fulfillment. Is it enough, for example, for a pope or council to claim the charism of infallibility for a particular doctrinal judgment? Could a pope or council not be mistaken in their judgment that these conditions have been fulfilled? Put differently, is it legitimate for theologians in particular to investigate whether *in fact* the requisite conditions for a solemn definition have been fulfilled?

If it is true that there is no *juridical* authority superior to the college and its head, nevertheless, the Church itself has a moral obligation to discern whether prescribed conditions have in fact been fulfilled.[67] In practice this process of verification will generally be undertaken by theologians. It will be their task to question whether that which was defined falls within the prescribed scope of dogmatic teaching (faith and morals), whether a pope and/or council was free of coercion, whether the definition was preceded by reasonable investigation of Scripture and tradition, and whether a true and not merely formal communion has been preserved by pope and bishops. Also important for this question of verification is Vatican II's insistence that in the instance of a solemn definition a reception by the faithful ultimately cannot be lacking. Should a presumably valid exercise of the extraordinary magisterium fail to be received over time by the whole people of God, that lack of reception (admittedly difficult to verify) could indicate that some other condition had not in fact been fulfilled, thereby rendering the definition invalid.

Conclusion

In this chapter I have considered the exercise of the extraordinary magisterium both in terms of its historical development and its contemporary contextualization in the light of Vatican II. It might be helpful to summarize several fundamental principles that frame a proper understanding of this particular exercise of doctrinal teaching authority.

It is the whole college of bishops that possesses supreme doctrinal teaching authority within the Church. While Vatican II did not say so explicitly, I agree with Rahner, Congar, and others who contend that

---

[67]Cf. Sullivan, *Magisterium,* 106–9; Dulles, *A Church to Believe In,* 138–42; Walter Kasper, "Zur Diskussion um das Problem der Unfehlbarkeit," *Stimmen der Zeit* 188 (1972) 368.

the unity of supreme authority demands that there be one formal subject for the concrete exercise of supreme teaching authority in the Church, the college of bishops. The council's consistent attempt to place traditional claims regarding the papacy in the context of episcopal collegiality supports this assumption.

This college can define doctrine with the charism of infallibility when it manifests this supreme authority in one of two collegial forms, explicitly through a formal act of the college of bishops (e.g., in a conciliar definition) or implicitly through a formal act of the bishop of Rome, who is always at the same time head of the college of bishops (e.g., an ex cathedra *papal definition).* Vatican II's treatment of the episcopacy constituted a break from the zero-sum ecclesiology that sees pope and college as competing loci of power and authority. As both member and head of the college, the pope always acts collegially, that is, in a way that symbolically manifests the *sensus* or "mind" of the college. This claim seriously relativizes any distinction between a solemn definition by the whole college of bishops (generally in an ecumenical council) and a solemn definition by a pope. Both demand clear expressions of manifest episcopal communion, which must be more than a formal obedience of bishops to pope. This collegiality assumes a real communion constituted by honest, open-ended conversation and mutual inquiry. While Vatican II reiterated the possibility of the pope exercising the charism of infallibility in a doctrinal judgment apart from the explicit participation of the college, it did not mean that this should be the norm. Going as far back as St. Thomas, we saw the common assumption that a pope would, in the normal course of affairs, act in concert with the whole college. Given the fundamental unity of these two manifestations of the extraordinary magisterium, and given ecumenical perceptions that an imperial style of papal ministry is deeply embedded in Roman Catholic doctrine, it will be important to stress the collegial dimension of any exercise of the extraordinary magisterium.

Episcopal collegiality is grounded in the communion of Churches. The collegial unity of bishops and pope as one supreme authority in the Church cannot be so presented as to portray the college as an external authority or "governing board" over the whole Church. The pope possesses authority to teach as bishop of the local Church of Rome and head of the college, and the bishops have authority to teach precisely as pastors of local Churches. The faith that is authoritatively proclaimed by the college of bishops cannot be separated from the faith that is lived by the Churches whose pastors the bishops are. The bishops have authority as bishops *within,* not *over* their Churches.

The infallibility of the episcopal college (in both of its collegial manifestations) is inextricably linked to the infallibility of the whole people of God. Vatican II's teaching that God's word is given to the whole Church suggests that infallible teaching acts formalize the faith of the whole people of God. It follows that more fully attending to the infallibility of the whole people of God will likely mean relativizing the role of propositional articulations of the faith. The interpretation of defined dogma will always look to the lived faith of the whole Church as the dogma's interpretive "horizon."

In part 3 of this volume I have considered the various exercises of doctrinal teaching authority in the Church. In the fourth part of this volume I wish to consider a topic I have already discussed in several contexts in the preceding chapters, namely the reception of doctrinal teaching by the faithful. The place of the faithful has often been the missing piece of the puzzle in previous theologies of doctrinal teaching authority. In chapter 8 I will consider the corporate role of the faithful in the reception of Church teaching and in chapter 9 the responsibility of the individual believer.

For Further Reading

The Infallibility of Ecumenical Councils

Bermejo, Luis. *Infallibility on Trial: Church, Conciliarity, and Communion.* Westminster: Christian Classics, 1992.

Burns, Patrick J. "Communion, Councils, and Collegiality: Some Catholic Reflections." In *Papal Primacy and the Universal Church.* Ed. P. C. Empie and T. A. Murphy, 151–72. Minneapolis: Augsburg, 1974.

Congar, Yves. "The Council as an Assembly and the Church as essentially Conciliar." In *Theologians Today: Yves Congar,* 103–28. London and New York: Sheed & Ward, 1972.

Dvornik, Francis. *The Ecumenical Councils.* Vol. 82 of 20th Century Encyclopedia of Catholicism. New York: Hawthorn, 1961.

Fransen, Piet. "The Authority of the Councils." In *Problems of Authority*, ed. J. M. Todd, 43–78. Baltimore: Helicon, 1962.

Huizing, Peter and Knut Walf, eds. *The Ecumenical Council.* Concilium 167. New York: Seabury, 1983.

Sullivan, Francis A. *Magisterium: Teaching Authority in the Catholic Church.* New York: Paulist, 1983, especially 84–90.

──────. *Creative Fidelity. Weighing and Interpreting Documents of the Magisterium.* New York: Paulist, 1996.

Papal Infallibility

Congar, Yves. "St. Thomas Aquinas and the Infallibility of the Papal Magisterium." *Thomist* 38 (1974) 81–105.

Dionne, J. Robert. *The Papacy and the Church: A Study of Praxis and Reception in Ecumenical Perspective.* New York: Philosophical Library, 1987.

Dulles, Avery. "A Moderate Infallibilism: An Ecumenical Approach." In *A Church to Believe In*, 133–48. New York: Crossroad, 1982.

Eno, Robert B. *The Rise of the Papacy.* Wilmington: Glazier, 1990.

Ford, John T. "Infallibility: A Review of Recent Studies." *Theological Studies* 40 (1979) 273–305.

Heft, James. *John XXII and Papal Teaching Authority.* Toronto: Mellon, 1986.

Jalland, Trevor. *Church and Papacy.* London: SPCK, 1944.

McSorley, Harry. "Some Forgotten Truths About the Petrine Ministry." *Journal of Ecumenical Studies* 11 (1974) 208–37.

Sullivan, Francis A. *Magisterium: Teaching Authority in the Catholic Church.* New York: Paulist, 1983, especially 90–118.

Tekippe, Terry, ed. *Papal Infallibility: An Application of Lonergan's Theological Method.* Washington: Univ. Press of America, 1983.

Tierney, Brian. *Origins of Papal Infallibility, 1150–1350.* Leiden: Brill, 1972.

Vatican I on Papal Infallibility

Butler, Dom Cuthbert. *The Vatican Council.* London: Longmans, Green, 1930.

Cwiekowski, Frederick J. *The English Bishops and the First Vatican Council.* Louvain: Publications Universitaires de Louvain, 1971.

Hennesey, James. *The First Council of the Vatican: The American Experience.* New York: Herder & Herder, 1963.

Newman and Gladstone: The Vatican Decrees. Notre Dame: Univ. of Notre Dame Press, 1962.

O'Gara, Margaret. *Triumph in Defeat: Infallibility, Vatican I, and the French Minority Bishops.* Washington: The Catholic Univ. of America Press, 1988.

Part Four
The Reception of Church Teaching

8

Receiving and Responding to the Word: Corporate Reception of Church Teaching

A central theme running throughout this work holds that all reflection on doctrinal teaching authority in the Church must begin with the affirmation that divine revelation, the word of God, has been given to the whole Christian community *qua* community. This emphasis on the whole community as the recipient of God's word and its implications for a theology of doctrinal teaching authority was, in general, not adequately integrated into the neo-Scholastic manuals' treatment of the topic. The documents of Vatican II gave this topic much more attention and it has become an important subject in postconciliar ecclesiology. For that reason, in addition to the traditional consideration of teaching authority in terms of its subject (Part 1), object (Part 2), and mode of exercise (Part 3), in the final part of this volume I wish to consider a fourth dimension of doctrinal teaching authority, namely the corporate and individual *reception* of doctrinal teaching. This chapter will attend to reception as an explicitly corporate or ecclesial process, while chapter 9 will consider one's individual response to Church teaching as a participation in ecclesial reception.

This appreciation of the whole Church, and not simply the college of bishops, as the recipient of God's divine revelation has been enhanced by the twentieth-century retrieval of two central concepts that have been discussed earlier in this volume: ecclesial reception, and the *sensus fidelium*.

The Indispensable Role of the People of God in "Receiving" God's Word

Scholarly study of the notion of ecclesial reception grew out of the flourishing studies in patristic and medieval theology in the 1940s, 1950s, and 1960s. The ecclesiological developments of Vatican II provided a new impetus for the study of this topic. Broadly speaking, ecclesial reception refers to the process by which some teaching, ritual, discipline, or law is assimilated into the life of the Church.[1] According to Edward Kilmartin, the patristic and medieval concept of reception was "a tributary of the dominant ecclesiology of that age: a communion ecclesiology."[2] In the Church of the first millennium "reception" involved the dynamic process by which local Churches accepted as their own a conciliar teaching, liturgical rite, or disciplinary practice, the origin of which came from beyond their own community. The process of ecclesial reception involved an active discernment by the Churches regarding the authenticity of that which was being "received." This process included not just the discernment that took place prior to the formal acceptance of a teaching, rite, or discipline but its assimilation into the life of the community as well. In

---

[1]The groundbreaking work on this topic was done by Alois Grillmeier and Yves Congar. Cf. Alois Grillmeier, "Konzil und Rezeption: Methodische Bemerkungen zu einem Thema der ökumenischen Diskussion der Gegenwart," *Theologie und Philosophie* 45 (1970) 321-52 and Yves Congar, "La 'réception' comme réalité ecclésiologique," *Revue des sciences philosophiques et théologiques* 56 (1972) 369–403. For an abbreviated English translation see Yves Congar, "Reception as an Ecclesiological Reality," in *Election and Consensus in the Church,* Concilium 77, ed. Giuseppe Alberigo and Anton Weiler (New York: Herder, 1972) 43–68. While Grillmeier's study focused on the reception of law, Congar viewed reception much more broadly as a fundamental ecclesial process. As an interesting aside, both of these theologians were created cardinal by John Paul II in the 1994 consistory in recognition of their lifelong service to the Church. For other notable studies on the topic see Hermann J. Pottmeyer, "Reception and Submission," *The Jurist* 51 (1991) 269–92; Thomas Rausch, "Reception Past and Present," *Theological Studies* 47 (1986) 497–508; Edward Kilmartin, "Reception in History: An Ecclesiological Phenomenon and Its Significance," *Journal of Ecumenical Studies* 21 (1984) 34–54; W. Hryniewicz, "Die ekklesiale Rezeption in der Sicht der orthodoxen Theologie," *Theologie und Glaube* 65 (1975) 250–66.

[2]Kilmartin, "Reception in History," 34.

other words, when a community accepted a particular doctrinal formulation, for example, the community itself was transformed in the process of making that doctrine its own. Reception meant not mere acceptance but transformation, both of the receiving community and that which was received.

When the Church of the late Middle Ages and Counter Reformation moved away from an ecclesiology of communion in favor of a more pyramidical or hierocratic view of the Church, the role of ecclesial reception diminished. As Congar observes:

> The notion of reception . . . is excluded (or even expressly rejected) when for all the foregoing there is substituted a wholly pyramidal conception of the Church as a mass totally determined by its summit, in which (quite apart from any consideration of a largely private spirituality) there is hardly any mention of the Holy Spirit other than as the guarantor of an infallibility of hierarchical courts, and where the conciliar decrees themselves become papal decrees "sacro approbante concilio."[3]

During the late Middle Ages the dynamic, theological understanding of reception was replaced by a view of reception governed by the juridical notion of obedience. To receive a doctrine in this view meant to be obedient to that which was commanded or imposed. Lost was the important difference between a law issued by command or decree and the gospel of Jesus Christ proclaimed in doctrinal form. The paradigm of command-obedience extended beyond its proper juridical sphere to influence the entire teaching ministry of the Church. It was the *ressourcement* of patristic studies in the 1940s that allowed contemporary ecclesiology to recover the earlier, more dynamic view of reception as it was experienced in the Church of the first millennium.

How does the patristic concept of reception inform our understanding of teaching authority in the Church? The primary consequence is that one can no longer artificially separate the ecclesial moment when a teaching is first promulgated, or a rite or discipline imposed, from its reception by the Churches. Congar insists that "reception is no more than the extension or prolongation of the conciliar process: it is associated with the same essential 'conciliarity' of the Church."[4] By correlating reception with conciliarity, Congar helps

---

[3]Congar, "Reception as an Ecclesiological Reality," 60.
[4]Ibid., 64.

direct our attention to the quality of ecclesial relationship that is essential for a proper understanding of the enunciation of God's word in the Christian community.

In an ecclesiology of communion the deposit of faith given to the Church is not so much a filing cabinet of propositional truths as it is a living word sustained by the life of the Church itself. God's word is enunciated in the proclamation of the Scriptures, in the life stories of the newly baptized, in the celebration of the liturgy, and in the reflection of believers struggling to incarnate the gospel in the workplace and in their homes. In other words, the emergence of God's word depends not simply on a discrete teaching act but on a particular set of communal relationships. When reception no longer means simply obedient submission but active appropriation, it can illuminate the interrelational foundations of ecclesial life. Terms like "reception," "conciliarity," and "communion," when fully developed and properly correlated one to another, negate any isolation of a discrete teaching transaction between teacher and learner from the to-and-fro movement of proclamation, reception, assimilation, and transformation, which constitutes the life of the Church. A true reappropriation of ecclesial reception will invariably shift focus from the teaching office considered in isolation to the quality of ecclesial life itself, in which the exercise of doctrinal teaching authority can only be a contributing even if necessary element.

The *Sensus Fidelium*

More recent theological literature has attended to another ecclesiological concept closely related to ecclesial reception, namely the *sensus fidelium.*[5] While this term would not always be employed ex-

---

[5] For a comprehensive assessment of the literature see John Burkhard, "*Sensus Fidei:* Theological Reflection Since Vatican II," *Heythrop Journal* 34 (1993) 41–59, 137–59. Cf. John Burkhard, "*Sensus fidei*: Meaning, Role, and Future of a Teaching of Vatican II," *Louvain Studies* 17 (1992) 18–34; Wolfgang Beinert, "Das Finden und Verkünden der Wahrheit in der Gemeinschaft der Kirche," *Catholica* 43 (1989) 1–30; Edmund J. Dobbin, "*Sensus Fidelium* Reconsidered," *New Theology Review* 2 (1989) 48–64; Jan Kerkhofs, "Le Peuple de Dieu est-il infaillible? L'Importance du sensus fidelium dans l'Église post-conciliaire," *Freiburger Zeitschrift für Philosophie und Theologie* 35 (1988) 3–19; Leo Scheffczyk, "Sensus Fidelium—Witness on the Part

plicitly, the fundamental concept, namely the inerrancy of the faith of the whole community of believers, can be traced back to the very origins of Christianity. According to Wolfgang Beinert the *consensus omnium,* or universal belief of the faithful, played an important role in the Church's preservation of apostolic tradition up through the Middle Ages. Like Kilmartin he credits this to the ecclesiology of communion dominant in the first millennium.[6] Since this ecclesiology did not isolate one part of the Church, for example, the hierarchy, from the life of the whole Church, a commitment to the importance of the testimony of the faithful was only natural.

However, even with the shift from this ecclesiology of communion to a more juridical conception of the Church during the late Middle Ages, the basic conviction endured regarding the centrality of the witness of all the faithful. Gustave Thils finds evidence of this conviction in the period from the sixteenth to the nineteenth century. While ecclesiology during the period between Trent and Vatican I was dominated by anti-Protestant polemics that stressed the legitimacy of the institutional dimension of the Church, important writers like Melchior Cano in the sixteenth century, Jacques Bossuet in the seventeenth century, C.-R. Billuart in the eighteenth century, and Giovanni Perrone, Johann Adam Möhler, and John Henry Newman in the

---

of the Community," *Communio* 15 (1988) 182–98; Heinrich Fries, "Sensus Fidelium: Die Theologie zwischen dem Lehramt der Hierarchie und dem Lehramt der Gläubigen," in *Theologe und Hierarch,* ed. J. Pfammater and E. Christen (Zürich: Benziger, 1988) 55–77; Herbert Vorgrimler, "From *Sensus Fidei* to *Consensus Fidelium,*" in *The Teaching Authority of Believers,* Concilium 180, ed. Johann Baptist Metz and Edward Schillebeeckx (Edinburgh: T. & T. Clark, 1985) 3–11; Wald Wagner, "Glaubenssinn, Glaubenszustimmung und Glaubenskonsenz," *Theologie und Glaube* 69 (1979) 263–71; J.-M. R. Tillard, "Sensus Fidelium," *One in Christ* 11 (1975) 2–29; William M. Thompson, "*Sensus Fidelium* and Infallibility," *American Ecclesiastical Review* 167 (1973) 45–86; Wolfgang Beinert, "Bedeutung und Begründung des Glaubenssinnes (Sensus Fidei) als eines dogmatischen Erkenntniskriteriums," *Catholica* 25 (1971) 271–303; John W. Glaser, "Authority, Connatural Knowledge, and the Spontaneous Judgment of the Faithful," *Theological Studies* 29 (1968) 742–51; Gustave Thils, *L'infaillibilité du peuple chrétien "in credendo": Notes de théologie posttridentine* (Paris: Desclée, 1963).

[6]Beinert, "Bedeutung und Begründung," 275. For other historical surveys of the notion of the *sensus fidelium,* see Thompson, "*Sensus Fidelium* and Infallibility"; Thils, *L'infaillibilité du peuple chrétien.*

nineteenth century would continue to insist on the ecclesiological significance of the witness of the faithful.

Newman's treatment of the topic deserves special attention because of the important role it played in his ecclesiology. In his essay *On Consulting the Faithful*[7] he developed a particularly historical and organic understanding of the *sensus fidelium*. His earlier study of the Arian controversy had already led him to the conclusion that at least in that one historical instance the orthodoxy of the Christian faith was preserved not by the episcopate but by the belief of the faithful. On this basis he felt it natural and wholly traditional that the ecclesiastical magisterium ought to consult the faithful on the substance of their belief before offering authoritative pronouncements. Newman possessed a subtle and complex appreciation for the dialectical movement of the Church's journey toward truth. This view prevented him from placing the testimony of the faithful and the authoritative teaching of the ecclesiastical magisterium in opposition. Jeremy Miller has characterized this movement in three distinct moments.[8] First there is the *articulation,* or expression, of the Christian faith in liturgy, devotional practices, religious art, and the like. The second moment is characterized as *pedagogy,* in which the ecclesiastical magisterium discerns that which is articulated in the faith of the baptized and authoritatively represents that faith in propositional form. The final moment is *reception,* in which the faithful either do or do not recognize the faith authoritatively proclaimed as their own. This more organic understanding of the *sensus fidelium* was similar at numerous points to the ancient ecclesiology of communion. This process of *articulation, pedagogy,* and *reception* suggests a spiral-like movement in the Church's traditioning process: *articulation* leads to *pedagogy* leads to *reception,* which in turn engenders a new articulation. This spiral-like movement can be helpful in dispelling the tendency toward a linear conception of Church teaching, which either starts with the deposit of faith, which first resides in the hierarchy and then is being dispensed to the faithful (the Roman Catholic tendency) or with the deposit of faith residing in the community and then being given formal expression in the teaching of the Church's ministers (the Protestant tendency).

---

[7] John Henry Newman, *On Consulting the Faithful in Matters of Doctrine,* ed. John Coulson (1859; reprint Kansas City: Sheed & Ward, 1961).

[8] Jeremy Miller, *John Henry Newman on the Idea of the Church* (Shepherdstown: Patmos, 1987) 151–52.

It is only after Vatican I, with the Ultramontane preoccupation with questions of papal authority, that we find a restriction in the scope and significance of the *sensus fidelium*.[9] During the period between Vatican I and Vatican II the testimony of the faith of all believers was (with important exceptions) reduced in many of the Latin seminary manuals to a passive mirroring of magisterial teaching.[10]

Vatican II, however, returned to a view of the *sensus fidelium* more reminiscent of Newman than the manuals. The council did not actually use the term *sensus fidelium* but spoke rather of a *sensus fidei*, referring to the sense or instinct of faith given to all the baptized. This notion is found in article 12 of *Lumen gentium*. The passage appears in the second chapter of the constitution on the people of God, *preceding* the chapters on the hierarchy and laity. This suggests one of the most important contributions of this term, namely, its focus on the witness of the whole Church before any consideration of specialized ecclesial roles.[11]

> The holy people of God has a share, too, in the prophetic role of Christ, when it renders him a living witness, especially through a life of faith and charity, and when it offers to God a sacrifice of praise, the tribute of lips that honour his name. *The universal body of the faithful who have received the anointing of the holy one, cannot be mistaken in belief.* It displays this particular quality through a supernatural sense of the faith in the whole people when "from the bishops to the last of the faithful laity," it expresses the consent of all in matters of faith and morals. Through this sense of faith which is aroused and sustained by the Spirit of truth, the people of God, under the guidance of the sacred magisterium to which it is faithfully obedient, receives no longer the words of human beings but truly the word of God; it adheres indefectibly to "the faith which was once for all delivered to the saints"; it penetrates more deeply into that same faith through right judgment and applies it more fully to life (*LG* 12, my emphasis).

Each believer, by virtue of baptism, has a supernatural instinct or sense of the faith that allows each to recognize divine revelation and to respond to it in faith. The infallibility of the whole people of God,

---

[9]Burkhard, "*Sensus fidei*: Meaning, Role, and Future," 19–23.

[10]Cf. Johann Baptist Franzelin, *De Divina Traditione et Scriptura*, 4th ed. (Rome: Congregation for the Propagation of the Faith, 1896) 104ff.

[11]Burkhard, "*Sensus fidei*: Meaning, Role, and Future," 26.

however, does not refer to the individual exercise of this *sensus fidei* but to the corporate belief of the whole people of God. Thus we must also speak of the sense of the whole faithful (*sensus fidelium*), namely, that which the whole people of God in fact believe. When the faithful are united in their belief, possessing a *consensus* regarding a matter of faith, we can speak of a *consensus fidelium*.[12] It is in this situation, when in fact all the faithful are united in their belief, that the charism of infallibility is operative.

The above conciliar passage lays emphasis on the faith of all the baptized "from the bishops down to the last member of the laity." It is important to resist the temptation to reduce the *sensus fidelium* to the laity. To submit to this would be to further exacerbate a tendency to play various sectors of the Church against one another. Including the clergy within the sphere of the *sensus fidelium* serves as an important reminder that even the authoritative teachers of the Church are also learners, members of the baptized who receive the teaching of Christ, are transformed by that encounter, and strive to live that gospel in their daily lives.

That the council did not conceive of the *sensus fidei* in some vague, passive sense is reflected in its conjoining of the *sensus fidei* to a more pneumatological approach to ecclesial ministry. Article 4 of *Lumen gentium* affirms the diversity of gifts, "hierarchical and charismatic," which both rejuvenates the Church and assists it in the fulfillment of its mission. This is reaffirmed later in article 12, which sees the renewal and building up of the Church accomplished by the gifts that the Spirit has apportioned to all believers. While there is no diminishment of the clear differentiation of ministries and gifts exercised in the Church, the emphasis is placed on their unity in the one Spirit. In article 12 and again later in article 35, *Lumen gentium* asserts that the prophetic office of Christ is fulfilled "not only through the hierarchy who teach in his name and by his power, but also through the laity whom he constitutes his witnesses and equips with an understanding of the faith and a grace of speech precisely so that the power of the gospel may shine forth in the daily life of family and society" (*LG* 35). It is impossible to underestimate the significance of this shift from a two-tiered Church to one characterized by mutual co-

---

[12]Here I follow Francis Sullivan's understanding of these terms. Cf. his *Magisterium: Teaching Authority in the Catholic Church* (New York: Paulist, 1983) 21–23.

operation and a rich diversity of gifts and ministries grounded in the common faith of baptism.

Ecclesial Reception and Juridical Validation

The implications of recent studies on ecclesial reception and the *sensus fidelium* have occasionally been resisted out of fear of a new Gallicanism or conciliarism. Ironically, this fear arises out of a largely juridical framework. The assumption is that in resurrecting the notion of reception theologians are attempting to impose the reception or consent of the faithful as a juridical requirement for a doctrinal teaching's authenticity. However, as contemporary theologians have insisted, reception is not concerned with the juridical validity or even veracity of a teaching but with its efficacy.[13] A teaching that has not been "received" is not, for that reason, necessarily false. The claim is, in fact, more empirical in character. A teaching that is not received is not efficacious; it has no transformative power within the community. In short, a nonreceived teaching becomes irrelevant to the life of the community. This may be the situation in which the Catholic Church now finds itself with respect to Pope Paul VI's encyclical *Humanae vitae*. Prescinding from the truth or falsity of the Church's official position on artificial contraception, it is an empirical fact that this teaching has not been received by large segments of the Church today. For many Catholics, Church teaching on the morality of contraception is not so much rejected as ignored. In this situation, the ecclesiastical magisterium must avoid the temptation to simply "shout louder" and instead engage in an honest inquiry after the underlying reasons for this nonreception. Is the resistance to this teaching rooted in nontheological factors, for example, cultural pressures, or is it theological in nature and a manifestation of the *sensus fidelium?*

Reception often involves a long historical process. Universal reception of a papal or conciliar teaching has frequently taken decades, if not centuries. Looking back to certain points in the history of the reception of a given doctrine, we can better recognize the prophetic character of those who continued to proclaim a teaching that had not yet been received. St. Athanasius's steadfast proclamation of the

---

[13]H. Bacht, "Vom Lehramt der Kirche und in der Kirche," *Catholica* 25 (1971) 144–67, see especially 157ff.

Nicene doctrine in the face of protracted opposition is a classic example of the prophetic quality of a teaching that, up to a certain point in time, had not yet been received universally. It remains to be seen whether current Church teaching like that on contraception belongs in the same category.[14]

Reception and Inculturation

If the notion of reception is to be theologically useful today, we cannot remain content with a historical retrieval of the patristic understanding of reception. In our modern situation the concept of reception takes on a new significance that was only dimly acknowledged before Vatican II. This new significance is due to the heightened appreciation of culture as a constitutive characteristic of human existence. In the Pastoral Constitution on the Church in the Modern World, *Gaudium et spes,* the bishops state: "It is a feature of the human person that [he or she] can attain to real and full humanity only through culture; that is, by cultivating the goods of nature and values. Wherever human life is concerned, therefore, nature and culture are very intimately connected." The council goes on to define precisely what it means by "culture":

> The term "culture" in general refers to everything by which we perfect and develop our many spiritual and physical endowments; applying ourselves through knowledge and effort to bring the earth within our power; developing ways of behaving and institutions, we make life in society more human, whether in the family or in the civil sphere as a whole; in the course of time we express, share and preserve in our works great spiritual experiences and aspirations to contribute to the progress of many people, even of the whole human race. Human culture thus necessarily takes on a historical and social aspect. . . . In this sense one can talk of a plurality of cultures. The variety of ways in which objects are utilised, labour is applied, the self is expressed, religion is practised, customary ways of behaving take shape, laws and juridical institutions are established, the sciences and arts develop, and beauty is pursued, all give rise to different conditions of life in common, and different expressions in the structuring of life's resources. In

[14]See John Thiel's thoughtful reflections on nonreception as an indication of what he calls "dramatically developing doctrine." John E. Thiel, "Tradition and Authoritative Reasoning," *Theological Studies* 56 (December 1995) 627–51.

this way the handing on of customs becomes an inheritance peculiar to each human community, and an identifiable historical environment is established to receive people of every race and age and to provide them with the resources to cultivate their human and social life (*GS* 53).

Human culture is not something strictly external, like a costume we choose to put on or take off at will; it pertains to the very substance of our lives. Human culture is realized in social institutions and customs, in the particular form of our work and play, in the way we grieve and the way we celebrate.

It follows, then, that far from being a matter indifferent to the life of faith, human culture enriches the Christian life. At Vatican II the bishops demonstrated a much greater appreciation for the plurality of human cultures as a manifestation of the plenitude of God's creation (cf. *LG* 13; *AG* 22). As the Church fulfills its mission in the proclamation of the good news of Jesus Christ to all nations, it recognizes that this saving gospel, the foundation of our Christian unity, must take shape in and through human culture. To some extent each culture will express the one faith in its own way. As Pope Paul VI put it in his apostolic exhortation *"On Evangelization in the Modern World," Evangelii nuntiandi,* "In the mind of the Lord the Church is universal by vocation and mission, but when she puts down her roots in a variety of cultural, social and human terrains, she takes on different external expressions and appearances in each part of the world" (*EN* 62). Pope John Paul II has made much the same point. "The synthesis between culture and faith is not just a demand of culture, but also of faith. . . . A faith which does not become culture is a faith which has not been fully received, not thoroughly thought through, not faithfully lived out."[15]

This emphasis on what has come to be known as "inculturation" is an important part of a contemporary understanding of the ecclesial dynamics of reception. However, "inculturation" has come to mean many different things to different people.[16] Robert Schreiter considers "inculturation" under the category of local theologies. According to

---

[15]*L'Osservatore Romano,* English ed. (June 28, 1982) 7.

[16]This consideration of inculturation draws from Robert Schreiter's *Constructing Local Theologies* (Maryknoll: Orbis, 1985) 6–21. Other important works on the topic include Stephen B. Bevans, *Models of Contextual Theology* (Maryknoll: Orbis, 1992); Anthony J. Gittins, *Gifts and Strangers: Meeting the Challenge of Inculturation* (New York: Paulist, 1989); Aylward Shorter, *Toward a Theology of Inculturation* (Maryknoll: Orbis, 1988); Anscar

Schreiter one can identify three different models of local theology
that operate from fundamentally different assumptions regarding the
encounter between faith and culture. The first model is a *translation
model* influenced by the dynamic-equivalence theory of biblical
translation. In this model the gospel message is first stripped of its
previous cultural accretions and then translated into modes of expression indigenous to the receiving culture. This approach assumes
a kernel-and-husk view of divine revelation, in which there is a universally recognizable kernel of divine truth overlaid with the husk of
cultural expressions. This model can admit, for example, that certain
doctrinal formulations contain cultural influences, but it assumes that
these can be readily identified and excised from the timeless inner
meaning of that doctrinal formulation.

Schreiter identifies two weaknesses with this model. First, its
understanding of culture assumes that there are readily identifiable
cultural patterns that can be decoded, rendering them immediately intelligible to someone foreign to that culture. This cultural analysis is
often superficial and does not recognize that some cultural patterns
may be unique to a given culture, significantly complicating the task
of translation. In these instances another culture may not possess a
cultural pattern or meaning that is "dynamically equivalent." The second weakness concerns the kernel-and-husk conception of divine
revelation. This view assumes a universalist, ahistorical, acultural articulation of the gospel message that is accessible beneath any historically and culturally conditioned expression of the gospel. As we
saw in chapter 4, contemporary hermeneutics has increasingly called
this assumption into question. To follow the metaphor, we never have
the kernel without the husk.

The kernel-and-husk theory reflects an inadequate understanding
of the incarnation. The view that the Word Incarnate simply took on
the appearance of humanity was condemned as heretical in the early
Church. The doctrine of the incarnation insists that the Word Incarnate was enfleshed in humanity, that it assumed the human condition
in its entirety. God's self-communication in the person of Jesus of
Nazareth cannot be abstracted from Jesus of Nazareth's historical ex-

Chupungo, *Liturgies of the Future: The Process and Methods of Inculturation* (New York: Paulist, 1989); Joseph Fitzpatrick, *One Church, Many Cultures: The Challenge of Diversity* (Kansas City: Sheed & Ward, 1987);
Anscar J. Chupungo, *Cultural Adaptation of the Liturgy* (New York: Paulist,
1982).

istence. It is in the life, preaching, death, and resurrection of this one Palestinian Jew that we have received the unsurpassable self-communication of God. It is not in spite of but *through* Christ's life and ministry in all its cultural and historical particularity that we encounter God's saving word. We encounter Jesus as the Word of God not by excising Jesus from his historical and cultural context but by engaging him in that context. The second model of inculturation is the *adaptation model*. This model focuses less on stripping the gospel message of its cultural accretions and attends more to the particularities of the receiving culture. However, while taking more seriously the unique characteristics of the receiving culture, this model still imposes philosophical and systematic theological categories that may be foreign to the receiving culture. These structures are often so fundamental as to escape notice. For example, Schreiter notes that "many Asian cultures can deal with contradictory data in a conjunctive (both/and) fashion that to Westerners, with their disjunctive (either/or) modes of thought, seems dangerously relativistic."[17] The basic structures of rationality can influence even a presentation of the gospel that seeks to be sensitive to the receiving culture.

Alongside the translation and adaptation models, Schreiter writes of a third model, concerned less with translation or adaptation than with context. The contextual model differs from the first two models in that its starting point is not the form of the gospel that is proclaimed but the defining context of the receiving culture. What are the important distinguishing features of this culture? What are the questions and issues that must be put to the gospel? Reflection on the receiving culture may stress the importance of preserving cultural identity in one instance and the importance of transformative change or liberation from indigenous cultural forces in another. Extended consideration of this model highlights a more important difference between this and the previous two models. Both the translation and adaptation models can be tainted with a paternalism in which those who bring the gospel to a particular culture are supposed to do the work of inculturation. In a contextual model the receiving community itself is responsible for the inculturation.

It is at this point that inculturation and the concept of reception meet. In a contextual model a particular community receives the gospel message as it is proclaimed by the teachers of the Church.

[17]Schreiter, *Constructing Local Theologies,* 10.

There is no predetermined translation or adaptation. Rather, a dialogue is effected between the pastoral agent, who has the task of proclaiming the gospel, and the community, which actively engages and appropriates that message within its own cultural milieu. A local theology emerges, not as the product of a creative adaptation or translation of the Christian faith by a pastoral agent but as the product of a community's living conversation with that which is proclaimed.

This third model abandons the kernel-and-husk view of the gospel that is communicated. Whenever we proclaim the gospel, whether to those who are hearing it for the first time or to established Christian communities, we must abandon any hope of presenting that gospel faith in some pristine transcultural, transhistorical mode. This admission of the culture-laden character of our presentation of the faith need not resign us to the twin extremes of ecclesial sectarianism on the one hand and cultural imperialism on the other. There is no other way to profess our faith. What is demanded is a style of proclamation that is more openly dialogical in character. One cannot anticipate in advance the outcome of such a conversation. In a true engagement between the Christian gospel and a particular culture a new faith will be born. Clearly this was the result of St. Paul's proclamation of the faith of a Jewish sect to a Gentile audience. Paul did not simply translate the one gospel; there was a new transformation of that one gospel message as it was proclaimed to a Hellenistic world. The concrete outcome of Paul's mission to the Gentiles could not possibly have been anticipated. And yet we know that in spite of this real transformation there were profound continuities. This tension between the two poles of continuity and change is the very engine of what Catholics call "tradition."

While theories of inculturation have generally emerged within the context of missiology, the basic principles help inform a contemporary understanding of ecclesial reception. Work on models of inculturation highlights the importance of an active engagement and dialogue between the one Christian faith and a particular community. It is not just that the community "hears" what is proclaimed by the authoritative teachers of the Church and then assimilates it into the life of the community. Often the interaction is initiated not by the teacher but by the community itself, which addresses its questions to the Christian tradition. Some Third World Churches ask what the gospel has to say to their experience of economic hardship. In the First World a member of the scientific community may wonder about the ethical limits of certain forms of genetic research and bring these questions into engagement with the faith she professes.

God's word for a particular community fully emerges only within the community as the fruit of a lively conversation between the questions, concerns, and preoccupations of a particular community and the gospel message as it is mediated by the tradition of the Church. This view of "reception" assumes the opposite of a trickle-down theory of revelation. God's word does not come to us through an ecclesiastical conduit but emerges from within the ecclesial life of a community in which a teaching's authoritative proclamation can only be one moment in a prolonged ecclesial process. That ordained leadership has a unique role to play within this communal conversation is not being challenged. That they are assisted by the Spirit in the authoritative articulation and judgment of the fruit of this ecclesial conversation is also not being questioned. But an adequate theology of reception must place the role of the authoritative teacher squarely within the context of the work of the Spirit in the larger process of ecclesial conversation. In that conversation authoritative teachers, theologians, and all the baptized have an essential contribution to make.

The Role of the Professional Theological Community in Ecclesial Reception

Within this process of ecclesial reception the professional theological community plays a distinctive and important role. Before the Second Vatican Council many ecclesiastical documents viewed the theology as an auxiliary service to the ecclesiastical magisterium. This was particularly evident in Pope Pius XII's *Humani generis* (1950). Theologians had the responsibility of faithfully explicating that which was proclaimed by the pope and bishops (see fig. 4). The theologian was often viewed as an official propagandist for the Church.

In 1975 The International Theological Commission issued a document entitled *Theses on the Relationship Between the Ecclesiastical Magisterium and Theology.*[18] This document reflected the important

---

[18]The English translation of this ITC document can be found in *The Magisterium and Morality,* Readings in Moral Theology No. 3, ed. Charles E. Curran and Richard A. McCormick (New York: Paulist, 1982) 151–70. For a helpful summary and analysis see the final chapter of Sullivan's *Magisterium,* 174–218.

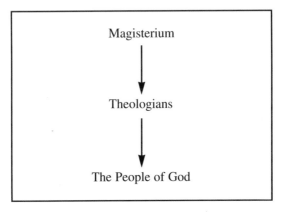

Figure 4

ecclesiological shifts that occurred at Vatican II and articulated a new vision of the relationship between the magisterium and theologians. Central to this document was its view of the theological task as a twofold mediation between the magisterium and the people of God.[19] With reference to the magisterium, the theological community tries to insure that the authentic teaching of the Church is communicated as clearly and effectively as possible. With respect to the people of God, the theological community discerns the unique insights of all the baptized and gives these systematic expression so that they can become part of the ongoing discernment process of the Church in general and the magisterium in particular. Since the people of God exist as a sacrament within the world, and its unique witness to the gospel reverberates in every sphere of "worldly existence" (e.g., work, family, leisure, politics), the twofold tasks of making Church teaching intelligible in the context of daily living and giving voice to the witness of the faithful require that the theologian be an astute interpreter of "the signs of the times."

Since the publication of the ITC document, two other ecclesiastical documents have appeared that explicitly address the relationship between the theological community and the magisterium. In 1989 the American bishops, in collaboration with the Catholic Theological Society of America and the Canon Law Society of America, promulgated the document *Doctrinal Responsibilities: Approaches to Promoting Cooperation and Resolving Misunderstandings Between*

[19]Sullivan, *Magisterium,* 192–93.

Bishops and Theologians.[20] This document drew heavily on the earlier ITC document. In 1990 the CDF issued its own "Instruction on the Ecclesial Vocation of the Theologian."[21] Though they are not equally successful in this regard, each of these three documents shares the new ecclesiological foundation established by Vatican II; all three documents situate the ministries of both the ecclesiastical magisterium and the theological community within the larger context of the people of God.[22] Drawing on an ecclesiology of communion, these documents all reflect the conviction that the word of God is the private possession of neither the magisterium nor the theologians but resides in the whole Church. Cardinal Ratzinger, in his commentary on the CDF instruction, drew attention to this fact:

> Looking at the articulation of the document, one is almost struck by the fact that we have not introduced it by speaking first about the magisterium, but rather about the topic of truth as a gift from God to his people. The truth of faith is not given to isolated individuals; rather through it God wanted to give life to a history and to a people. The truth is located in the communitarian subject of the People of God.[23]

[20]NCCB, *Doctrinal Responsibilities: Approaches to Promoting Cooperation and Resolving Misunderstandings Between Bishops and Theologians* (Washington: USCC, 1989).

[21]CDF, "Instruction on the Ecclesial Vocation of the Theologian," *Origins* 20 (July 5, 1990) 117–26. Many theologians have argued that in spite of its title, the CDF instruction did not adequately attend to the properly ecclesial context of the vocation of the theologian. John Boyle contrasts the instruction's treatment of the theologian as "loner" with John Henry Newman's understanding of the work of the *schola theologorum,* the theological community. The CDF document has also been criticized for its inadequate treatment of theological dissent, its avoidance of more correlational theologies, and its implicit assumption that the seminary professor be the norm for considering the theologian's relationship to the magisterium. See John P. Boyle, *Church Teaching Authority: Historical and Theological Studies* (Notre Dame: Univ. of Notre Dame Press, 1995) 142–60, 171–75; Francis A. Sullivan, "The Theologian's Ecclesial Vocation and the 1990 CDF Instruction," *Theological Studies* 52 (1991) 51–68; Joseph Komonchak, "The Magisterium and Theologians," *Chicago Studies* 29 (November 1990) 307–29; Ladislas Örsy, "Magisterium and Theologians: A Vatican Document," *America* (July 21, 1990) 30–32.

[22]See ITC, *Theses,* 2 and 3; CDF, "Ecclesial Vocation of the Theologian," nos. 4 and 5; NCCB, *Doctrinal Responsibilities,* 3.

[23]Joseph Ratzinger, "Theology Is Not Private Idea of Theologian," *L'Osservatore Romano,* English ed., 27 (July 2, 1990) 5.

Ratzinger sees in the CDF document a shift from a "'magisterium-theology' dualism" to a "triangular relationship: the People of God, as the bearer of the sense of faith and as the place common to all in the ensemble of faith, Magisterium and theology."[24] This triangular relationship (see fig. 5), I believe, better reflects the proper role of the community of theologians in the process of ecclesial reception.

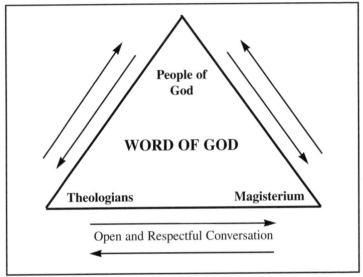

People of
God

WORD OF GOD

Theologians   **Magisterium**

Open and Respectful Conversation

Figure 5

The CDF describes the role of the theologian in this way:

> His role is to pursue in a particular way an ever deeper understanding of the word of God found in the inspired Scriptures and handed on by the living tradition of the church. He does this in communion with the magisterium, which has been charged with the responsibility of preserving the deposit of faith.[25]

The theological community seeks this "deeper understanding" of God's word by employing the appropriate scholarly tools along two axes. The first path to this deeper understanding is diachronic, as the theologian looks to what David Tracy calls the great "classics" of the

---

[24]Ibid.
[25]CDF, "Ecclesial Vocation of the Theologian," no. 6.

tradition (e.g., the Scriptures, post-biblical doctrinal statements, theological treatises, ritual actions, and symbols) for manifestations of the apostolic faith. The proper application of the scientific tools for historical study will be critical to the successful retrieval of the apostolic faith as it is encountered in its many and diverse historical expressions. At this point specialists in biblical and historical studies will have a particularly significant contribution to make. The second path is synchronic and involves the discovery of God's word as it is manifested in the *sensus fidelium* and in the subtle movements of God's Spirit in the world today. This path was emphasized in Vatican II's Pastoral Constitution on the Church in the Modern World:

> It is for God's people as a whole, with the help of the holy Spirit, and especially for pastors and theologians, to listen to the various voices of our day, discerning them and interpreting them, and to evaluate them in the light of the divine word, so that the revealed truth can be increasingly appropriated, better understood and more suitably expressed (*GS* 44).

Later, in article 62, the council again affirms the responsibility of the theologian to bring to the Church insights drawn from modern culture and scientific study.

> Although the church has contributed much to the advancement of culture, it is a fact that for contingent reasons the relationship between culture and christian formation is not always without its difficulties. Such difficulties are not necessarily harmful to a life of faith and can even stimulate a more accurate and deeper understanding of faith. In fact, recent studies and discoveries in science, history and philosophy give rise to new enquiries with practical implications, and also demand new investigations by theologians. Moreover, while respecting the methods and requirements of theological science, theologians are invited continually to look for a more appropriate way of communicating doctrine to the people of their time.

It will be the task of systematic and pastoral theologians to provide a coherent and intelligible articulation of this apostolic faith as it has emerged through their theological inquiry along both of these axes. It is primarily by seeking this deeper understanding of God's word both diachronically and synchronically that the theological community fulfills its important role in the process of ecclesial reception.

Finally, I should note that all three postconciliar documents affirmed, again in differing degrees, the critical dimension of the theological enterprise. The International Theological Commission writes:

[T]he theologian's task of interpreting the statements of the past and present magisterium, of putting them into the context of the whole of revealed truth, and of seeking a better understanding of them with the aid of the science of hermeneutics, brings with it a function that is in some sense critical. This criticism, of course, must be of the positive, not the destructive kind.[26]

It is the recognition of this critical task more than anything else that differentiates this view of the theological vocation from that dominant immediately before Vatican II. There is an acknowledgment here, however tentative, that constructive theological criticism need not be a manifestation of disloyalty but a genuine service to the Church.[27]

The ministry of theologians shares with the ministry of the bishops a common commitment to the word of God, but the work of the theological community is by its nature more tentative and experimental. While the principal responsibility of the ecclesiastical magisterium is to safeguard the integrity of the apostolic faith, the work of the theological community is concerned with deepening the Church's apprehension and assimilation of that faith. The differences between these two responsibilities suggest that even with the best of intentions a certain tension between the two may exist. While all three documents acknowledge that tension may be inevitable and even beneficial,[28] the American bishops in particular are to be commended for trying to develop concrete guidelines for handling these tensions in an open and respectful manner.

Conclusion

Theologies of revelation and theologies of the Church go hand-in-hand. For almost a century between the two Vatican councils Catholic theology operated out of a basically two-tiered, pyramidical ecclesiology. Perhaps the clearest expression of this view of the Church is found in the passage which I quoted earlier from *Vehementor nos*, a 1906 encyclical of Pope Pius X:

It follows that the Church is essentially an *unequal* society, that is, a society comprising two categories of persons, the Pastors and the

[26]ITC, *Theses*, 8.2. See also CDF, "Ecclesial Vocation of the Theologian," no. 9; NCCB, *Doctrinal Responsibilities*, 7.
[27]CDF, "Ecclesial Vocation of the Theologian," no. 30.
[28]Ibid., no. 25.

flock, those who occupy a rank in the different degrees of the hierarchy and the multitude of the faithful. So distinct are these categories that with the pastoral body only rests the necessary right and authority for promoting the end of the society and directing all its members towards that end; the one duty of the multitude is to allow themselves to be led, and, like a docile flock, to follow the Pastors (8).[29]

This ecclesiology rested on a distinction first articulated by sixteenth-century theologian Thomas Stapleton between a teaching Church *(ecclesia docens)* and a learning Church *(ecclesia discens* or *ecclesia docta)*. Within this framework the learning Church was inevitably reduced to a passive receptacle of that revelation given actively to the hierarchy. A pyramidical conception of the Church engendered a trickle-down theory of revelation. God's word is given immediately to the hierarchy of the Church and only mediately, through the hierarchy, to the whole Christian community.

Throughout this volume, I have insisted that the ecclesiological developments of Vatican II challenge both this pyramidical ecclesiology and its related understanding of revelation. In fidelity to the ecclesiological trajectory evident in the Vatican II documents, I have sketched out an ecclesiology of communion as a foundation for the consideration of doctrinal teaching authority. It may be helpful to develop a little more fully the theological foundations of this ecclesiology.

As I noted in the introduction, the Church, as a sacrament of divine communion, can be thought of as an icon of the Trinity.[30] It is a relational entity that mediates, as sacrament, the life of Trinitarian communion. Consequently, it should be possible to derive from Trinitarian theology a set of grammatical rules that would govern the structures and life of the Church. That which we hold for the triune life of God ought to apply by analogy to the Church as ecclesial communion. Therefore, I would like to consider three statements from Trinitarian doctrine that each engender an ecclesial corollary.

1. Trinitarian doctrine holds that the being of God is hypostatic or personal. God is fundamentally tripersonal. There is no abstract divine essence that can be discovered "behind" the Trinitarian persons.

---

[29]English translation from Claudia Carlen, ed., *The Papal Encyclicals* (New York: McGrath, 1981) 3:47–48. The full Latin text can be found *ASS* 39 (1906) 3–16.

[30]For an extended development of the Church as an icon of the Trinity see Bruno Forte, *L'Église: Icône de la Trinité* (Paris: Médiaspaul, 1985).

Furthermore, Trinitarian doctrine reminds us that the divine persons are constituted by relations. Consequently, Trinitarian doctrine teaches us that God's very being is personal and relational. God is being-as-communion.[31] This relational view of the being of God permeates the Scriptures and in particular the Johannine community's dynamic understanding of God as love. This basic theological insight yields the following ecclesial corollary: *The Church is constituted by the life of communion. Just as Trinitarian persons are relational and cannot be conceived apart from their divine relations, so too the Church is constituted relationally.* Because humankind is created in the image and likeness of God, human persons are also constituted as personal and relational beings. Humans are made for communion. We believe that this life of communion is proclaimed and celebrated in word and sacrament within the Church. Through our membership in the Church we discover our true identity as creatures made for communion. Consequently, within the Church there can be no autonomous loci of power and authority. The exercise of power and authority in the Church can only be understood relationally.

2. The doctrine of the Trinity tells us that the Trinitarian persons are both differentiated and egalitarian. Within the triune life of God there is differentiation of persons (the Unoriginate Origin is not the Logos, the Logos is not the Spirit), but there is no subordinationism. This yields a second ecclesial corollary: *Within the Church there is a differentiation of relations or ordines but there can be no hierarchy in the ontological (e.g., pseudo-Dionysian) understanding of the term.* Vatican II insisted that the Church is a *communio hierarchica.* However, this need not be understood as demanding a pyramidical, topdown structure.[32] An ecclesiology of communion grounded in the triune life of God admits the existence of a stable differentiation of ecclesial relations and ministries; it does reject any differentiation or

[31]John D. Zizioulas, *Being as Communion* (Crestwood: St. Vladimir's Seminary Press, 1985). For a consideration of Trinitarian doctrine as generative of a relational grammar for the Christian life see Catherine Mowry LaCugna, *God for Us: The Trinity and Christian Life* (San Francisco: HarperCollins, 1991), especially part 2.

[32]See Walter Kasper's admission of the ambiguities inherent in this term in *Theology and Church* (New York: Crossroad, 1989) 156–59. In the *nota praevia* attached to *Lumen gentium,* the term appears as a way of distinguishing ecclesial *communio* from some liberal democratic understanding of a collective that would lack any essential structure, order, or principle of authority.

ordering that subordinates one relation or ministry to another. The sacrament of baptism establishes the most fundamental ecclesial relation in which every believer is given a supernatural instinct for the faith and the responsibility to proclaim that faith in word and deed. The baptismal call of all believers to pass on the apostolic faith is given sacramental specification in the sacrament of orders. Episcopal consecration, in particular, establishes a distinct and necessary ecclesial relation between the bishop and the local Church in which the bishop is empowered to give normative expression to the apostolic faith of the whole community. The proper exercise of that ministry depends in good part on the maintenance of a right relationship between bishop and Church.

3. Trinitarian relations are characterized by mutuality and reciprocity. Within the divine life of God there is a fundamental to-and-fro movement or interpenetration *(perichoresis)* among the divine persons. This insight yields, in turn, a third ecclesial corollary: *Within the life of the Church all relationships are mutual and reciprocal.* The dynamism of the life of the Spirit is multidirectional within the various ecclesial relations that constitute the Church. This is particularly true of the relationships between the magisterium and theologians, the magisterium and the whole people of God, and that between theologians and the whole people of God. In each relationship there must be a real recognition that both conversation partners will serve, at various moments, as teachers and learners.

In faith and baptism every believer submits to the revelatory and salvific power of the Christ event. The meaningfulness of that revelatory event is discovered by the Christian community in the complex relations and activities that constitute the life of the community. Just as the pyramidal ecclesiology of the late Middle Ages and Counter Reformation engendered a trickle-down view of revelation, so an ecclesiology of communion engenders a theology of revelation grounded in the living word received and sustained within the whole Christian community. John Boyle has captured this ecclesiological foundation well:

> What I have been describing, then, suggests a view of the church as *community of religious and moral discernment* in which a dialogue exists between the proposition and explication of the Christian faith and its implications by authoritative teachers and the reception of that teaching by the church community—which also possess the gifts of the Spirit. It is the experience and reflections of the community which

in turn produce further insights and discernment by the community. The community thus stimulates discernment by the authoritative teachers and a new, perhaps modified proposition of the Christian faith and its implications.[33]

This vision of the Church suggests that we are in fact a "community of reception," in which reception is not so much a juridical act of acceptance as it is an ongoing process in the life of the Church.[34]

If terms like "communion" and "reception" are to be more than spiritual buzz words, they must become enfleshed in the life of the Church. This insight is suggested in a much overlooked postconciliar document, *Communio et progressio,* the 1971 instruction on the means of social communication.[35] This pastoral instruction, promulgated only six years after the close of the council, recognized the integral connection between ecclesial communion and human communication.

> In the Christian faith, the unity and brotherhood of man are the chief aims of all communication and these find their source and model in the central mystery of the eternal communion between the Father, Son and Holy Spirit. . . . Communication is more than the expression of ideas and the indication of emotion. At its most profound level, it is the giving of self in love (8, 11).

This document suggests that the Church as a communion is called to be, at the same time, a "community of communication."[36] True ecclesial communion will be manifested in concrete processes of communication and dialogue. When the teaching ministry of the Church does not flow out of clear processes for open conversation and dialogue[37] at all levels, its juridical authority may remain, but it will be

[33]Boyle, *Church Teaching Authority,* 168.

[34]Michael J. Scanlon, "Catholicism and Living Tradition: The Church as a Community of Reception," in *Empowering Authority: The Charisms of Episcopacy and Primacy in the Church Today,* ed. Patrick J. Howell and Gary Chamberlain (Kansas City: Sheed & Ward, 1990) 1–16. See also Pottmeyer, "Reception and Submission," 290.

[35]Austin Flannery, ed., *Vatican Council II: The Conciliar and Post Conciliar Documents* (Northport: Costello, 1992) 293–349.

[36]Klaus Kienzler, "The Church as Communion and Communication," in *The Church and Communication,* ed. Patrick Granfield (Kansas City: Sheed & Ward, 1994) 95.

[37]Hermann Pottmeyer, "Dialogue as a Model for Communication in the

difficult to acknowledge such teaching as an authentic expression of the corporate faith of the Church.

The Roman Catholic Church today is in desperate need of concrete guidelines for sustaining this kind of open-ended conversation and dialogue. For example, the CDF instruction "Some Aspects of the Church Understood as Communion" offered a rich theology of ecclesial communion but offered little if any guidance for how this communion can be nourished and sustained through concrete actions and structures within the Church.[38] Specific guidelines are important precisely because open conversation and dialogue is bound to bring with it a certain amount of disagreement and conflict. Without clearly agreed upon guidelines one very human response to disagreement and conflict is to short-circuit the conversation and demonize one's opponents. German theologian Otto Hermann Pesch warns of this danger and proposes a few rudimentary guidelines that could be helpful.[39] Pesch notes that true ecclesial dialogue "excludes any compulsion and any prohibition of thought." Official interventions should be undertaken "only as a last resort" and there should be no condemnations "if it is not clear beyond a shadow of doubt that there is heresy

---

Church," in *The Church and Communication,* 97–103. When I use the term "conversation" here, I mean it in the way in which it is used by hermeneutical theologians like David Tracy: "Conversation is a game with some hard rules: say only what you mean; say it as accurately as you can; listen to and respect what the other says, however different or other; be willing to correct or defend your opinions if challenged by the conversation partner; be willing to argue if necessary, to confront if demanded, to endure necessary conflict, to change your mind if the evidence suggests it." *Plurality and Ambiguity: Hermeneutics, Religion, and Hope* (San Francisco: Harper & Row, 1987) 19. Paul Lakeland has applied Jürgen Habermas' communication theory to an understanding of teaching authority within the Church. He contends that the life of the Church must be constituted by such open-ended, disciplined conversation—what Habermas calls "communicative action." It is in and through this communicative action that revelation emerges within the community. Paul Lakeland, *Theology and Critical Theory: The Discourse of the Church* (Nashville: Abingdon, 1990).

[38]CDF, "Some Aspects of the Church Understood as Communion," *Origins* 22 (June 25, 1922) 108–12.

[39]Otto Hermann Pesch, "The Infallibility of the Papal *Magisterium*: Unresolved Problems and Future Perspectives," in *Hans Küng: New Horizons for Faith and Thought,* ed. Karl-Josef Kuschel and Hermann Häring (New York: Continuum, 1993) 13–42 at 34–36.

and that believers are being led astray." There must be a willingness "to leave a controversial question temporarily open if agreement has not been reached." Anyone in a position of conflict with ecclesial authorities should be able to rely on "a legal and fair procedure which safeguards personal honor and dignity." Finally, appropriate ecclesial discipline must be carried out in a manner that "corresponds to what is seemly in dealings with adults." The full reality of the Church as a communion cannot be realized until concrete rules such as these are universally operative in ecclesial conversation.

Up to this point, I have focused on the reception of Church teaching by the whole Christian community. Yet within this corporate reception each believer strives to make his or her own the teaching of the Church. This more individual "reception" of Church teaching raises important questions regarding the response that is "owed" to that teaching. The final chapter will consider that fundamental issue.

For Further Reading

Ecclesial Reception

Congar, Yves. "Reception as an Ecclesiological Reality." In *Election and Consensus in the Church.* Concilium 77. Ed. Giuseppe Alberigo and Anton Weiler, 43–68. New York: Herder, 1972.

Kilmartin, Edward. "Reception in History: An Ecclesiological Phenomenon and Its Significance." *Journal of Ecumenical Studies* 21 (1984) 34–54.

Pottmeyer, Hermann J. "Reception and Submission." *The Jurist* 51 (1991) 269–92.

Rausch, Thomas. "Reception Past and Present." *Theological Studies* 47 (1986) 497–508.

The Sensus Fidelium

Burkhard, John. "*Sensus Fidei*: Meaning, Role, and Future of a Teaching of Vatican II." *Louvain Studies* 17 (1992) 18–34.

_____. "*Sensus Fidei:* Theological Reflection Since Vatican II." *Heythrop Journal* 34 (1993) 41–59, 137–59.

Dobbin, Edmund J. "*Sensus Fidelium* Reconsidered." *New Theology Review* 2 (1989) 48–64.

Glaser, John W. "Authority, Connatural Knowledge, and the Spontaneous Judgment of the Faithful." *Theological Studies* 29 (1968) 742–51.

Metz, Johann Baptist, and Edward Schillebeeckx, eds. *The Teaching Authority of the Believers*. Concilium 180. Edinburgh: T. & T. Clark, 1985.

Scheffczyk, Leo. "Sensus Fidelium—Witness on the Part of the Community." *Communio* 15 (1988) 182–98.

Thompson, William M. "*Sensus Fidelium* and Infallibility." *American Ecclesiastical Review* 167 (1973) 45–86.

Tillard, J.-M. R. "Sensus Fidelium." *One in Christ* 11 (1975) 2–29.

Reception and Inculturation

Bevans, Stephen B. *Models of Contextual Theology*. Maryknoll: Orbis, 1992.

Chupungo, Anscar J. *Cultural Adaptation of the Liturgy*. New York: Paulist, 1982.

_____. *Liturgies of the Future: The Process and Methods of Inculturation*. New York: Paulist, 1989.

Fitzpatrick, Joseph. *One Church, Many Cultures: The Challenge of Diversity*. Kansas City: Sheed & Ward, 1987.

Gittins, Anthony J. *Gifts and Strangers: Meeting the Challenge of Inculturation*. New York: Paulist, 1989.

Shorter, Aylward. *Toward a Theology of Inculturation*. Maryknoll: Orbis, 1988.

Schreiter, Robert. *Constructing Local Theologies*. Maryknoll: Orbis, 1985.

The Relationship Between the Magisterium and Theologians

Buckley, Michael J., Margaret Farley, John T. Ford, Walter Principe, and James H. Provost. *Report of the Catholic Theological Society of America Committee on the Profession of Faith and the Oath of Fidelity*. Washington: CTSA, 1990.

Congregation for the Doctrine of the Faith. "An Instruction on the Ecclesial Vocation of the Theologian." *Origins* 20 (July 5, 1990) 117–126.

Curran, Charles E., and Richard A. McCormick, eds. *The Magisterium and Morality*. Readings in Moral Theology No. 3. New York: Paulist, 1982.

Örsy, Ladislas. *The Church: Learning and Teaching.* Wilmington: Glazier, 1987.

_____. "Magisterium and Theologians: A Vatican Document." *America* (July 21, 1990) 30–32.

_____. *The Profession of Faith and the Oath of Fidelity: A Theological and Canonical Analysis.* Wilmington: Glazier, 1990.

Spohn, William. "The Magisterium and Morality." *Theological Studies* 54 (March 1993) 96–100.

Sullivan, Francis A. "The Magisterium and the Role of Theologians in the Church." In *Magisterium: Teaching Authority in the Catholic Church,* 174–218. New York: Paulist, 1983.

_____. "The Theologian's Ecclesial Vocation and the 1990 CDF Instruction." *Theological Studies* 52 (1991) 51–68.

9

Receiving and Responding to the Word:
Personal Reception of Church Teaching

After the promulgation of Pope Paul VI's encyclical on birth regulation, *Humanae vitae* (1968), the American bishops responded by publishing their own pastoral letter, "Human Life in Our Day."[1] In that document the bishops reaffirmed papal teaching while at the same time reminding Catholics of three things. First, the bishops carefully explicated Church teaching on the primacy of conscience, citing both Cardinal John Henry Newman and St. Thomas Aquinas (nos. 37–45). Second, by affirming that *Humanae vitae* was an exercise of noninfallible papal teaching, they acknowledged the traditional distinctions regarding degrees of magisterial authority in Church pronouncements (nos. 46–48). Finally, they reiterated the norms for licit theological dissent (nos. 49–54) that had long been part of the Catholic tradition.

Of course one could find considerations of all three of these topics in most of the seminary manuals used only a decade earlier. However, discussion of these matters had hitherto been conducted only among clergy and theologians. Ordinary Catholics seldom heard anything from the pulpit regarding the Church's teaching on conscience and the possibility of dissent. With the American bishops' letter and similar responses from other episcopal conferences,[2] these distinctions

[1] NCCB, "Human Life in Our Day," in *Pastoral Letters of the United States Catholic Bishops,* ed. Hugh J. Nolan (Washington: USCC, 1983) 3:164–94.

[2] Similar approaches can be found in statements of the episcopal conferences of Austria, Belgium, Canada, CELAM, France, Indonesia, Netherlands,

were explicitly brought to the attention of many of the Catholic faithful. In the two and a half decades since *Humanae vitae,* discussion regarding the kind of response the faithful owe to Church teaching has become one of interest to a public much broader than clergy and theologians.

Individual and Ecclesial Reception

One shortcoming of many considerations of this topic is the tendency to separate the response of an individual believer to Church teaching from his or her social and ecclesial context. That is, many pose the following kinds of questions: What is the appropriate response of the individual believer to Church teaching? Under what conditions may an individual believer withhold assent from a particular teaching? Under what conditions may a theologian publicly dissent from a particular Church teaching? How do we weigh the authority of the individual conscience against the authority of the ecclesiastical magisterium? I have deferred consideration of these questions until now precisely because they are often addressed from the perspective of the individual believer in a way that overlooks the important fact that as Christians, we do not profess a private faith. The act of faith, while certainly personal in character, is also communal. Just as it is a mistake to isolate discrete teaching acts of the magisterium from the life of the Church, so too is it misguided to isolate the response of the individual believer to Church teaching from the corporate reception of Church doctrine by the whole people of God. The character and significance of an individual's response to church teaching both influences and is influenced by the ecclesial community. The response of the active Christian committed to an ecclesial community cannot be the same as the response of a Christian who lives on the periphery of an ecclesial community.[3] This is the im-

---

Scandinavia, Switzerland, and West Germany. These statements may be found in John Horgan, ed., Humanae vitae *and the Bishops: The Encyclical and the Statements of the National Hierarchies* (Shannon, Ireland: Irish Univ. Press, 1972). For an analysis of these ecclesiastical responses see Joseph A. Selling, *The Reaction to* Humanae vitae: *A Study in Special and Fundamental Theology* (Ann Arbor: Univ. Microfilms, 1979).

[3]I intentionally am using the more inclusive term "Christian," since it seems unavoidable, following what Vatican II has taught regarding the real if imperfect communion that exists between the Roman Catholic Church and non-Catholic Christians, that all Christians participate in varying degrees in

portant point made by many who resent the presentation of Gallup polls as if their findings constituted the *sensus fidelium*. Such polls fail to acknowledge the importance of ecclesial context.

Vatican II wrote of the *sensus fidei* as the supernatural gift by which every baptized believer is able to recognize God's word. This sense or instinct for the faith, however, is actualized within a particular context. For example, how one responds to the Church's teaching on capital punishment will be influenced considerably by social and ecclesial context. The response of an individual only marginally affiliated with a Christian community and influenced by the ethic of retribution common to our Western society is likely to differ from the response of a believer active within an ecclesial community that takes the countercultural values of Jesus Christ seriously.

Not only is the individual response to Church teaching influenced by social and ecclesial contexts, but the individual's response also *contributes* to the Christian community's ongoing appropriation of God's word. The individual's assent to Church teaching has communal implications. Each personal response to a doctrinal teaching is drawn into the communal character of the Church itself and contributes to the shape of the Church's corporate witness to God's word. Because an individual's assent to Church teaching is truly personal, every personal assent will be unique. The believer's response to doctrinal teaching cannot be reduced to a question of mere assent or dissent, to affirmation or negation. Since God's word is a living, salvific word that addresses us as persons, our response to that word as it is mediated in various ways in Church teaching will be irreducibly personal and therefore unique in character. It follows, then, that this unique and personal assent, when drawn into the life of the community, will make a unique contribution to that community's corporate consciousness and Christian witness.

Imagine two Roman Catholics, both of whom give an affirmative assent to Church teaching on the objective moral evil of abortion. For one Catholic the unique character of their assent includes the conviction that this assent demands acts of civil disobedience. Consequently, this person's personal assent to the Church's teaching will be

---

the *sensus fidelium*. It must be added, furthermore, that for one who believes that the Holy Spirit is manifested beyond the boundaries of the Church, no voice can be overlooked as a possible manifestation of the Spirit, even if we cannot speak of the nonbeliever as participating, strictly speaking, in the *sensus fidelium*.

reflected, perhaps, in a decision to engage in nonviolent civil disobedience. Another Catholic also assents to Church teaching on abortion, but this person's assent takes on its particular character within the framework of a certain set of convictions regarding the distinction between religious and public morality and the importance of legal democratic processes in a free society. The second individual would prefer to focus on legislative remedies to economic and social crises that force women into situations in which abortion appears to be the only option. Both Catholics "assent" to Church teaching, but the character of their assent differs considerably. Moreover, both of these personal responses are drawn up into the communal consciousness of the Church and shape the Church's own corporate witness, for good or ill. This is confirmed by the way in which the media perceives the Roman Catholic position on abortion. This perception has been shaped by the public character of those Catholic pro-life advocates who participate in acts of civil disobedience. Consequently, many in the media are led, incorrectly, to identify more extreme forms of pro-life protest with the "Catholic position" on the matter.

In conclusion, before attending to the specific character of the personal response of a believer to Church teaching, it is important to acknowledge the communal character of this response. Each individual response to doctrinal teaching participates in the communal process of doctrinal reception discussed in the last chapter.

Reflections on the Proper Response of the Believer to Church Teaching

In chapter 4 I considered four different categories of Church teaching that have emerged in recent ecclesiastical documents. If the distinctions between these categories are significant, as I have contended, then there ought to be corresponding distinctions in the kind of response that the believer is to give to each category of Church teaching (the reader may wish to review ch. 4 before proceeding). I will consider each of these responses below.

An Assent of Faith to Definitive Dogma

Throughout this volume I have returned again and again to the influence of a propositional model of revelation on Catholic theology. This model tends to reduce divine revelation to a set of discrete "truths" that provide "information" about God. It follows from this theology of revelation that faith will be understood primarily as an intellectual assent to these divine truths. Following the tentative new developments in the documents of Vatican II, I have employed a different conception of revelation. This view accents the unique, salvific, and participatory character of divine revelation. If God's word comes to us as both a personal address and an invitation, then faith must correspond to this more relational and personal view of God's divine self-communication. In this context faith will include not just an intellectual assent to the truth of what is communicated but a sense of trust, commitment, and personal self-disposal. Faith is our fundamental response to God's personal address and invitation to the life of communion.[4]

In scholastic theology one often made a distinction between the formal and material objects of faith. According to this schema the formal object of faith is God as God is revealed to us through Christ and in the Spirit. The material object of faith denotes, then, those particular truths articulated in propositional form that attempt to communicate something of that God who can be known only in the unique modality of saving relationship. Aquinas wrote that, as the formal object of faith, God was the first truth manifested in Scripture and Church doctrine, both of which proceed from that first truth.[5] Elsewhere he insisted that "the act of the believer does not terminate in the propositions but in the reality, for we do not formulate propositions except in order to know things by means of them, whether in science or in faith."[6] For example, I do not believe primarily in the doctrine of the Trinity, I believe in the triune God. Any consideration of the act of faith as an assent to a particular proposition must be careful to remember that this is but one, and indeed secondary, aspect of a much more comprehensive account of faith. While the rest of this chapter will attend to the question of one's response to particular doctrinal

[4]For a detailed analysis of various understandings of the act of faith see Roger Aubert, *Le problème de l'acte de foi* 2nd ed., (Louvain: Warny, 1960). For a more recent review of the theological literature on understandings of faith in fundamental theology, see Avery Dulles, *The Assurance of Things Hoped For: A Theology of Christian Faith* (New York: Oxford Univ. Press, 1994). For a recent approach to models of faith from a philosophical and comparative religions perspective see William Lad Sessions, *The Concept of Faith: A Philosophical Investigation* (Ithaca: Cornell Univ., 1994).
[5]Thomas Aquinas, *Summa theologiae* 2a 2ae, q. 5, a. 3c.
[6]Ibid., q. 1, a. 2, ad 2.

propositions, this must be understood in the light of the primary understanding of faith as one's fundamental and personal self-disposition before God.

Recall that dogmas are those teachings that the ecclesiastical magisterium has taught infallibly as divinely revealed. As such these teachings communicate, however imperfectly, God's offer of salvation. The response of the believer to these teachings is appropriately called by Vatican II an "assent" or "submission of faith" *(obsequio fidei)* because the believer, through the internal testimony of the Spirit, recognizes in this particular teaching that saving word that demands no less than total surrender. In scholastic theology it was said that the motive for one's act of faith was the authority of divine revelation itself. The believer is moved to an act of faith by the very truthfulness of God. Some manualists referred to the stance of the believer in this instance as that of "metaphysical certitude."[7] While one can question the value of this kind of abstract language, the central point should not be lost. The basis for my certitude is the very truthfulness and trustworthiness of God. In faith I respond to the word of God *mediated* by a particular dogma.

How are we to assess, however, the situation in which a baptized believer is unable to offer an assent of faith to a particular dogma? Roman Catholicism has traditionally held that due to the central role dogma plays in the articulation of God's saving word, membership in the Church of Jesus Christ would be called into question by the obstinate and public denial of dogma.[8] This kind of formal rejection is

[7] Cf. Marcelino Zalba, *Theologiae moralis compendium* (Madrid: BAC, 1958) 1:360, as cited in John P. Boyle, *Church Teaching Authority: Historical and Theological Studies* (Notre Dame: Univ. of Notre Dame Press, 1995) 86.

[8] Karl Rahner writes that "if there is to be any question of heresy, then it must be a matter of a *truth* which, precisely *as* truth, is significant for salvation." Karl Rahner, "What is Heresy?" in *Theological Investigations* (Baltimore: Helicon, 1966) 5:470. In light of this, the reader might recall the distinction proposed in chapter 4 between proclamatory and confirmatory dogmas. There I suggested that it is these proclamatory dogmas that communicate God's saving truth, while confirmatory dogmas are those dogmatic teachings that confirm, often through historical exemplification (e.g., the Marian dogmas) saving truth communicated in other proclamatory dogmas. If this distinction is legitimate, then it is possible for a person to be unable to give an assent of faith to a particular dogma without being excluded from the

called "heresy."[9] However, formal heresy is in fact quite rare. The actual stance of most Roman Catholics to at least some of the dogmatic teachings proposed by the Church falls between explicit affirmation or rejection. Karl Rahner has put the matter quite well in his apologetic work, *Our Christian Faith:*

> A normal Christian, who cannot be asked to engage in lengthy theological studies, may quite properly, in relation to the Church's general consciousness of its faith, make emphases and select. This is quite possible without requiring a positive rejection of what is left to one side in such a selection. . . . Today Christians in their situations certainly have the duty and the right, when making such a selection, to concentrate on the most fundamental issues of the Christian faith and to leave much else to one side because they cannot yet fit it in.[10]

Similarly, Avery Dulles writes:

> Few if any believers explicitly know everything that the Church, through its magisterium, has taught and teaches as divinely revealed. For the ordinary believer, who is not an expert on the history of doctrine, it suffices to adhere explicitly to the central truths of Christianity. These are well known from familiar passages in Scripture, from Christian preaching and catechesis, from the creeds (which summarize the central articles of faith), and from the liturgy (which celebrates the great mysteries of faith in the annual cycle of feasts and seasons).[11]

Many Catholic Christians, secure in their fundamental profession of faith in Jesus Christ, will simply never find reason to consider explicitly many teachings that have dogmatic status. Questions regarding the existence of angels, the belief in purgatory, or the matter of what constitutes an "integral" confession as taught by the council of Trent will never trouble them. Furthermore, the quality of their faith should not be judged deficient because of this fact. After all, it was generally only in response to a particular threat or challenge to the

---

Church of Christ if that dogma were merely confirmatory of dogmatic content articulated in other proclamatory dogmatic formulations.

[9]Again it is Rahner who is compelled to further qualify the judgment of heresy: "The Christian judgment of heresy does not deny that in certain circumstances a person who explicitly rejects a particular truth may possess this truth implicitly (just as the converse is possible)." Ibid., 476.

[10]Karl Rahner and Karl-Heinz Weger, *Our Christian Faith: Answers for the Future* (New York: Crossroad, 1981) 134–35.

[11]Dulles, *Assurance of Things Hoped For,* 192.

faith that the Church saw fit to define certain dogmas in a formal way. For many today the questions that gave rise to certain dogmatic statements may no longer be pertinent. It should not surprise us, consequently, if the status of a given dogmatic determination, born out of questions or controversies quite removed from the life of a given believer, may not present a pressing claim on their faith. In this situation the stance of the believer can hardly be characterized as obstinate and public rejection.

The Firm Acceptance of Definitive Doctrine

As I noted in chapter 4, the explicit delineation of this second category of Church teaching is much more recent. The 1989 Profession of Faith mandated by the CDF consisted of the Niceno-Constantinopolitan Creed, followed by three additional paragraphs. The second additional paragraph reads as follows: "I also firmly embrace and hold all and each that are definitively proposed by the Church concerning the doctrine of the faith and morals."[12] However awkwardly formulated, this passage apparently refers to those teachings which, strictly speaking, are not revealed but "which are so intimately linked with it [divine revelation] that for practical purposes they stand and fall together."[13] Because these teachings are not divinely revealed we cannot respond to them with an assent of faith.[14] These teachings are proposed "in a definitive way," meaning presumably, that they are proposed infallibly as irreversible teachings. Consequently, the view of the CDF appears to be that if one cannot give to these teachings an assent of faith, nevertheless that assent must be more than that owed to nondefinitive doctrine. The profession of faith employs the phrase to "firmly embrace and hold," to describe this response. Similarly, the Vatican instruction explains that these teachings "must be firmly accepted and held" (no. 23). Dulles speaks simply of a "firm assent."[15]

---

[12]This is the translation of Ladislas Örsy, *The Profession of Faith and the Oath of Fidelity: A Theological and Canonical Analysis* (Wilmington: Glazier, 1990) 21.

[13]Ibid., 26.

[14]However, one sometimes finds the appropriate response characterized as *ecclesiastical faith* to distinguish it from divine and Catholic faith. See Yves Congar, "Faits dogmatiques et 'foi ecclésiastique,'" in *Sainte Église: Études et approches ecclésiologiques* (Paris: Cerf, 1964) 357–73.

[15]Avery Dulles, *The Craft of Theology: From Symbol to System* (New York: Crossroad, 1992) 110.

Unfortunately, one can infer little from these formulations regarding the particular features of this assent save that it must in some way be distinguished from both the assent of faith and that assent owed to nondefinitive, authoritative doctrine. I have considered some of the ambiguities inherent in this category of Church teaching in chapter 4. The ambiguity certainly is not dispelled when it comes to the question of the response owed to such teaching. It is interesting that there is no reference to this kind of response in the 1983 Code of Canon Law, which speaks only of the assent of faith and the *obsequium* owed to authoritative doctrine.[16]

However one understands the distinctive character of this category and the response owed to it, I find no evidence in tradition that the denial of definitive doctrine was viewed as heresy in the modern sense of the word. Consequently, unlike the case of definitive dogma, the obstinate denial of a definitive doctrine would not necessarily place one outside the Roman Catholic communion.

A "*Religious* Obsequium *of Intellect and Will*" *to Nondefinitive Authoritative Doctrine*

The majority of ecclesiastical pronouncements on matters of doctrine, particularly regarding the moral life, fall in the category of nondefinitive, authoritative doctrine. This refers to that teaching that the pope and bishops propose when assisted by the Holy Spirit but without recourse to the charism of infallibility. Because these doctrines are not proclaimed infallibly, the Catholic Church recognizes the remote possibility of error. While they may or may not be closely related to divine revelation, the Church's refusal to propose the teaching "definitively" means that it is either unable (because the material content of the teaching does not fall within the scope of either divine revelation or that which is necessary to guard and defend divine revelation) or is not yet ready to bind itself irrevocably to the revelatory character of this teaching. What kind of response are Catholics to give to such teaching?

First, as Ladislas Örsy has observed, in the response that any believer is called upon to give to a particular teaching, "the commitment . . . of the individual person must be of the same degree as the

---

[16]Cf. cann. 750, 752. See Michael J. Buckley and others, *Report of the Catholic Theological Society of America Committee on the Profession of Faith and the Oath of Fidelity* (Washington: CTSA, 1990) 81–82.

commitment . . . of the Church."[17] When the ecclesiastical magisterium does not propose a particular doctrine definitively, the faithful cannot be expected to give an assent of faith to such teaching. Örsy has highlighted the serious epistemological difficulties inherent in this category of assent. For authoritative doctrine is not proclaimed as an article of faith, nor is it proposed as self-evident by the application of human reason. "But, and this is our question, how can the human mind affirm that a proposition is true when its truth is neither witnessed by the Holy Spirit (that which is divinely revealed), nor supported by rational evidence?"[18]

Vatican II, unfortunately, offered little to help resolve the matter.[19] *Lumen gentium* 25 holds that Catholics are to give to authoritative doctrine a religious *obsequium* of intellect and will. The proper translation of the term *obsequium* has received a great deal of attention. While Sullivan finds acceptable Flannery's translation of the term as "submission," Bishop B. C. Butler prefers rendering *obsequium* as "due respect."[20] For his part Örsy contends that there is no one obvious translation of the term in English. Its meaning may vary depending on its application. At one point *obsequium* may demand mere respectful listening, and at another it may require a faithful submission.[21] For Örsy, *obsequium* as used in the conciliar texts connotes a

[17]Örsy, *Profession of Faith and the Oath of Fidelity,* 32.

[18]Ibid., 35.

[19]Karl Rahner was one of the first commentators to note the inadequacies of Vatican II's treatment of this in *Lumen gentium* 25. See Karl Rahner, "Dogmatic Constitution on the Church, Chapter III," in *Commentary on the Documents of Vatican II,* ed. Herbert Vorgrimler (New York: Crossroad, 1989) 208–10; idem, "Theologie und Lehramt," *Stimmen der Zeit* 198 (1980) 373; idem, "Dream for the Church," in *Theological Investigations* (New York: Crossroad, 1981) 20:136.

[20]Francis Sullivan, *Magisterium: Teaching Authority in the Catholic Church* (New York: Paulist, 1983) 159; B. C. Butler, "Infallible: Authenticum: Assensus: Obsequium. Christian Teaching Authority and the Christian's Response," *Doctrine and Life* 31 (1981) 77–89.

[21]Örsy contends that this term must be classified as a "seminal locution." "Seminal locution is an expression which conveys an insight into the truth but without defining it with precision; it needs to be developed further. It is a broad and intuitive approach to a mystery that leaves plenty of room for future discoveries." Ladislas Örsy, *The Church: Learning and Teaching* (Wilmington: Glazier, 1987) 85.

particular kind of attitude or stance of loyalty and respect toward the Church and its teaching. The precise form this attitude will take depends on "the person to whom *obsequium* must be rendered, or on the point of doctrine that is proposed as entitled to *obsequium*."[22]

In the council's description of the proper response owed to authoritative doctrine, one should note the explicit mention not only of the will but of the intellect as well. John Boyle, in an important study seeking to place the term *obsequium* in its historical context, finds that in much of the Catholic Christian tradition the term *obsequium* had a predominantly obediential character that downplayed the role of the intellect in seeking after truth. From the period of the Middle Ages, the understanding of *obsequium* was influenced by the Pauline passage: "We destroy arguments and every pretension raising itself against the knowledge of God, and take every thought captive in obedience to Christ *[obsequium Christi]*, and we are ready to punish every disobedience, once your obedience is complete" (2 Cor 10:5-6).[23] The fact that it was common in certain scholastic ecclesiological tracts to locate the power to teach in the power of jurisdiction further encouraged the adoption of the juridical model of command and obedience. In this model the accent is placed on the will directing the intellect to assent.

Yet the proclamation of Christian doctrine belongs to a category wholly different from the promulgation of legislation. In the case of Church legislation obedience demands only that there be no conflict with some more vital moral obligation. To take a mundane example from civil society, when driving on the highway I may come across a 55 mph speed limit sign. I do not inquire after the "truth" of this law but merely whether I can obey it without violating some other greater priority (e.g., bringing my wife, in the final stages of labor, to the hospital). However, in the proclamation of Christian doctrine I must inquire after the *truthfulness* of this teaching as well. The character of Church doctrine demands that one strive toward an *internal* assent.

Many theologians share Boyle's concern that recent ecclesiastical statements have accentuated the obediential character of the *obsequium* of intellect and will owed to authoritative doctrine.[24] The emphasis is

---

[22]Ibid., 89.

[23]Boyle assigns two chapters to the historical and theological context of the phrase *obsequium mentis et voluntatis* in *Church Teaching Authority*, 63–94.

[24]See Hermann Pottmeyer, "Reception and Submission," *The Jurist* 51 (1991) 269–92. Pottmeyer finds evidence of this more obediential interpretation both in

placed on the formal authority of the bishops and/or the pope rather than on the arguments adduced in support of a particular teaching. The difficulty is that in the case of authoritative doctrine we are concerned with the possibility of error, however remote. Given the possibility of error, where giving assent becomes problematic the proper response of the faithful certainly must include a critical assessment of the arguments the Church proposes in support of its teaching.

One helpful interpretation of the unique *obsequium religiosum* demanded for authoritative doctrine is offered by Francis Sullivan.[25] According to Sullivan this religious *obsequium* involves an obedience of *judgment,* which engages will and intellect in a particular way. This obedience of judgment does not mean that the intellect must find a particular teaching to be self-evidently true. To limit our capacity to assent to such self-evidently true propositions would be to exclude the role of the will in our act of assent. We must be free to assent to a proposition even when its truthfulness is not logically compelling. This is something that we do in many areas of our lives. We are accustomed to accepting as true many judgments or statements of fact without recourse to logical demonstration. Frequently we are content simply to rely on the authority of others, even when we are fully aware that those whom we rely on may err in what they present to us as true. Much the same point was made in a statement by the then West German bishops written in 1967 to those commissioned to preach the faith:

> At this point a difficult problem arises, calling for realistic discussion. It is one which today more than formerly threatens the faith of many Catholics or their attitude of free and unreserved trust towards the teaching authorities of the Church. We refer to the fact that in the exercise of its official function this teaching authority of the Church can, and on occasion actually does, fall into errors. . . . The first point to be recognized resolutely and realistically is that human life, even at a wholly general level, must always be lived "by doing one's best according to one's lights" and by recognized principles which, while at the theoretical level they cannot be recognized as absolutely certain, nevertheless command our respect in the "here and now" as valid norms of thinking and acting because in the existing circumstances they are the best that can be found. This is something that everyone

---

the CDF instruction "The Ecclesial Vocation of the Theologian" and the Profession of Faith and the Oath of Fidelity.

[25]Sullivan, *Magisterium,* 162–66.

recognizes from the concrete experience of his own life. Every doctor in his diagnoses, every statesman in the political judgments he arrives at on particular situations and the decisions he bases on these, is aware of this fact. . . . In such a case the position of the individual Christian in regard to the Church is analogous to that of a man who knows that he is bound to accept the decision of a specialist even while recognizing that it is not infallible.[26]

This letter of the German bishops appears to confirm the legitimacy of assenting to the truthfulness of a teaching while at the same time acknowledging the possibility of error.

Yet what of the situation in which a believer begins to doubt the truthfulness of a teaching? In this instance it is no longer a matter of the truth value of a teaching not being *compelling*. Rather, in this instance the teaching may appear to the individual as dubious. Since what we are considering here is authoritative doctrine, the possibility of error, however remote, does exist. Following Sullivan's analysis, the intellect cannot be commanded to assent to a proposition that appears to it as false. The submission of intellect to a teaching means, practically, that when one cannot automatically and without pause give an assent to the truth of authoritative doctrine, formal inquiry into the Church's teaching will be not only legitimate but necessary. In this instance a religious *obsequium* of intellect and will means considering not only the teaching itself but the arguments and explanations proposed in defense of the teaching. Often difficulties in arriving at an internal assent to a doctrine emerge because of misunderstandings regarding the teaching itself. A careful study of the Church's presentation of the doctrine may help overcome serious doubts.

However, the assent to authoritative doctrine also involves a moral component. Since the arguments in favor of a teaching are rarely *compelling,* one's moral disposition can influence the willingness to give assent. Let us take the example of the moral norm prohibiting adultery. A person's capacity to assent to this teaching may be influenced by whether or not they are currently engaged in or desirous of engaging in an adulterous relationship. An authentic *obsequium* of intellect and will to Church doctrine demands a careful examination of

---

[26]This statement can be found reprinted in *Dissent in the Church,* Readings in Moral Theology No. 6, ed. Charles E. Curran and Richard A. McCormick (New York: Paulist, 1988) 129–32.

conscience. The individual must accept the possibility that his or her difficulties with a particular teaching may have their root in the fear of that moral conversion that internal assent may demand.

Finally, a person's capacity to assent to a teaching is often influenced by the testimony and authority of others. This was the point made in the letter of the West German bishops when they employed the analogy of the doctor-patient relationship. A person might experience chest pains and visit a cardiologist out of fear of a heart attack. However, that person can acknowledge the greater expertise of the cardiologist and accept on his testimony the judgment that what was experienced was nothing more than heartburn. This depends, however, on a stance of basic respect for the authority of the doctor's testimony. In the same way, one's disposition to accept the truth of a Church teaching will be partly influenced by the presence or absence of respect for the faith insight of the whole Christian community and the trustworthiness of the ecclesiastical magisterium in its doctrinal pronouncements.

To conclude, I have found helpful Richard McCormick's summary formulation of this response: to give an *obsequium* of intellect and will to authoritative doctrine means to engage in a "docile personal attempt to assimilate the teaching, an attempt that can end in 'inability to assimilate' (dissent)."[27] This attempt at personal assimilation is, in its own way, an act of reception in which the believer honestly strives to make the Church's teaching his or her own. This demands (1) an honest attempt to properly understand what the magisterium teaches, (2) a careful consideration of the arguments the magisterium and theologians adduce in support of (and in opposition to) Church teaching, (3) an examination of conscience to discern whether one's inability to give an internal assent is due to fear of conversion, and (4) a proper respect for the authority and general trustworthiness of the Church and its authoritative teachers in the proclamation of Church doctrine.[28] There may well be instances when, even after fulfilling

[27]Richard A. McCormick, *Corrective Vision: Explorations in Moral Theology* (Kansas City: Sheed & Ward, 1994) 85.

[28]The question of respect for Church authority is a difficult one. Certainly there have been periods in the history of the Church when the actions and attitudes of Church officeholders were such that respect for their authority may have been difficult. Even today there are critics of the hierarchy who have questioned its trustworthiness, at least in certain spheres of Church teaching (e.g., issues related to women and sexuality). Since we are dealing here with

these four conditions, an individual believer may not be able to assimilate this teaching into his or her religious stance. In other words, the believer is unable to arrive at a true internal assent. This withholding of assent, sometimes called legitimate dissent, must be viewed as a valid exercise of the fundamental obligation of all believers to seek after truth and to accept the consequences of that search. Furthermore, this withholding of assent *does not* remove one, as in the case of heresy, from full participation in the Roman Catholic communion.

While the Vatican II documents make no explicit mention of the possibility of legitimate dissent, the council's theological commission did consider the question. Three different *modi* were offered to the theological commission regarding the possibility of legitimate dissent. One *modus* posed the question of an "educated person [who], confronted with a teaching proposed non-infallibly, cannot, for solid reasons, give his internal assent."[29] In response, the commission rejected the proposed emendation, but on the grounds that the matter was already addressed in the "approved manuals." Joseph Komonchak's important study of these manuals confirms the fact that the possibility of legitimately withholding assent from an authoritative doctrine was considered possible.[30]

It would be a serious mistake to see the permissibility of withholding assent in these carefully defined circumstances as a mere act of condescension to human weakness and error. Nor can legitimate dissent be equated with disobedience as some would have it. Because the magisterium itself grants the possibility of error in the proclamation of authoritative doctrine, the dissent of believers may positively

---

the exercise of Church teaching authority in the proclamation of authoritative but nondefinitive doctrine (consequently there is no question of an infallible assistance of the Holy Spirit), it is certainly possible, at any point in history, for the actions and ideological biases of Church officeholders to seriously weaken any claims to respect on the part of the faithful. After all, it is exceedingly difficult to determine the limits beyond which the Holy Spirit would not allow human sinfulness to affect the credibility of the Church's teaching office.

[29] *Acta synodalia,* vol. III/8, 88.

[30] Joseph Komonchak, "Ordinary Papal Magisterium and Religious Assent," in *The Magisterium and Morality,* Readings in Moral Theology No. 3, ed. Charles E. Curran and Richard A. McCormick (New York: Paulist, 1982) 67–90.

assist the Church in recognizing its error and moving forward in pursuit of the "plenitude of truth." One can think of numerous past "dissenting theologians" like Yves Congar, Karl Rahner, or John Courtney Murray whose "dissenting positions" eventually nudged the ecclesiastical magisterium toward a new formulation of Church teaching. This possibility cannot, in principle, be denied to the ordinary believer. Though without the professional credentials of the theologian, the believer possesses a supernatural instinct of the faith and therefore can contribute to the Church's corporate discernment of God's word. In other words, we must acknowledge the real possibility that legitimate dissent itself may be a manifestation of the Spirit in bringing the whole Church to truth.

Conscientious Obedience to Prudential Admonitions and Applications of Church Doctrine

It is difficult to characterize the appropriate response to this final category of Church teaching. As I noted in chapter 4, this category includes a variety of ecclesiastical pronouncements, some of which warn of dangerous theological trends and opinions (e.g., the CDF's statements on liberation theology), others of which simply determine the concrete discipline of the Church (e.g., the number of holy days of obligation to be celebrated in the liturgical calendar). It may even be possible to include some specific or concrete moral norms in this category. The general response one owes to such pronouncements can be described as conscientious obedience. In these instances it is possible to render an external assent to a law or judgment while questioning the advisability, prudence, or even correctness of that law or judgment. This act of obedience is called "conscientious" because it is conditioned by the exercise of one's own conscience and prudential judgment that the demands of a particular Church law or pronouncement are not superseded by more important claims on human action.

To some, the careful articulation of these various responses to Church teaching is an exercise in hairsplitting. Many faithful Catholics will go through their entire lives without ever being troubled with the doctrinal positions of the Catholic Church. They will, with equal vigor, profess their belief in the real presence of Christ in the Eucharist, the saving work of Christ on the cross, the prohibition of artificial contraception, and the law of celibacy for priests. Yet there are many Catholics today who find it difficult to accept unconditionally all that the Catholic Church proclaims in its doctrine and church discipline. All Catholics have a right to know that ecclesiastical pronouncements differ significantly, not only in their content but in their authoritative character. They must also know that their response to Church teaching can and should be correlated to the particular character of the teaching itself. What is at stake here is nothing less than a proper understanding of what constitutes Church membership and the fact that, in Catholic teaching, not all disagreement with ecclesiastical pronouncements necessarily separates one from the Roman Catholic communion. The following table is intended to help summarize the four categories of Church teaching and the response owed to each.

LEVELS OF CHURCH TEACHING	RESPONSE OF THE FAITHFUL
Definitive Dogma	**Assent of Faith** [The believer makes an act of faith, trusting that this teaching is revealed by God]
Definitive Doctrine	**Firm Acceptance** [The believer "accepts and holds" these teachings to be true]
Nondefinitive, Authoritative Doctrine	***Obsequium* of Intellect and Will** [The believer strives to assimilate a teaching of the Church into their religious stance, while recognizing the remote possibility of Church error]
Prudential Admonitions and Provisional Applications of Church Doctrine	**Conscientious Obedience** [The believer obeys (the spirit of) any Church law or disciplinary action that does not lead to sin, even when questioning the ultimate value or wisdom of the law or action]

Figure 6

Conclusion

In the end, one's response to Church teaching can never be reduced to a simple matter of assent or dissent. To the extent that one's response to Church teaching is a truly personal response, the definitive character of that response is ultimately disclosed only in the concrete shape of a believer's life. Just as the true nature of Church doctrine is only discovered within the context of a rich Christian tradition that passes on God's word in innumerable forms, the true nature of the Christian's response to that doctrine is interwoven in the daily life of Christian discipleship. It is there, in the ongoing struggle to remain faithful as followers of Jesus, that we give our most profound answer to God's invitation to saving communion which is faithfully if imperfectly communicated to us in Christian doctrine.

For Further Reading

Boyle, John P. "Obsequium mentis et voluntatis," and "Authoritative, Non-Definitive Teaching and the Principle of Probabilism." In *Church Teaching Authority: Historical and Theological Studies,* 63–94. Notre Dame: Univ. of Notre Dame Press, 1995.

Buckley, Michael J., Margaret Farley, John T. Ford, Walter Principe, and James H. Provost. *Report of the Catholic Theological Society of America Committee on the Profession of Faith and the Oath of Fidelity.* Washington: CTSA, 1990.

Butler, B. C. "Infallible: Authenticum: Assensus: Obsequium. Christian Teaching Authority and the Christian's Response." *Doctrine and Life* 31 (1981) 77–89.

Congregation for the Doctrine of the Faith. "The Ecclesial Vocation of the Theologian," *Origins* 20 (July 5, 1990) 118–26.

Curran, Charles E., and Richard A. McCormick, eds. *Dissent in the Church.* Readings in Moral Theology No. 6. New York: Paulist, 1988.

Dulles, Avery. *The Assurance of Things Hoped For: A Theology of Christian Faith.* New York: Oxford Univ. Press, 1994.

Komonchak, Joseph. "Ordinary Papal Magisterium and Religious Assent." In *The Magisterium and Morality.* Readings in Moral Theology No. 3, ed. Charles E. Curran and Richard A. McCormick, 67–90. New York: Paulist, 1982.

Örsy, Ladislas. *The Church: Learning and Teaching.* Wilmington: Glazier, 1987.

_____. *The Profession of Faith and the Oath of Fidelity: A Theological and Canonical Analysis.* Wilmington: Glazier, 1990.

Pottmeyer, Hermann. "Reception and Submission." *The Jurist* 51 (1991) 269-92.

Spohn, William. "The Magisterium and Morality." *Theological Studies* 54 (March 1993) 96–100.

Sullivan, Francis A. "The 'Secondary Object' of Infallibility." *Theological Studies* 54 (1993) 536–50.

_____. "The Non-Definitive Exercise of Papal and Conciliar Teaching Authority." In *Magisterium: Teaching Authority in the Catholic Church,* 153–73. New York: Paulist, 1983.

_____. "The Theologian's Ecclesial Vocation and the 1990 CDF Instruction." *Theological Studies* 52 (1991) 51–68.

_____. "Some Observations on the New Formula for the Profession of Faith." *Gregorianum* 70 (1989) 552–54.

Conclusion: Some Reflections
on Doctrinal Teaching Authority in the
Church of the Third Millennium

As we approach the end of almost two thousand years of Christianity, it is impossible to overlook the startling contrasts between the first two millennia. The first thousand years of Christianity's existence was by no means without feuds and conflicts. Nevertheless, the first millennium of Christianity can still be characterized by substantial ecclesial unity. The same cannot be said of the second millennium. The schism between East and West formalized in 1054, the fissures in the Church that followed the sixteenth-century reformations, the departure of Old Catholics in the late nineteenth century, and the formal schism that exists now in the twentieth century for members of the Society of St. Pius X, followers of the late Archbishop Marcel Lefebvre, all suggest that the second millennium of Christianity has been one of division. What is in store for the third millennium? Is there an opportunity for a new Christian unity, and if so, what would it look like? The ecumenical movement has labored over this question during the last thirty years. Such notions as "reconciled diversity," "conciliarity," and now "*koinonia*/communion" have been proposed as models for conceiving a unity among the various Christian traditions that does not compromise their distinctive identities.

It is difficult to imagine a formalized unity among the Churches that does not include some shared understanding of doctrinal teaching authority. Even so, Roman Catholics cannot afford the hubris of thinking that their structures and understandings of authority *in toto* and as presently constituted provide the only viable possibility. If there lies in the future of Christianity a formalized unity among some of the various Christian traditions, no one can know at this point what precise form the structures and manner of exercise of ecclesial authority will take. However, there are two things that are incumbent upon Roman Catholicism if it is to contribute to that future unity.

First, it must come to the table of ecumenical dialogue with a coherent understanding of its own view of doctrinal authority, one that flows from the best of its ecclesiological tradition. This volume has tried to contribute to that enhanced self-understanding. Second, it must address the tangible gap many perceive between Catholicism's *vision* of ecclesial authority and its concrete structures and practice. This was the concern of the bishops at Vatican II when, regarding the Catholic's obligations to the cause of ecumenism, they wrote:

> Catholics, in their ecumenical work, must assuredly be concerned for other Christians, praying for them, keeping them informed about the church, making the first approaches towards them. But their especial duty is to make a careful and honest appraisal of whatever needs to be renewed in the catholic household itself, in order that its life may bear witness more faithfully and clearly to the teachings and ordinances which have come to it from Christ through the hands of the apostles (*UR* 4).

I believe that this Catholic life includes, among other things, the concrete ecclesiastical structures for teaching and governance. For example, it helps little to teach of the ministry of the bishop as pastor of souls and servant of communion in the local Church when almost 50 percent of Roman Catholic bishops possess titular sees that no longer exist. Similarly, it does little good to speak of the papacy as a ministry safeguarding the unity of faith and communion if the other Christian communions look to the papacy and still see imperial and monarchical trappings.

Pope John Paul II, in his call for the preparation of a Jubilee Year, has challenged Christians and particularly Catholics to engage in a thoroughgoing examination of conscience:

> This then is one of the tasks of Christians as we make our way to the year 2000. The approaching end of the second millennium demands of everyone an examination of conscience and the promotion of fitting ecumenical initiatives so that we can celebrate the great Jubilee, if not completely united, at least much closer to overcoming the divisions of

the second millennium. . . . An examination of conscience must also consider the reception given to the council [Vatican II], this great gift of the Spirit to the church at the end of the second millennium. To what extent has the word of God become more fully the soul of theology and the inspiration of the whole of Christian living, as *Dei Verbum* sought? . . . In the universal church and in the particular churches, is the ecclesiology of communion described in *Lumen Gentium* being strengthened? Does it leave room for charisms, ministries and different forms of participation by the people of God, without adopting notions borrowed from democracy and sociology which do not reflect the vision of the church and the authentic spirit of Vatican II?[1]

In his apostolic letter the pope was careful to avoid calling the Catholic Church *qua* Church to this kind of examination of conscience. Sinfulness and error were only attributed to the "sons and daughters" of the Church. But surely the examination of conscience he called for must have a corporate and ecclesial dimension. It must be legitimate to ask how we can, *as a Church*, in preparation for the coming millennium, strengthen the ecclesiology of communion and further the cause of Christian unity. As I noted in the introduction, this call for an examination of conscience was given a new specificity in the Pope's encyclical on ecumenism, in which he called for further study regarding the nature of teaching authority in the Church.

In response to the Pope's challenge, it seems appropriate to conclude this volume on doctrinal teaching authority in the Church with a partial and somewhat tentative set of reflections on ways in which this ecclesiology of communion could be strengthened with respect to the structures and manner of exercise of doctrinal teaching authority in the Catholic Church.

The Relationship Between the Local Bishop and the Local Church

An ecclesiology that properly attends to the Eucharistic foundations of the Church will highlight the essential role of the local Church and its bishop in the life of ecclesial communion. It is the bishop who functions as the center of unity within the local Church. That bishop symbolically represents the faith consciousness of his

[1]John Paul II, "As The Third Millennium Draws Near" *(Tertio millennio adveniente)* nos. 34, 36, *Origins* 24 (November 24, 1994) 410–11.

Church in his participation in the college of bishops. It is here in the relationship between bishop and local Church that the greatest opportunities can be found for the testimony of the *sensus fidelium* to influence the formal teaching of the Church. The reciprocal character of the relationship between bishop and local Church is frequently obscured, however, by many of the concrete ecclesiastical structures and practices that shape the exercise of episcopal ministry today.

Formal Ordinations

When Vatican II settled in the affirmative the hitherto open question regarding the sacramentality of the episcopate, it was acting in consonance with an ecclesiology of communion.[2] It reflected an ancient commitment to the episcopate as an ecclesial structure essential to the life of the Church, and it set aside that trajectory begun in the eleventh century that divorced the episcopate from pastoral ministry and viewed the bishop in largely administrative terms. Unfortunately, the sacramental character of episcopal consecration is today undermined by the practice of formal ordinations, that is, the ordination to the episcopate of Church officials who will not be assigned a pastoral charge to an existing local community. These bishops may serve as nuncios, apostolic delegates, prelates of Roman congregations, or as auxiliary or coadjutor bishops. Yet for them the only vestige of a real pastoral charge to a local community comes by way of the ancient practice of assigning a titular see, that is, the assignment of title to a Church which has lapsed or was suppressed.

This practice has its origins in the twelfth century when, after the Turkish conquest of large sections of the Christianized Mediterranean and Europe, Rome continued to appoint bishops to sees under Turkish rule and then assigned these bishops to assist ordinaries of large dioceses elsewhere. In the sixteenth century this practice was expanded at the Fifth Lateran Council to extend the assignment of lapsed or suppressed sees to all bishops without a local Church in order to correct, if only in name, earlier abuses in episcopal appointments. In 1882 the Congregation of Propaganda replaced the more ancient title of such bishops, *episcopus in partibus infidelium*, with

²The material that follows appeared in an earlier article of mine, "Ecclesiology of Communion and Ecclesiastical Structures: Towards a Renewed Ministry of the Bishop," *Église et Théologie* 24 (1993) 185ff.

the phrase "titular bishops," in deference to the civil governments of the countries where the titular sees were located. According to the *Annuario pontificio* of 1991 there are well over fifteen hundred titular sees, though some are currently vacant.

Granting titular sees to bishops who will not serve as pastoral leaders to local Churches obscures an authentic theology of the episcopate in two ways. First, it trivializes the relationship between a bishop and his local community, which, from the perspective of a *communio* ecclesiology, is essential to episcopal identity. How can one speak meaningfully of a bishop's "communion" with a nonexistent community?[3] Second, it transforms what is properly a sacramental ministry within the Church into an honorary or administrative title.[4] Furthermore, the theological and sacramental structure of the church as a *communio hierarchica* risks being eclipsed by a bureaucratic or administrative structure. This eclipse reinforces the impression, widespread in many quarters, that such ecclesial structures are more concerned with rank and domination than with ecclesial service.

The Appointment of Bishops

No ecclesiastical practice exerts a more significant influence on the life of the local Church than the concrete manner in which bishops are appointed. Chapter 2 discussed the ancient practice of locally electing bishops. Few realize that our current practice of papal appointment is a relatively modern one and that the 1983 Code of Canon Law still makes provision for local election (cf. can. 377.1). In spite of this, the possibility of enhanced participation of the local

---

[3] Auxiliary and coadjutor bishops must be distinguished from other titular bishops. These bishops do have pastoral responsibility, albeit under the authority of a local ordinary, to a particular community. This pastoral relationship to a particular community on the part of auxiliaries and coadjutors would seem then, to render the assignment of a titular see unnecessary.

[4] The ordination rite itself warns against this view of the episcopacy when in the suggested homily for the principal consecrator the rite says: "The title of bishop is one not of honor but of function, and therefore a bishop should strive to serve rather than to rule. Such is the counsel of the Master: the greater should behave as if he were the least, and the leader as if he were the one who serves." "The Ordination of a Bishop," in *The Rites of the Catholic Church*, vol. 2 (New York: Pueblo, 1969) no. 18.

Church in the appointment of a bishop is often condemned as a plank in a misguided reformist platform bent on the "democratization of the Church." It is dismissed as simply one among many modern innovations bent on secularizing the Church. But the explicit involvement of the local Church in episcopal appointment is rooted in both sound ecclesiology and ancient tradition; it is hardly a modern innovation.

The ministry of the bishop is characterized by a twofold relationship. The bishop not only brings the one apostolic faith to his people, but he bears their unique celebration of the faith back to the universal Church. This representative relationship requires a real reciprocity between bishop and community. Once again, the bishop is both a teacher and a listener. The circumvention of the real participation of the whole community in the appointment of a bishop can impair that reciprocal relationship in the same way that a circumvention of the participation of neighboring bishops in the ordination of the local bishop would weaken and even undermine the local Church's relationship to the Church universal. While the integrity of the latter relationship is protected zealously by Church custom, the former relationship has been seriously weakened.

The slogan "the Church is not a democracy," as with many slogans, does contain a half-truth; the Church cannot succumb to a strictly liberal democratic conception of its constitution, viewing all authority as residing first in the people and then, only in delegated fashion, in the clergy. However, support for the election of bishops no more requires seeing the bishop as a "delegate" of the people than does papal appointment of a bishop require a view of a bishop as vicar of the pope. Since it is the Holy Spirit who is the transcendent subject of the life of the Church, there is no reason why the same Spirit, which now works through direct appointment by the Holy See, may not work through some form of local election.

Local participation in episcopal appointments should not be identified with that understanding of election that has its roots in political liberalism. In the latter case each individual votes according to his or her particular interests and commitments. The understanding of "election" in political liberalism is that of an aggregate polling of individual preferences. However, an ecclesiological commitment to local participation of the faithful in the election of a bishop requires a different dynamic. The people of God submit themselves to the guidance of the Spirit in a process of corporate discernment that is intent upon serving the will of God in the community's corporate choice of a candidate. One could easily imagine the adaptation of canonical structures like diocesan synods for the purpose of episcopal election.[5] Would such a process of local election be free of "politics"? Clearly not. But then few would deny the political considerations involved in the current practice. Anyone aware of Church history knows that the Spirit is able to work in the midst of sometimes scandalous manifestations of political infighting and intrigue.

The election of the bishop by the local community is an alternative means of episcopal selection that may reflect the democratic tendencies of our modern age, but much more, it is a practice in keeping with our most ancient ecclesial insights regarding the bishop's immersion within the local believing community.

Structures of Communion in the Local Church

In an ecclesiology of communion there can be no autonomous entities within the Church. If every ecclesial reality manifests itself only in and through communion with others, then this communion ought to find expression in the concrete life of the local Church under the pastoral leadership of the bishop. Beyond the question of episcopal appointment, an ecclesiology of communion invites us to consider how this life of communion between bishop and flock can be sustained *after* the bishop's ordination/installation. There are numerous means for giving institutional expression to this communion between bishop and people that go beyond the practice of episcopal visitations to parishes. Article 27 of *Christus Dominus* suggests two concrete structures that have the potential of furthering communion at the local level: presbyteral councils and pastoral councils. The 1983 Code of Canon Law requires the establishment of diocesan presbyteral councils (can. 497) and encourages the establishment of both diocesan and parochial pastoral councils (cann. 511, 536). If diocesan pastoral councils are established, canon 512 stresses the importance of lay membership as representatives of the people of God. As a permanent ecclesiastical structure within the local Church, pastoral councils

[5]Effective models of discernment in the choice of religious leadership are already being employed in many consecrated religious communities. For a contemporary consideration of the manner of episcopal appointment and papal election see Gustave Thils, *Choisir les évêques? Elire le pape?* (Paris: Lethielleux, 1970).

possess a still largely untapped potential for realizing communion within the local Church by providing a body through which the bishop may both consult and instruct the faithful.

Another institutional structure contained in the 1983 code is the diocesan synod. While the 1917 code had mandated that such synods (which, by tradition were limited to clerical participation) be held every ten years, this was largely ignored. The ten-year requirement was therefore dropped in the 1983 code, with the frequency of convocation left to the bishop. What is more significant in the new code however, is the expansion of membership in the diocesan synod; canon 460 defines a synod as "a group of selected priests and other Christian faithful of a particular Church." Canon 463.2 lists "lay members of the Christian faithful" among those whose attendance is now required at a diocesan synod. Diocesan synods, again largely ignored in many dioceses, can facilitate broad-based participation on the part of the faithful in decisions made for the good of the Church. Both pastoral councils and diocesan synods have the advantage over episcopal visitations in that they provide a context in which real, sustained dialogue over issues relating to the local Church may be conducted in a fruitful manner.

Regarding the assimilation of the teaching of Vatican II into the daily life of the Church, Edward Schillebeeckx writes: "During the 1970s and above all during the 1980s, precisely those elements in Vatican II which were 'new' in comparison to the post-Tridentine life of the church and its ecclesiology *have not been given any consistent institutional structures* by the official church."[6] The translation of Vatican II's ecclesiology of communion into the Church's institutional life must be considered one of the foremost responsibilities of Church leadership today. It is useless to speak of a real communion within the Church if there are no concrete manifestations of communion in which authentic conversation and consultation can take place.[7]

Renewal of the Exercise of Episcopal Collegiality

The same concrete manifestations of communion that are necessary within the local Church are also necessary in the communion of Churches. In the thirty years since the close of the Second Vatican

[6] Edward Schillebeeckx, *Church: The Human Story of God* (New York: Crossroad, 1990) xiv. Emphasis mine.
[7] Ibid., 190–92.

Council, one can identify several developments intended to enhance the authority of the college of bishops. The revised Code of Canon Law gives to the bishops an authority unprecedented since the first centuries of the Church. Episcopal conferences have become increasingly important, as has the world synod of bishops. Nevertheless, there remain real impediments to the full and proper exercise of the authority given to the college of bishops.

Episcopal Conferences and the World Synod of Bishops

The tremendous potential of both episcopal conferences and the world synod of bishops has not been realized. Serious questions regarding the doctrinal teaching authority of both conferences and the world synod have been raised. I treated both in some detail in chapter 6, but here I would like to raise some more specific questions.

One criticism of episcopal conferences that deserves attention is the complaint by some that the work of episcopal conferences is largely administrative in nature and therefore does little to foster the communion of the Churches. This criticism has some merit. First, the relatively short meetings of the episcopal conferences make extended deliberation over important issues unlikely. Many votes have to be conducted by mail when there is not a quorum at the bishops' meetings. Votes by mail are conducted without the benefit of conversation and communal deliberation, important components in the process of ecclesial discernment. Furthermore, the limitation of membership in these conferences to bishops limits the possibility for input on the part of the faithful. In response to this criticism, it is worth noting that the 1983 code considers episcopal conferences in the section on particular Churches and their groupings. There the treatment of conferences (cann. 447–59) is preceded by a consideration of other structures that express the communion of certain groupings of local Churches, for example, particular councils (cann. 439–46). These councils, so fundamental to the life of the early Church, have largely been neglected in modern times in favor of episcopal conferences.[8] These councils, which do have a properly deliberative role and include a much greater representation of the people of God, including

---

[8]Historically, this may have been due to the restrictions increasingly placed on particular councils by the Holy See in reaction to the use of these councils by Febronian and Gallican sympathizers. The nineteenth century did see an increase in the convocation of such councils, evidenced in the important role played by the plenary councils of Baltimore in the United States.

the laity, may serve as a more apt expression of ecclesial communion among the Churches of a given region. The collegial character of the work of episcopal conferences might be more readily evident if it were conducted in conjunction with the frequent convocation of plenary councils.[9]

A second expression of episcopal collegiality is the world synod of bishops instituted by Pope Paul VI. As currently structured the episcopal synods are hampered as instruments of collegiality. The papacy and the Roman curia have considerable influence in the appointment of delegates to the synod and the determination of the agenda. Furthermore, the practice of having the pope rather than the synod itself write a summary document, a shift of responsibilities that first occurred with the 1974 synod on evangelization, seriously weakens its collegial dimension. The synod has become a highly orchestrated affair that provides only limited opportunity for episcopal discussion of preassigned topics. Consequently, it has not fulfilled the hopes of many of the council members who had envisioned a structure able to give expression to conciliar teaching on episcopal collegiality.

Episcopal collegiality is the visible or external expression of the communion of the Churches. As such, the interaction of the bishops should give testimony to the faith insight of the Churches. The underlying assumption of the principle of collegiality is that the bishops, including the bishop of Rome, benefit from this interaction. If bishops and pope are learners as well as teachers, collegial interaction must be so conducted as to encourage the learning process that must precede any formal teaching act. Ideally, episcopal synods would facilitate that learning process by providing a forum for the free exchange of ideas and the frank consideration of the most pressing issues in the Church today. In order to better accomplish this, it may be necessary to restructure episcopal synods in ways that would encourage episcopal initiative in raising questions of concern for the universal Church. The agendas should be determined by the bishops themselves, and rules of procedure should be established that would encourage honest discussion and debate.

---

[9]Cf. James H. Provost, "Episcopal Conferences as an Expression of the Communion of Churches," in *Episcopal Conferences: Historical, Canonical, and Theological Studies*, ed. Thomas Reese (Washington: Georgetown Univ. Press, 1989) 282f.; Hervé Legrand, "Synodes et conseils de l'après-concile," *Nouvelle revue théologique* 98 (1976) 193–216.

The Relationship Between the College of Bishops, the Roman Curia, and the College of Cardinals

Born in the twelfth century as a kind of papal court for an imperial papacy, the Roman curia has functioned for nine centuries as the bureaucratic arm of the papacy. Like most bureaucratic structures, the curia has proven itself over the centuries to be remarkably resistant to reform.[10] Following the conciliarist controversy, which set the authority of the pope against the authority of the bishops, the curia, as an administrative arm of the papacy, frequently served a policing function and consequently has come to be viewed with suspicion by some bishops and theologians.

At Vatican II many bishops called for a reform of the curia in keeping with the renewed appreciation of the Church as communion.[11] Numerous proposals were made in this regard. Some suggested the creation of a special council of bishops after the close of Vatican II that would assist the pope in the pastoral care of the Church universal (this suggestion eventually led to Pope Paul VI's creation of the world synod of bishops). Others suggested that a special congregation be created within the curia that would consist of representative bishops and would have authority over the other congregations. The general call for reform, however, elicited the objection that since the curia was a papal institution it was not within the competence of the council to consider its reform. In this view the Roman curia was just like the curia of each individual bishop. Against this view, Cardinal Alfrink insisted that the curia served not only the pope but the college

---

[10]Of course attempts at curial reform have been undertaken periodically, most notably by Pius X. See his *Sapienti consilio, AAS* 1 (1909) 7–19; Paul VI, *Regimini Ecclesiae universae, AAS* 59 (1967) 885–928; and John Paul II, *Pastor bonus, AAS* 80 (1988) 841–932. However, each of these attempts failed in achieving a fundamental restructuring of the curia in light of sound ecclesiological principles. Cf. I. Gordon, *De Curia Romana renovata, Periodica de re morali et liturgica* 58 (1969) 59–116; Peter Huizing and Knut Walf, *The Roman Curia and the Communion of Churches,* Concilium 127 (New York: Seabury, 1979), for essays that treat the question of curial reform. On the most recent attempt at curial reform, see James Provost, "*Pastor Bonus*: Reflections on the Reorganization of the Roman Curia," *The Jurist* 48 (1988) 499–535.

[11]Karl Mörsdorf, "Decree on the Bishops' Pastoral Office in the Church," in *Commentary on the Documents of Vatican II,* ed. Herbert Vorgrimler (New York: Crossroad, 1989) 2:173–75, 210–13.

of bishops. Alfrink's understanding seemed to follow from the council's teaching that the whole college shared with the pope supreme authority over the whole Church (cf. *LG* 22). In substantial agreement with Alfrink, Karl Mörsdorf writes: "The order in the Church was not first the Pope then the Curia and after that the bishops, but first the college of bishops, i.e., the Pope with the other bishops, and then the Curia as the executive instrument of the college of bishops though also of the Pope."[12] This latter view seems to be reflected in *Christus Dominus:*

> In the exercise of his supreme, full and immediate authority over the entire church, the Roman pontiff makes use of the various departments of the Roman curia. These departments, accordingly, operate in his name and with his authority for the good of the churches and in the service of the sacred pastors. These departments have unquestionably given outstanding assistance to the Roman pontiff *and to the pastors of the church.* Nevertheless it is the express wish of the conciliar fathers that they should be reorganised in a way more appropriate to the needs of our own times and of different regions and rites (*CD* 9, emphasis mine).

Unfortunately, the 1983 Code of Canon Law (can. 360) deleted reference to the "pastors" and speaks only of the curia's service to the Churches. In fact, both Vatican II and the new Code of Canon Law have failed to resolve satisfactorily the thorny complex of canonical and ecclesiological questions regarding the function and authority of the Roman curia.

Canon 361 stipulates that the term "Apostolic See," or "Holy See," includes not only the pope but the Roman curia without, however, clearly developing the theological foundations of the relationship between the papacy and the curia. Over sixty-five years ago Pope Benedict XIV stipulated that the work of the curia was not legislative in nature but would be confined solely to the execution of papal legislation.[13] This distinction between the pope and bishops as legislators and the curial dicasteries as executors was important, and the debates at Vatican II suggest that the bishops wished to highlight this distinc-

[12]Ibid., 174.

[13]Cf. J. Schmidt, "The Juridic Value of the *Instructio* Provided by the Motu Proprio '*Cum Iuris Canonici*' September 15, 1917," *The Jurist* 1 (1949) 289–316; James Provost, "The Legates of the Roman Pontiff," in *The Code of Canon Law: A Text and Commentary,* ed. James A. Coriden, Thomas J. Green, and Donald E. Heintschel (New York: Paulist, 1985) 300.

tion. In practice, however, the distinction has been ignored, with the result that the congregations of the Roman curia have virtually replaced the college of bishops as the principal legislators of the Church. Ancient canonical principle does allow for the delegation of the pope's own power of jurisdiction to curial offices. While canon law envisions the participation of the Roman curia in papal governance of the Church, there is reason to question whether the curia can similarly participate in the doctrinal teaching authority of the pope. This authority cannot be delegated because it is his by virtue of his episcopal office as bishop of Rome (see ch. 2). Peter Huizing and Knut Walf confirm this view:

> The theological "sacral" character of the papal office rests on the sacramental character of his ordination as a bishop. It is not possible to delegate this sacramental character of the papal authority to a functionary whose authority ultimately rests upon an administrative appointment. Nor is it possible to bestow this authority on an institution, the existence and power of which depends upon administrative structures and appointments.[14]

This raises important questions regarding the status of curial documents that address doctrinal concerns. In canon law most curial documents require papal approval. This approval can take either of two forms: documents offered in common form have only the general approval of the pope for the publication of the document. Documents promulgated in special form are documents the content of which the pope has made his own. Such documents must include some explicit declaration of this special form of approval. These documents would appear to derive their authority from the papal teaching office itself. In any event, the growing proliferation of curial pronouncements coupled with a widespread ignorance regarding the canonical distinction between common form and special form has created a great deal of confusion and has had the effect of granting, in the practical order, an authority to some curial documents that may be unwarranted ecclesiologically. This question clearly deserves more attention than it has received to date.[15] Much like the practice of formal

---

[14]Peter Huizing and Knut Walf, "Editorial," in *The Roman Curia and the Communion of Churches,* xii.

[15]Ladislas Örsy writes: "I do not know of any thorough study from a theological point of view of the power of the Roman curia. In general it is said

ordinations, the current exercise of curial authority risks obscuring the sacramental origin of the supreme authority given to the college of bishops and its head, the bishop of Rome.

Closely related to the Roman curia is another ecclesiastical institution of medieval invention, the college of cardinals. The title of cardinal originated in the Church of Rome in a number of different contexts. The *cardinal-presbyter* was a priest assigned to an ancient parish in Rome that had jurisdiction over one of the shrines built over the tombs of martyrs (e.g., St. Mary Major, St. Peter's Basilica). Priests responsible for presiding at the liturgies of these shrines were known as "cardinals." Similarly, the *cardinal-bishop* was a bishop from a neighboring town who occasionally performed episcopal functions at the Lateran, the episcopal cathedral of the Church of Rome. As the bishop of Rome acquired civil responsibility for the city of Rome, key clergy assigned to administer social services throughout the city were given the title *cardinal-deacon*. Eventually, these various cardinals became chief advisors to the bishop of Rome.[16] Soon the responsibilities of these cardinals expanded to include serving as papal envoys and legates. After the reforms of Pope Leo IX and Pope Gregory VII in the eleventh century, these cardinals were constituted as a canonical college, or chapter, and in 1179 they were made sole electors of the bishop of Rome, thereby eliminating the traditional role of the clergy and laity in papal election. Cardinals would soon hold all key leadership positions within the Roman curia. Numerous theories developed in the Middle Ages that suggested that this college of cardinals was divinely instituted. Through much of the Middle Ages the college of cardinals possessed much more ecclesiastical power than the college of bishops.

---

that it is the arm of the pope in governing the church, which of course is true. An ambivalence that would deserve serious study is in the situation that the pope cannot hand over to anyone his charism of infallibility (fidelity to the message) but he can let others participate in his power to govern (jurisdiction)." Ladislas Örsy, *The Church: Learning and Teaching* (Wilmington: Glazier, 1987) 52 n. 8.

[16]James Provost, "The Cardinals of the Holy Roman Church," in *The Code of Canon Law: A Text and Commentary,* 286ff.; Giuseppe Alberigo, *Cardinalato e collegialità: Studi sull'ecclesiologia tra l'XI e il XIV secolo* (Florence: Vallecchi, 1969); Yves Congar, "Notes sur le destin de l'idée de collégialité épiscopale en occident au moyen âge (VIIe–XVI– siècles)," in *La collégialité épiscopale: Histoire et théologie* (Paris: Cerf, 1969) 99–129.

In spite of significant reforms by Pope Sixtus V (1586), Innocent XII (1692), and the more recent attempts at reform by Pope John XXIII and Pope Paul VI, the college of cardinals remains one of the most powerful and influential of all ecclesiastical institutions. According to canon 349 of the new Code of Canon Law, there are three principal tasks of the cardinalate, (1) the election of the bishop of Rome, (2) advising the pope, and (3) assisting the pope in special tasks related to the pastoral care of the universal Church. The objections raised against the role of the college of cardinals are much like those raised against the Roman curia. The college of cardinals is a medieval invention that has, in significant ways, co-opted the authority of the college of bishops, which is not a medieval invention but which, according to Church teaching, is divinely instituted and shares in the papal responsibility for the pastoral care of the universal Church. The principal result of redirecting responsibility for participating in the pastoral care of the universal Church to the college of cardinals has been a system of governance that marginalizes the college of bishops, undermines a real exercise of episcopal collegiality, and consequently diminishes the ecclesiological significance of the life of the local Church as a contribution to the Church universal.[17] A reinvigoration of Vatican II's vision of episcopal collegiality and an ecclesiology of communion cannot occur without a fundamental shift of responsibility for assisting the pope in the pastoral care of the universal Church back to the college of bishops where, *according to church teaching,* it belongs.

A Clearer Presentation of the Gradation of Authoritative Church Teaching

In contemporary preaching and catechesis there is often little attempt to communicate to the faithful the important distinctions present in our tradition regarding the gradation of authority in Church teaching. André Naud has referred to the ecclesiastical reluctance to make these distinctions as *le mal catholique,* the Catholic malady.[18] The title of Naud's book bears discussion. Naud writes of *le magistère incertain,* which might be translated as the "uncertain" or

[17]This point was made by Yves Congar in his *Ministères et communion écclésiale* (Paris: Cerf, 1971) 109–17.

[18]André Naud, *Le magistère incertain* (Montreal: Fides, 1987) 23–45.

"doubtful" magisterium.[19] But *incertain* can also mean "indistinct" or "blurred." Naud makes use of both senses. He contends that alongside the infallible magisterium properly exercised in the Church, there is another "uncertain" magisterium that teaches with less authority and must honestly acknowledge the possibility of error. From this point of view the recognition of an "uncertain" magisterium is good and necessary. Naud also sees evidence of *le magistère incertain* in the sense of a magisterium with an unfortunate tendency to blur the necessary distinctions in its exercise of authority. This tendency has done a real disservice to the life of the Church. In this volume I have tried to develop the importance of Naud's first understanding of an uncertain magisterium by clearly delineating those instances when the ecclesiastical magisterium exercises less than an infallible teaching authority. At the same time I have identified the real dangers of an "uncertain" magisterium that overlooks important distinctions. The attitude of many that informing the faithful of the various distinctions in the authority of Church doctrine will only bring confusion and widespread dissent needs to be named for what it is: an inexcusable ecclesiastical paternalism.

Less Reliance on Formal Authority

Pope Pius XII's 1950 encyclical *Humani generis* concludes with the following statement:

> And if the Supreme Pontiffs, in their official documents, deliberately pass judgment on a matter hitherto controverted, it is evident to all that, in accordance with the mind and intention of the same Pontiffs, that question can no longer be considered a subject for free debate among theologians.[20]

This statement reflects the excessive reliance on formal authority that had come to dominate the Roman Catholic Church in the years between Vatican I and Vatican II. It assumes a theology of the magisterium influenced much more by canon law than ecclesiology. Intellectual doubts or questions give way in the face of a formal decision to cease all inquiry in the name of obedience. Obedience to Church office supersedes obedience to truth. The theologian and the

[19] Ibid. For his summary treatment of the title of his book see his epilogue, 263–65.

[20] Pius XII, *AAS* 42 (1950) 568.

ordinary believer are expected to respond to the authority of the officeholder more than to the authority of what is taught.

At Vatican II the closing statement from *Humani generis* was included in the preparatory draft document on the Church. However, at the request of several bishops the statement was deleted because of a sense that it imposed unjustifiable restrictions on the theological enterprise. The removal of this text is but one example of the way in which the council initiated a shift in the Church's understanding of the nature and exercise of authority. This shift was anticipated in Pope John XXIII's opening address at the beginning of the council. The pope observed that the Church has always vigorously opposed errors and that

> frequently she has condemned them with the greatest severity. Nowadays, however, the Spouse of Christ prefers to make use of the medicine of mercy rather than that of severity. She considers that she meets the needs of the present day by *demonstrating the validity of her teaching rather than by condemnations* (emphasis mine).[21]

The pope knew well the danger of relying too exclusively on formal authority. If a particular teaching of the Church and the arguments adduced in support of it are not persuasive, simply "ratcheting up" the authoritative status of the teaching, or arbitrarily closing off debate, will not substitute for persuasive argumentation and dialogue. Michael Scanlon writes:

> The authority or effective power of the gospel is *in* the gospel. The gospel does not get its authority from the office of the official preacher or teacher. Formal authority works when it is in possession, i.e., when it is unquestioned because presupposed. But once questioned, all authorities must render an *apologia* to legitimate their claims. . . . Such appeals [to formal authority] are more and more otiose. The oft noted pragmatism of ecclesiastical leaders should realize this fact by now— simply put, it doesn't work! And—to move from a judgment of fact to a judgment of value—it shouldn't work! Appeals to formal authority should heed the practical economy of Ockham's razor![22]

---

[21]The English text is found in Floyd Anderson, ed., *Council Daybook, Sessions 1 and 2* (Washington: NCWC, 1965) 25–29, citation at 27.

[22]Michael J. Scanlon, "Catholicism and Living Tradition: The Church as a Community of Reception," in *Empowering Authority: The Charisms of Episcopacy and Primacy in the Church Today*, ed. Patrick J. Howell and Gary Chamberlain (Kansas City: Sheed & Ward, 1990) 4.

In spite of the new approaches evident at Vatican II, the excessive reliance on formal authority continues in some ecclesiastical circles. Church leadership must recognize that a sustained and exclusive reliance on formal authority at the expense of reasoned argumentation and debate will ultimately marginalize and diminish the Church's teaching authority.[23]

The Proper Employment of Theological Consultation

For at least one hundred years prior to the Second Vatican Council one could discern a disturbing pattern of popes and bishops consulting exclusively "court theologians." When the International Theological Commission was created under Pope Paul VI, many hoped for new developments in theological consultation in which the Holy See and all the bishops would consult internationally respected theologians belonging to different schools of thought. The pope had envisioned that the commission would serve a consultative role not only to the pope himself but to the CDF. This important papal initiative must be expanded. A frequent consultation of theologians representing divergent views on a matter need not threaten the legitimate authority of those who hold Church office. Unfortunately, in the last fifteen years the diversity of views represented by the ITC membership has diminished considerably, and some fear a return to the practice of limiting Vatican consultation to "court theologians."[24]

In spite of the American media's attempt to paint the relationship between bishops and theologians in terms of conflict and confrontation, the situation in North America offers a much more positive model for the collaboration between bishops and theologians. The NCCB frequently draws on the work of top theologians in this country

---

[23]Examples of this return to the reliance on exclusively formal authority is reflected in the Pope's position on artificial contraception and the ordination of women. In 1987 John Paul II stated that "what is taught by the Church on contraception does not belong to material freely debatable among theologians." *L'Osservatore Romano,* English ed. (July 6, 1987) 12. The Pope made a similar pronouncement regarding the ordination of women in "Ordinatio sacerdotalis," *Origins* 24 (June 9, 1994) 50–52. See Richard R. Gaillardetz, "An Exercise of the Hierarchical Magisterium," *America* 171 (July 30–August 6) 19–22.

[24]Distinguished theologians like Karl Rahner, Yves Congar, and Walter Principe resigned from the commission, in part to protest inappropriate curial/papal suppression of theological diversity on the commission.

and often consults with the appropriate professional theological associations. Respected American theologians like Michael Buckley and Joseph DiNoia have served on the bishops' theological staff. The pope and the Roman curia can only profit from the broader horizons offered by this kind of theological consultation across the ideological spectrum.

The aim of this volume was relatively straightforward—to consider the doctrinal teaching authority of the Church from the perspective of Vatican II's retrieval of an ecclesiology of communion. I have taken this notion of communion, with its incorporation of principles of conciliarity, collegiality, ecclesial reception, and the *sensus fidelium,* and reconsidered the concrete structures of the Church's teaching office, the object of doctrinal teaching, the manner in which doctrinal authority can and ought to be exercised, and the reception of doctrinal teaching by both the individual believer and by the whole Christian community.

Two fundamental presuppositions have informed this study. The first is Vatican II's insistence that God's word has been given to the whole Christian community in Jesus Christ by the power of the Holy Spirit. Any understanding of the structures and exercise of doctrinal teaching authority will be distorted or defective to the extent that it does not fully account for this basic conviction. God's word is not in the possession of a privileged few within the Church, however much Catholics may insist on an apostolic ministry with the privileged responsibility of safeguarding the authentic proclamation of that word. Second, the authoritative structures and exercise of doctrinal teaching authority must be governed by the requirements of an ecclesiology of communion. That ecclesiology insists on the relational character of the Church, in which there are no autonomous loci of power and authority.

As a Roman Catholic theologian, I affirm the necessity of a doctrinal teaching office in the life of the Church. But the nature and exercise of this doctrinal authority must be governed by the gospel of Jesus Christ and the conceptions of authority that flow from the life of ecclesial communion. A renewed teaching authority, one that is properly situated and exercised within the Church as a communion, can only help the Church to enter its third millennium of existence with what Pope John XXIII called "the simple and pure lines that the face of the Church of Jesus had at its birth."[25]

---

[25]Quoted in Xavier Rynne, *Vatican Council II,* single volume version (New York: Farrar, Straus, and Giroux, 1968) 8.

Subject Index